Rich Johnson's
Guide to Trailer Boat Sailing

Casting Off In a Small Boat

Rich and Becky Johnson

Rich Johnson's
Guide to Trailer Boat Sailing

Casting Off In a Small Boat

Dedication

We dedicate this book to Eric, Ryan and Shane — the three Eagle Scouts who inspired the name of our boat *Three Eagles*. And to Sharlene, who, although she isn't an Eagle Scout is certainly our little angel.

Table of Contents

Foreword

Trailer sailors are the luckiest breed of nautical people. If we want to, we can spend one weekend on a lake in the great north woods, and the next weekend in coastal waters. We can tow the boat south in the winter and sail among the Florida Keys, then head northwest when the weather warms and cruise the San Juan Islands. We can spend a whole winter in the Sea of Cortez, if we had the time, then load the boat on the trailer and head for a pristine glacier-fed lake in Canada for the summer. And along the way between our destinations, we can slide the boat into any number of bays or lakes or rivers to test the wind and spend the night camping on board. The choice is ours, and we enjoy alternatives not available to sailors with non-trailerable boats.

Indeed, I was talking with a world cruising sailor one day, discussing the newly built 60-footer he and his wife intended to launch for a planned circumnavigation. This was their second time around, owning a large custom-built boat intended for blue water cruising. When he asked what kind of boat Becky and I sail, I winced as I told him, "It's a MacGregor 26X, just a little trailerable pocket cruiser."

To my great surprise, he turned to his wife and said, "Someday that's what I want to have. A boat we can trailer around the country."

I was stunned. Until then, I thought people with big yachts had it all, but this couple taught me there's a lot to be said for the flexibility of sailing a trailerable boat. We have the option of keeping our boat in a marina part of the year, or we can avoid paying marina fees during the off-season and park the boat at home on the trailer. That way we don't pay any fees and the boat is unaffected by bottom fouling. Having the boat in the back yard puts it right at hand for doing projects, but it's always poised for taking off down the road toward the next adventure.

Without a doubt, that is the biggest benefit of owning a trailerable sailboat; you can sail on waters anywhere in the country. On a recent trip, we stopped at a large lake with a nice marina and launch ramp. While walking the docks, we met a couple lounging in the cockpit of their Hunter 33 and struck up a conversation. It turns out they bought their boat from a previous owner in Florida, then had it trucked west to this lake, which was their home port. And there they stayed. Every winter, they had to have a big truck come to haul the boat out before the lake froze. Every spring they had the big truck come back to launch them again. All winter long, the boat sat "on the hard" in a cradle. And every time the boat was moved it cost them money.

We sailed the lake that day, stayed overnight in a slip, and left the next day for another destination, pulling our boat behind our pickup. This is the life of a trailer sailor. These boats offer tremendous flexibility, but to take full advantage of it we must learn how to get the most out of our boats and the tow vehicles that pull them. And that's the purpose of this book — to explore the technical details of owning and using a trailerable sailboat. Along with all the technical stuff, Becky and I will share with you some of our own adventures in trailer sailing. So, turn the page and let the fun begin.

Introduction
The Adventure Begins

Somewhere in my life, a seed was planted and it grew until it became a sailboat. I can thank my buddy Steve for preparing the soil. He fed me full of stories about his sailing adventures and left me dreaming about boats. There was the time he took his family to Flathead Lake in Montana and sailed out onto the deep blue. At midday, the wind died, leaving the sails limp. Without a breeze, the sun bore down until everyone decided to go for a swim. They all jumped overboard and were splashing around when, suddenly, Steve heard the slatting of the mainsail and looked up to see the wind had returned and the boat was sailing away on its own. It's interesting how fast a man can swim when swept over by full panic. He caught a trailing rope, managed to pull himself aboard and sailed back to pick up his family — a wiser man.

Before we jump all the way to the conclusion that Steve became entirely wise, we should study another of his misadventures (he has had many). The family was visiting Mission Bay in Southern California. Steve got the urge to take the family sailing on the bay. The day was hot and, while they were sailing, Steve's wife (who will remain nameless for the sake of our friendship) wanted to go for a swim.

Steve said, "Just hang onto this rope, jump overboard, and I'll tow you around." Sounded good to Dana (Oops, dang! Now she'll never talk to me again), so that's what she did. It worked for a while, but then the wind picked up and the boat started moving faster and faster, until the water peeled off her swimsuit. Before he could get the boat stopped, Steve trolled his naked wife past a cheering crowd of boaters. Amazingly, Dana is still married to Steve, and stranger yet, she still goes sailing with him. A wonderfully forgiving woman.

And so it was, Steve's stories got me started thinking about hoisting a sail and heading for the horizon. But it was only a lazy dream, because I never did anything about it. Then I began work on a novel in which the hero knew how to sail. Realizing I couldn't write this portion of the story with any authority, I began researching. My study led into dusty regions of the library, where I found books about sail making, boat design, keels, rigging, and other such esoterica. I read by day, and dreamed by night. I subscribed to *Cruising World, Sail,* and *Sailing* to vicariously tap into the lives of others who were "out there" doing what I desperately wanted to do. I read their tales and drooled over their photographs. The obsession got so bad I even signed up for *Practical Sailor,* a technical publication that doesn't even have any pictures!

Then it happened—I found myself spending more and more time in the classified section of the magazines, and I could deny it no longer; I was subconsciously shopping for a sailboat.

I had no business shopping for a sailboat. At the time, we lived at an elevation of 6200 feet near the base of the Teton Mountains in eastern Idaho. Water is frozen solid half the year, and sometimes the reservoirs are drained nearly dry in the springtime to supply agricultural needs downstream. This was not sailing country.

Still, you know how an obsession gnaws at you one day at a time until you surrender. Not wanting to be gnawed at for too long, I surrendered early to save a lot of unnecessary pain. No matter if we didn't live in ideal sailing country, because I had read about TRAILERABLE sailboats.

Suddenly, my research had a focus. I quit reading the classified section of the magazines, where I mostly saw large fixed-keel boats that needed to be tied to a dock, someplace like Seattle or Miami or Norfolk, where the water never freezes. From that point, I concentrated on trailerable sailboats, comparing all the vital specifications, boat and trailer construction, cabin layout and amenities, ease of trailering, versatility, price vs. features, etc. Then I logged onto a variety of owner-based websites to see what owners said about their boats. When the dust cleared, Becky and I decided a MacGregor 26X best suited our needs.

The dealer nearest our home was a fellow named Paul in Salt Lake City. He sent us a brochure, which I memorized, and a video we watched over and over until it wore out. We also reviewed our budget. We didn't want to go into debt to buy a sailboat, so we looked around to see what we could sell to come up with the money. In the end, we sold a tent trailer and a classic Thunderbird we planned to restore someday. That wasn't enough, so we scratched up a bit more cash to close the gap.

Let's look at the issue of buying new versus used. In many parts of the country, it's fairly easy to find a good used boat that, with little or no work, can be put back into service. But, at the time, we lived in remote eastern Idaho where a sailboat had never even been *seen*, much less placed on the market for sale. If you wanted to buy a used snowmobile, our town was the place to go — but not for a sailboat. We had no opportunity to walk the docks or drive around to inspect and compare trailerable sailboats, determine how much work it would take to put an older boat back into commission, etc. For us, it made more sense to buy a new boat.

With the funds secured, we placed our order. Paul told us if we went to the factory in Costa Mesa, California and picked up the boat ourselves, we could save a few hundred dollars of delivery charges. We decided to do that. Besides, I figured by going to pick up the boat I could take a tour of the factory and see firsthand how our boat was built.

Our son Ryan joined me for a trip to California to take delivery of the boat. Our two oldest kids had already fled the nest — Sharlene was married and had children of her own, living in Southern California — and Eric had joined the Navy and was serving in Hawaii. Shane, our youngest son, was still in school, so Becky stayed behind to manage the homefront. The heroic voyage to rescue our boat from the factory was left to Ryan and me.

Becky and I didn't know the name of our boat when we set off to take possession of her. It wasn't until months later we finally decided on the moniker *Three Eagles* as a tribute to our three sons who all earned their Eagle rank in the Boy Scouts.

After a two-day drive, Ryan and I followed Paul's directions and a map to the factory. Anxious as we were, we arrived before any of the workers, and had to cool our heels in the parking lot, staring at a line of freshly built boats behind the security fence.

"Which one do you think is ours?" I asked. It was a rhetorical question that didn't matter, except to satisfy my own curiosity. All the boats were exactly the same. Still, I wanted to know which one to stare at the hardest.

Finally, company employees arrived, opened the office doors and the gate to the production lot, and we went inside. The office people knew we were coming — Paul had made all the arrangements. We signed the papers, handed over a check, and asked if we could take a tour of the plant. "Sure," the lady behind the desk smiled.

"Come right this way."

She handed us over to the official tour guy, who led us through the factory while explaining every step of the production process. We observed as molds were waxed and then sprayed with gelcoat. We saw fiberglass being hand laid. At a later stage, we witnessed a fresh hull being pulled from its mold. Right on cue, the hull liner and all the rest of the pieces that go inside showed up, and the various components were bonded into place. Finally, the deck was lowered onto the hull, the deck flange covered with bonding compound, and the whole thing bolted together with stainless steel hardware every few inches.

Actually seeing the production of a boat identical to our own gave me great comfort in knowing how much care was taken to ensure everything was done properly. Even though it was a long drive (about a thousand miles each way), it was worth the trip just to see how the boat was built.

Next stop was the boat parking lot, where we finally came face to face with *Three Eagles*. The factory guy showed us through the boat, went over the inventory of rigging pieces we would install later on as we set up the mast for the first time, and helped us get hitched up.

Out of the parking lot we went, hung a left, hung a right, another left, and then eventually we merged with traffic on the freeway. At the first stoplight I became sold on trailer brakes, when all the taillights ahead of us suddenly went red. The boat and trailer stopped easily and in complete control. Wiping the sweat from my palms, I waited for the semaphore to turn green, smiled at Ryan and felt the thrill known to every first-time boat owner.

I've heard the stories: the happiest two days in a boat owner's life are the day he buys the boat and the day he sells it. That one was laid on me by a friend in Newport Beach, California (adjacent to Costa Mesa) where Ryan and I spent the night before picking up our boat. Brian just laughed at our excitement about being new boat owners, then told me one day I'd enjoy selling the boat every bit as much as I loved buying it. I didn't like the joke as much as he did, and answered back that the happiest two days in the life of a hot rodder were the days he bought and sold his roadster. Brian, an avid roadster enthusiast, lost his smile about then. The good news is, after all these years, we're still happy boat owners and Brian still loves his roadster—so trite sayings don't always ring true.

The first night on our way home, we stopped at our daughter

Sharlene's house out in the Mojave Desert. I wanted to get an early start the next morning to avoid the heat of the day going over the infamous car-fire-hell known as the Baker Grade, between California and Nevada. We left at 1:00 a.m. and crossed the mountains in the darkest and coolest part of the night. Just before dawn, we cruised through Las Vegas before traffic got nasty. A couple hours later, we pulled over to sleep at a rest area not far from St. George, Utah. Ryan crawled into the boat's cabin, cleared a spot among the inventory of stuff and fell asleep. I stretched out across the bench seat of our F-150 pickup and was gone in a heartbeat. I dreamed of sailing.

Late afternoon of the next day, we pulled into the driveway at home. Even though we were tired from the trip, I couldn't wait to get the mast up. We sorted through all the rigging hardware, laid it out on the driveway, studied the owner's manual, and went to work. Carefully reading the instructions twice before we installed anything, we proceeded. At first, it was all a mystery to me — shrouds and stays, halyards and sheets, chainplates and tension adjusters. But before long, the mast was up, the boom attached, and we stood back to admire our work.

That's when the neighbors started arriving. Not only neighbors who lived next door, but neighbors who lived across the valley. Everybody's a neighbor in Teton Valley, Idaho, no matter how far away they live.

"What's that?" was the most common question.

"It's a sailboat," was my most common answer.

"What's it doing here?"

"It's ours."

"You gotta be kidding!"

"Nope. We're going to sail on Palisades Reservoir. Soon as it thaws out, and before it freezes over again."

"Well, that'll give you about seventeen good days of sailing each year," the neighbor said with a grin.

"Yeah," I had to agree, although the season is usually a bit longer than seventeen days. "But you see the trailer it's sitting on? We can take this boat to Florida and sail the Keys in February," I said smugly.

"Heck, you can't even get out of this valley in February, unless you're on a snowmobile," he chuckled.

He had a point. We'd have to plan ahead for winter escapes, but we didn't let that dampen our enthusiasm.

We practiced raising and lowering the mast, using a neat bit of rigging that allows one person to raise or lower the mast alone. We left the mast erect for two solid weeks, sitting right there in front of the house. I did that for two reasons—one, I thought it was a good idea to allow the rigging to stretch itself out. And two, I just liked to look at it. This was the biggest oddity Teton Valley had ever seen—a fully rigged sailboat. School kids came by to gawk at it. Some folks couldn't help making the obvious Noah jokes.

It took a couple weeks before our dealer could schedule time to help us officially commission the boat. Commissioning a boat is what happens when it is made ready for its initial launch. During the waiting period, we purchased a Honda 9.9-horsepower longshaft outboard motor as auxiliary power. There are some sailors, I've heard, who pride themselves in being able to go everywhere under sail power alone. I'm not one of them. I figure a quiet, clean-burning 4-stroke will help us get where we need to go when the wind is either too strong or too weak. It also helps maneuver around a dock or a marina without the wreckage caused by mismanaging the sails.

On the appointed day, Ryan and I lowered the mast, secured everything for travel and towed the boat several hours south to Bear Lake, which straddles the Idaho/Utah border. Paul met us in the parking lot of the marina, and we laid everything out on the ground—mast, boom, spreaders, sails, rigging, everything. Paul's job was to inspect our installation to make sure we did it right. I figured we'd done it right, because for two solid weeks the mast didn't fall down in our driveway. Turns out Paul agreed, and he congratulated us for our good work. We'd ordered the optional roller furling system, so Paul showed us how to install that on the headstay, then how to attach a sail and roll it up. Once everything was ready to go, the mast went back onto its step, the boom was connected, and we were ready to get the boat wet.

Thanks to the design of the trailer, and the fully retractable centerboard, our boat slid into the water without any of us having to get our feet wet. While I parked the truck and trailer, Paul and Ryan walked the boat to the deep end of the dock. I scrambled aboard, and we lowered the motor, the centerboard and the rudders and we were ready to go.

As we motored out beyond the breakwater, Paul showed us how to open the valves to fill the water ballast tank. Ten minutes later, the "basement" was full of water, so we closed the valves. There we were, sitting in the middle of a liquid turquoise paradise, ready to hoist the sails. The dream was about to come true.

First, Paul took the helm and handled the lines, to show us how it was done. Ryan and I nodded, as if we understood, and Paul asked if we had any questions.

"Nope," I said. "Looks pretty simple."

"Okay," Paul replied, looking at me, "do you want to take the helm?"

"Sure."

Paul put Ryan in charge of the sheets (sail control lines), and sat back ready to offer advice. I slid behind the wheel, told Ryan to ease the sheet because I wanted to go on a beam reach. The sheet eased, and I cracked off the wind a few degrees, staring intently up at the mainsail to make sure we kept the sail trimmed properly for our angle on the wind.

Paul looked at me quizzically. "You're making this look too easy. I thought you said you never sailed before."

"I've never been on a real sailboat before." I grinned. "But I've been sailing every night for the past two years."

We cruised up and down Bear Lake on every point of sail. Hard on the wind, we found the boat displayed an aggressive weather helm, trying to turn directly into the wind, and we had to fight the wheel. Paul showed us that by pulling the centerboard back about one-quarter, and by easing the mainsheet a bit, the weather helm is reduced.

We spent a couple hours with Paul, before he felt comfortable leaving us to our own devices. On the way back to the marina, Paul took the helm as Ryan and I lowered the main, furled the headsail, stowed the sheets and generally made the boat shipshape. I paid close attention as Paul docked the boat. He made it look so easy, as the fenders lightly caressed the soft rub bumper on the dock. Ryan and I left him there, then turned back out onto the lake to continue our first ever sailing adventure, fully confident we, as commander and crew, could handle anything that came up.

Right!

I've been told by other sailors that if you can sail the high mountain lakes, you can sail anywhere. I believe that's true. Wind is fluky on these lakes, as it seems to either die altogether or roar with a vengeance out of a canyon. Ryan and I managed to find every type and quality of wind in the hour after Paul left. Sailing north with the wind at our back and the boom eased out as far as it could go, the wind suddenly shifted 180 degrees. I felt it before I saw it and lunged for the mainsheet as the boom roared across the cockpit in an accidental jibe. It passed so close above me I felt the wind as the boom whistled past my head. Unfortunately, I couldn't catch the sheet in time, and the full force of the shifting wind against the sails sent us heeling over to starboard far enough to drive the end of the boom into the water.

Man, I felt stupid! An accidental jibe is among the most dangerous things that can happen, which is why running dead downwind is such a precarious point of sail. And there I was, only an hour into being a new skipper, and I'd already driven us into harm's way.

Ryan's eyes were big and he had an adventurously worried look on his face as he mouthed the words, "Whoa, dad, that was wild."

I was sorry to have exposed my son to risk. But, as it turned out, Ryan and I would face even greater excitement (read danger) on a future voyage — one that made an accidental jibe look like a walk in the park. These are the experiences that teach us the most immediate and lasting lessons. You've heard the saying, "What doesn't kill you will strengthen you." Well, one accidental jibe was enough to teach us to never let that happen again. The wind can shift unexpectedly, especially on a mountain lake where the shape of the landscape turns and funnels the wind in weird and unpredictable ways. That little episode taught us to be aware of what the wind is doing at all times.

Becky loves sailing. In fact, when we're out, she is the one who is normally at the helm while I handle the sheets. She will always be my co-captain and my favorite sailing companion. She's a good sport and has a wonderful sense of humor, but there's a limit to the size of the adventure she wants to experience. In fact, there have been a couple of "adventures" Ryan and I had when we were dang glad Becky wasn't with us. Our accidental jibe was one of them, and you'll read about another one later on. Having heard of water-soluble marriages, I am careful to try to keep certain unacceptable things from happening while she's on board.

Wife-friendly sailing means we reef and furl early, keep a hand on the mainsheet so we can dump air to prevent heeling beyond the comfort zone (15 degrees is okay...25 is pushing it), and we are always willing to drop sails altogether and use the motor. For us, the whole object of sailing is to have fun, and if someone on board is scared out of their wits, they're not having fun.

But let's get back to day-one of sailing on Bear Lake. There was a lot of wild and crazy stuff yet to come for Ryan and me. After the accidental jibe, we decided to take a breather and gather our noodles. We furled the headsail, stowed the main and motored back toward the marina. It was getting late, and we had to figure out how to fix dinner and then spend the night on the boat.

Everything went well as we entered the breakwater. People milled around on their boats as we approached the dock and made a perfect landing. Ryan hopped off the boat and tied the docklines fore and aft, and I shot a smug look at a guy getting ready to go out in his little fishing boat. We were getting good at this — we docked perfectly the first time. With a bit of an attitude in my step, I walked up to the office to rent a slip for the night.

The harbormaster took my money and showed me a map of the guest slips. Ours was halfway down and to the right. Back on board, I had Ryan release the docklines and we backed away from the dock. Then the fun began. At least it was fun for those other people standing around watching. For us, it was agonizing and embarrassing.

Without warning, something went terribly wrong with the steering (maybe it was the nut behind the wheel?). The boat went every direction except where I wanted it to go. We did one full donut in front of the launch ramp, which seemed to please the fisherman I had smiled smugly at earlier. I lost count of the other spectators whose mouths were either agape or laughing hysterically as I fought to discover how to control the boat.

What I didn't understand at the moment was that a rudder has no effect on the boat's direction until there is a hearty flow of water over the rudder's surface. I swung the wheel left and right, expecting the boat to obey instantly, but all we did was go in circles. One other thing I didn't fully understand was the concept of "lag" in the steering. Sailboats don't respond like a sports car, especially when they're barely moving in the confines of a marina.

At one point, we spun close to one of the finger docks that separate the slips. It wasn't the one we wanted, but by then I was ready to accept anything.

"Ryan," I shouted, "jump to that dock and we'll walk the boat to the right slip."

"Okay, dad," he answered, and positioned himself on the foredeck at the lifelines, ready to jump.

With too much momentum, we raced past the end of the dock,

and Ryan leaped into space. He actually landed on the dock, but was pulled off because the boat was moving too fast. There he was, poor boy, clinging to the lifelines as if his life depended on it, his feet dancing across the water as we headed for the next piece of dock.

For some unknown reason, at that moment, I made eye contact with every single person in the marina. I swear I did. And they all made eye contact back. In their eyes I saw looks of pity.

Soon, we were about to crash into another bit of dock, and Ryan, still clinging with a white-knuckle death grip, tried to get his feet on it. He managed one toe on the wood before we drifted away again, did another donut and headed for the slips on the other side of the fairway.

"Please, Dad," Ryan begged, "get next to the dock. I can't hold on much longer."

I could only nod silently, praying for a higher force to take over and guide us to a safe landing. And then it happened. The boat finally lost momentum, straightened out and came to a stop at the end of a slip. It was a miracle, and I looked up and said "Thanks." Ryan struggled up onto the platform, peeled his fingers off the lifelines, looked at me and shook his head. Then a big grin spread across his face and we both broke out laughing. In the background, I think I heard applause, but I'm not entirely sure.

"Dad," he finally said. "We gotta work on our landings."

"You mean you're going to stick with me, after that?" I laughed.

"Oh yeah," he said. "But let's not do it that way again."

"Well," I smiled, "I was curious about the strength of the lifelines. It was a good test."

Rather than try to drive the boat to the correct slip, we each grabbed a dockline and walked her around. Wisdom began to set in. I realized that some days you're the dog, and some days you're the hydrant. But we lived to tell about it.

* * * *

That's how it all started. A lot of water has gone under the keel since then, and the lessons we've learned were not always easy or fun, but always an adventure. You'll read about some of our escapades in the chapters to come—some are funny, some are scary. Hopefully, you'll catch the spirit of sailing a trailerable boat and discover the soul-satisfying joy that comes from the magical experience of exploring under sail.

Part One

Getting Started ... All About the Boat

Chapter One
The Right Boat

Boy, here's a dangerous subject. Reminds me of the ongoing Ford vs. Chevy argument I used to have with my dad when I was a teenager. But we need to spend a little time talking about this issue. (No, not Fords and Chevys!) If you've owned a sailboat before, or any boat, for that matter, you might have formed some opinions about the things you would like to see different on your next boat. If you've never owned a boat before, we'll give you our opinions about what works and what doesn't. At least what works for us and what doesn't. Take it all with a grain of salt (tastes better that way) and when you go boat shopping you'll have something extra to think about.

The West Wight Potter is an example of a small trailerable sailboat that can take you on great adventures. These fine pocket cruisers feature a small galley, porta potty, and four berths.

Photo credit:
International Marine

What Do You Want To Do?

There are different reasons for going sailing. Some folks like to go racing, some like long-term cruising, and some are perfectly satisfied just going out for part of a day to have a picnic on the boat and play around for a few hours. I guess we ought to declare our party affiliation right up front, because it won't be long before our personal prejudices become obvious anyway.

We're cruisers. Oh, to be sure, we are also racers, but not officially. Whenever we find ourselves on the same course with another sailboat, the race is on. Becky thinks it's funny the way I start muttering in a terrible rendition of a pirate's accent things like, "Yo ho, let's run 'er down and board 'er and plunder their pantry and steal their women." Well, I have to admit I do find myself in trouble when I get to the part about stealing the women. But the race is on anyway. We claw forward, tack for tack, trimming sails, trying to gain ground inch by inch. The funniest part is, the other boat is probably unaware that a race is going on. But it doesn't matter ... we're racing.

One of my favorite unofficial race memories is the time we were sailing home from Port Ludlow, Washington through Oak Bay, heading for the narrow passage leading to Port Townsend Bay. Another boat approached from an angle, obviously lining up for the same passage three miles distant. We had room to play. This time Becky started muttering as she gripped the wheel, and a killer grin spread across her face. The race was on. The breeze was up and I should have reefed, but Becky drove hard on the wind and buried the lee rail as we heeled past our normal fun-o-meter limit.

Our two boats crossed paths. We were well ahead, but they were a bigger (faster) boat, a ketch with two masts and lots of canvas up in the wind and they were coming fast. Eventually they tacked and we immediately tacked and, in our minds, the duel ensued. We matched them tack for tack, and at every crossing they gained ground. Becky clenched the wheel harder, pinched a little tighter into the wind, asked for more sail trim and I winched until the sheet was like an iron rod.

"Aarrrgh!" she exclaimed in obvious emotional pain after fifteen minutes of hard sailing. "They're going to pass us!"

"It's okay, honey," I tried to calm her. "We're cruisers, remember?"

"Not today, we're not!" her eyes were wild with adrenaline. "Can't we squeeze a little more out of the mainsail?"

For the life of me, I've never seen such enthusiasm for going fast. It was like being in the cockpit of an America's Cup boat. We lost, of course. The other boat was twice our size, flying acres of sail, and ... probably didn't even realize a race was under way. As she passed us, her smiling crew waved and lifted their drinks in a friendly toast. Who knows, maybe they enjoyed the chase too.

So there you have it; we're cruisers, most of the time, unless an opportunity for an unofficial race presents itself. But that is different from being a REAL racer. Real racers don't have a boat like ours. And real cruisers don't have boats like the real racers. And that's the point of this chapter. What kind of boat do you want? It all depends upon what you want to do with it.

Cruisers vs. Racers

When we go cruising, we like to be comfortable. Even on a relatively small trailerable sailboat, we can still be comfortable — sort of. The important things to cruisers are having a place to sleep, a dinette table to double as a nav station, a galley, perhaps even an enclosed head (bathroom). There should be enough storage space to stow food and water and clothing and supplies for at least an overnight or maybe even an extended voyage of a week or more. A cockpit dodger (sort of like a windshield), a bimini for a sun shade, and a full cockpit enclosure are strictly cruiser items. Not every cruising boat has all these features, but the more features you have, the greater your comfort level.

Pure racers, on the other hand, couldn't care less about creature comforts. If you've ever hung out with racers, you know they don't even care whether or not they're warm or well fed or have a place to pee when the need arises. All they care about is going fast. The faster the better. And speed can be measured in reverse proportion to weight, so race boats are light, and no extra goodies are brought aboard to make the crew comfortable.

Cruisers don't worry so much about windage (wind resistance created by a tall cabin), but racers do. That's why a race boat is low and sleek, while a cruise boat might look a little more boxy. You see, cruisers like to be able to stand up in the cabin (or at least hunch over but still be somewhat upright), but racers are willing to crawl on their belly though a minimalist cabin that's actually just storage space for extra sails.

You get the picture. The whole philosophy of a cruiser is different than the racing mindset. And so are the boats they sail. So we're back to the old question; what kind of sailing do you want to do?

Of course there are compromise boats that try to straddle the line and be both cruiser and racer. These boats are typically called (what else?) cruiser/racers. They go relatively fast, but not as fast as an honest racer, and they offer a modicum of creature comforts, but not like a real cruising boat. Keep in mind we're talking about trailerable sailboats here — in the realm of larger yachts, some cruiser/racer type boats offer livability in a go-fast vessel. But for us, size and weight are the limiting factors, so our cruiser/racers offer fewer amenities than larger boats.

The kind of boat you choose depends upon your own personal motivation. Since our motivation is primarily cruising, with only an occasional fast run against the enemy, we tend to lean toward more comfort and are willing to sacrifice speed to get it.

This issue of comfort is another piece of dangerous ground. My definition of comfort and Becky's definition of comfort are not the same. When I talk about our boat being comfortable, she says, "Hey, I wouldn't exactly call that comfort." So I'm willing to concede that comfort is a relative term.

To me, comfort is being able to stretch out my 6'1" frame in a straight line when sleeping. Yes, it would be more comfortable if I could also stand fully upright inside the cabin, but I'm willing to take what I can get. I can stand in the companionway when the hatch is open, but the rest of the time I hunch over or find a place to sit.

Becky can stand upright almost everywhere inside the cabin, but when she moves forward and bumps her head on the descending cabin roof, that violates her definition of comfort. We can both sleep fully stretched out — she in the forepeak berth and me in the aft berth beneath the cockpit. The galley isn't perfect, and neither is the head, but at least we have these amenities. And we'll talk more about each of these things a little later. I only mention them here because all these things are considerations when you buy a boat.

Now let's examine some of the practical and technical considerations about boat choice.

- **Ballast** — Trailerable sailboats come in four ballast versions: unballasted (small, lightweight sailing dinghies, often used for one-design racing); ballasted shoal-draft fixed keel (still trailerable, but not easily); swing keel (like a centerboard, but with a heavily ballasted keel); and water ballasted (a "basement" compartment floods with water to serve as ballast).

The whole purpose of ballast is to counteract the force of the wind on the sails. Without ballast, the wind will just knock the boat over. It's interesting to see what happens to a fixed-keel boat when the keel breaks off and the ballast suddenly goes missing. Almost immediately, the boat goes into a graceful tumble to one side, eventually laying the mast in the water while the crew scrambles to climb onto what used to be the bottom of the now overturning hull. We've seen this in even the most celebrated international races, like the run-up to the America's Cup, for example.

Unballasted boats are intended for people who enjoy athletic sailing, because whoever is onboard is regarded as movable ballast, a.k.a. railmeat. I have served as railmeat many times on someone else's racing boat. Even big yachts with heavily ballasted lead keels use railmeat when the breeze is up, the helmsman is driving hard into the wind and the racing is tough. Some lightweight trailerable racing sailboats are equipped with trapezes into which the crew members fit themselves so they can hang way out over the water on the windward side to enhance the "railmeat" ballast factor. It's fun and exciting, if you're up to it.

Ballasted boats with relatively short fixed keels can be trailered, but are not easy to get in and out of the water. Doing so requires submerging the trailer to a great enough depth to float the boat and allow the boat's keel to slide on or off the trailer without interference. This means the trailer has to be sunk several feet deeper than the draft of the boat. In order to do so, the trailer will either have an extendable tongue (so you can keep letting the trailer back farther and farther into the water), or you must use a winch and cable to ease the unhitched trailer down into deep water while the tow vehicle is still at the water's edge. I've helped owners of these sailboats launch, and it's a time-consuming, often difficult, chore that ties up the ramp long enough for waiting boaters to start forming a lynch mob.

Swing keel boats have ballasted keels, that are raised and lowered with a winch and cable that is mounted somewhere on the boat. When in the up position, the keel hides inside a "trunk" in the boat's hull, and is out of the way during the launch or loading process. Once the boat is out into deep water, the keel can be lowered until the ballast is deep, where it will do the most good.

Water ballasted boats (like ours), have a compartment in the "basement" that can be flooded when the skipper wants to take on ballast, or can be left empty if ballast isn't required. This arrangement has both pros and cons. On the pro side: it allows you to dump the ballast so the boat doesn't weigh so much on the trailer. This makes towing easier and eases the burden on your trailer. It also permits the skipper to adjust the sailing weight of the boat for motoring (a lighter boat will go faster and consume less fuel under power). Finally, water ballast cannot break and fall off the boat, leaving you unballasted.

On the con side: Because the ballast is actually contained inside the lower part of the hull, the counterforce benefit of the ballast is reduced. Ideally, to make the boat stiff (stand up powerfully against the force of wind on the sails), the ballast should be at the greatest possible distance beneath the hull. That's why some racing boats have all their lead in a bulb at the extreme lower end of the keel. But water ballast lives inside the bottom of the hull, where it contributes the least possible counterforce effort. This makes for a relatively tender boat (easily pushed over under the force of the wind). One other possible (but almost unheard of) downside to a water ballasted boat is that the ballast tank could leak water into the main hull, if the tank were damaged in some way.

One final word about ballast. A boat with permanent, heavy ballast can sink if the vessel takes on water, while a boat without ballast or with water ballast can be made unsinkable by installing foam flotation in buoyancy chambers of the hull. Something to think about.

• **Keels, Centerboards and Daggerboards** — While ballast counteracts the force of the wind on the sails to keep the boat upright, something else is needed under the hull to keep the wind from pushing the boat sideways through the water. That's where keels, centerboards or daggerboards come into play. Entire books can be written about the relative virtues of various shapes, sizes and configurations of these underwater appendages, but all we're going to discuss here is what you, as a prospective boat owner, need to know in order to make your choice.

Keels are either fixed or adjustable, as we discussed above. Fixed keels make launching and loading a pain, but are fairly trouble-free otherwise. However, if you plan on sailing in shoal waters, a boat with an adjustable keel allows you to sneak into shallower water closer to the beach before dropping anchor.

Centerboards are like swing keels, except they aren't ballasted. Our boat has a centerboard weighing only about 60 pounds. When the centerboard is down, it resembles a vertical wing underwater, and extends to a depth of about 6 feet. When the board is up, the boat drafts about 18 inches, and we can actually beach the boat. We've done this at times, such as on trips to Lake Powell where we anchor right on the sandy beaches. One of the great advantages of a centerboard is it can be designed to automatically kick up if you suddenly find yourself in water that's too thin. When the board makes contact with the ground or deadhead (partially submerged log), it releases itself and pivots up into its trunk without damage. The centerboard also offers the flexibility of having only a portion of the "keel" down. We can lower it half way, or three-quarters, depending upon sailing conditions. Adjusting the board in this way shifts the underwater center of lateral resistance, which is helpful at keeping the boat from tending to round-up (steer itself too hard into the wind) under certain wind conditions.

Daggerboards are somewhat like centerboards, except rather than pivoting up and down, they slide vertically up and down in their trunk. Some boat designers claim daggerboards are the most efficient appendages—an aspect more important for racers than cruisers. A drawback to the daggerboard is that it doesn't pivot, so damage might occur if the boat goes aground hard.

Confession time: I have inadvertently used our centerboard as a primitive depth-sounder once or twice, so I know this business of going aground can happen easily.

• **Tiller or Wheel**—Whether you choose a boat steered with a tiller or a wheel depends upon two things: how comfortable you are about learning to steer in a way many people think of as backward; and how much room you need in the cockpit.

Honestly, steering with a tiller isn't difficult to learn. It's like riding a bicycle; after a while the actions become second nature. But, that's Rich speaking. If you ask Becky, the ONLY way to steer a boat is with a wheel. In fact, that was one of her Big Four criteria when we bought our boat. (The other three were: the boat had to be unsinkable, self-righting, and have an enclosed head).

A tiller is convenient because it can be either tilted up out of the way or entirely removed, so it doesn't encroach on the cockpit. On the other hand, wheel steering is permanent and can be an obstruction in the middle of the cockpit. We've learned to live with

Wheel steering was a prerequisite for Becky when we were shopping for a boat. It makes it easy to steer, with no need to learn a new driving technique.

The view from behind the wheel is as familiar as driving a car.

Many trailerable sailboats have tillers instead of wheels
for steering. After a short learning period, steering
with a tiller becomes second nature and requires
almost no concentrated thought.

Photo credit: International Marine

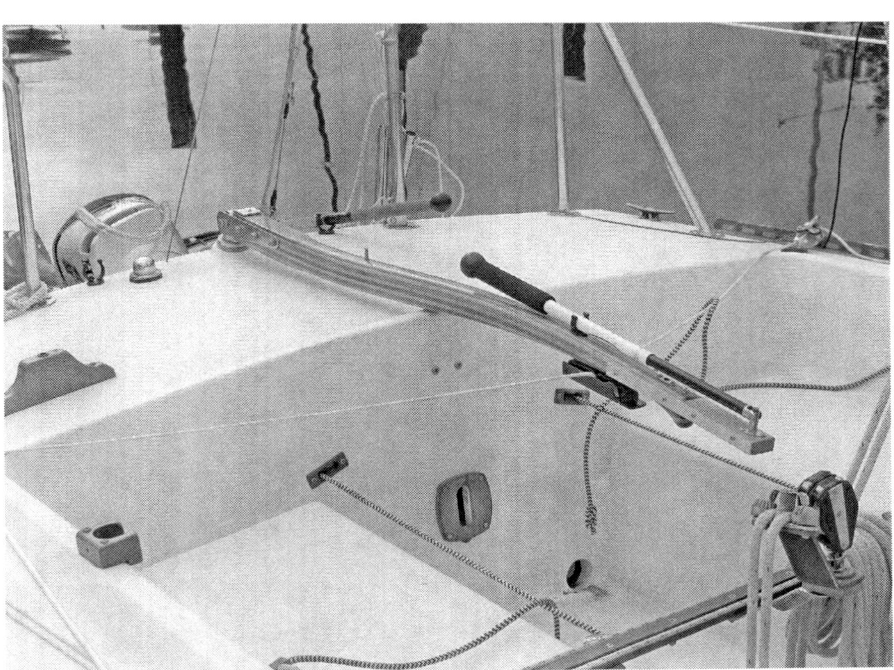

The tiller takes up a lot less space
in the cockpit than a wheel on a steering pedestal.

with the obstruction and don't find it terribly inconvenient to have to move around the steering pedestal, but when we have friends or relatives aboard, traffic jams occur. However, while sailing, it is VERY easy to steer the boat because it steers like a car.

- **Outboard / Inboard** — Most trailerable sailboats with motors are equipped with a small outboard, but others offer the option of an inboard powerplant. As with most things, you'll need to consider the pros and cons of each.

Outboards offer the convenience of easy serviceability, because they hang out there in mid-air, unobstructed by any enclosure. However, because they hang out there unobstructed by any enclosure, they are also prone to being stolen. If you're going to have an outboard motor hanging on the transom or a mounting system, make sure it's thru-bolted with security hardware, or at least be sure the attachment clamps are locked together with a padlock after being thoroughly tightened. Outboards come in 2-stroke and 4-stroke versions, and you must check local laws before making the purchase, because some 2-strokes are falling out of favor because of environmental contamination.

Inboard engines are not likely to be ripped off, because they're tucked away where nobody can easily get to them. But, because they are tucked away where nobody can easily get to them, they're more difficult to service, and a major overhaul requires an enormous amount of work to remove the engine. Changing the oil and filter can be a royal hassle, and heaven help you if the cooling system runs amok. And when you do service the engine, you face the possibility of dripping something the Admiral won't like on the carpet or furniture. Three other problems with inboard engines are heat, noise and fumes that invade the living space.

- **Gas / Diesel**

Diesel engines are generally hardier than their gasoline counterparts. The fuel sometimes costs less than gasoline, and the engines are more efficient (so you go farther on a gallon). As far as safety is concerned, diesel fuel will burn, but doesn't create explosive fumes. And diesel engines create less carbon monoxide, helping reduce the chance of accidental CO poisoning.

On the other hand, diesel engines are noisy and stinky. They also require careful attention to the service schedule, especially in the areas of fuel filtration and oil and filter changes.

Gasoline is the fuel of choice for outboards, because of the scarcity of diesel-powered outboard motors. Yanmar makes one, but it's almost nonexistent in the U.S. market. Gasoline fuel tanks must be vented to the outside (can't be enclosed below deck), and filling the tank is more dangerous because of possible spark-ignited fire or explosion. You have to be extra careful with gasoline.

- **Cockpit** — The size and configuration of your boat's cockpit can make all the difference when it comes to comfort and convenience while either cruising or racing. Racing boats typically have large, open cockpits so the skipper can invite lots of railmeat (human ballast) aboard. Cruising boats often have smaller cockpits, because that arrangement makes room for a bigger cabin. While we give a lot of importance to the cabin, we don't want to shortchange the cockpit. We like to be able to invite friends aboard. It's also nice to be able to lie down and stretch out on the cockpit bench, where we can look at the stars until we fall asleep, or so one can relax while someone else is at the helm.

- **Deck Layout** — The layout of the deck should be convenient and safe to move around. You need an easy method of moving from the cockpit to the cabin roof, with anti-skid tread on all areas where you walk. A toe rail all around the edge of the deck is a real nice benefit when the boat is heeled and you have to be on deck for some reason. The toe rail helps keep your feet from sliding into the deep. Likewise, the boat should be equipped with strong lifelines and stanchions all the way around.

  Examine deck hardware to make sure you have enough cleats in all the right places so you can tie up at the dock conveniently. Ideally, the boat should have fore and aft cleats as well as midship cleats on both sides. Up to a point, larger cleats are better than smaller ones, because they allow you to use larger docklines that will be more secure when the weather is nasty and the boat bucks against its mooring. Remember the bow cleats are also going to be used for tying up to a mooring buoy or for anchoring, so they need to be stout.

- **Sail Handling** — Most trailerable sailboats are sloops, having only one mast, one mainsail and a single headsail. Racers and cruisers are likely to have more than one headsail; the most popular choices being a 100% jib, a 130% to 150% genoa, and perhaps some kind of light-air sail such as a spinnaker.

Traditionalists and racers are more likely than cruisers to forego the use of roller furling for the headsail, preferring instead to hank (clip) on whatever sail they need from a large collection stuffed below decks. Cruisers, however, are more prone to keep the genoa wrapped up on the roller furling system and unroll whatever amount of sail they think is appropriate for the wind conditions.

Rolled-up sails on a furling system are not as efficient as a hanked-on sail. This is because the shape of the furled sail is altered as it is rolled up, so it can no longer present the optimum airfoil to take full advantage of the wind. Racers care about this. Most cruisers don't care much, and would rather lose a bit of efficiency and speed than risk their lives scrambling around on the foredeck trying to remove the old sail and replace it with something else.

In our opinion, a safety concern is at work here. The less a person leaves the cockpit to go forward on deck while underway, the safer it is. The cockpit is a relatively secure place, but a wet and slippery foredeck, while the boat is moving around and riding over waves, is not. And that's why cruisers tend to prefer roller furlers; so they can control the size of the headsail from the comfort and safety of the cockpit. If the wind pipes up suddenly, all you have to do is ease the sheet and draw in the furling line, and the sail rolls up like a window shade. When it's the right size, cleat the control lines and you're done.

• **Livability**—When you're thinking about buying a boat, try to actually spend some time aboard. Go below and imagine yourself living there. Ask yourself a long list of questions. How's the headroom? Does this boat make me claustrophobic? How easy is it to negotiate the companionway steps? Are there things to grab hold of so I can move about safely while under way?

Sit at the dinette and imagine enjoying a meal there, playing games at the table, spreading a chart and nav tools for navigation work. Take a seat on the settee to see how comfortable you feel. Can you easily lie down there to catch a quick nap, or will you have to depend on the bunk areas for sleeping?

Stand at the galley and pretend you're preparing dinner and washing dishes. Is the sink large enough to be useful? Are there handy places to stow utensils, spices, pot holders, hand towels, wash cloths, plates and cups and stuff like that? Figure out where you're going to store the food (especially the cold storage) and how convenient it will be to access when needed. On our boat, we have a large Coleman cooler beneath one of the dinette seats just opposite the galley. I removed the cooler lid hinges from the back and installed them on one end so the cooler opens more conveniently.

Crawl into the bunks — are you able to stretch out and get comfortable? How difficult is it to get in and out of bed?

What about the head ... can you actually maneuver inside? I don't fit comfortably inside our enclosed head, but the important thing is that Becky does. *Guys, you better come to grips with one thing — any feature of the boat that's important to your First Mate needs to be important to you if you want her to enjoy sailing with you.*

Check out all the storage compartments and imagine stowing clothing, food supplies, spare parts for the boat, and miscellaneous gear you're are likely to need on a voyage.

In the end, you have to ask the big question (and not be afraid of the answer): Will this arrangement work day in and day out? If it won't, you have only a few options — keep shopping until you find the perfect boat (hint: it doesn't exist), change your expectations (you cannot expect a boat to be as convenient and comfortable as your home), or give up on the idea of sailing. The last one is a rotten option, and we highly recommend you not give up.

- **Towability** — Your boat must be matched to the capability of your tow vehicle. The nice thing about a trailerable sailboat is you can take it anywhere you want to go ... but only if the tow vehicle is up to the job. If you want a large, heavy boat, you might need to buy a stronger tow vehicle to handle the weight and dimensions of your boat. I'll go into depth about choosing a tow vehicle in another chapter, but keep in mind this is an important (and perhaps expensive) factor in making your boat selection.

After all this research and consideration, you're likely to end up with a list of a few boats that most closely fit your needs. Now talk with owners of the type of boats you're considering and ask for their honest opinions (avoid those who have a For Sale sign on the boat). If possible, try to arrange to crew aboard boats that are on your list of candidates to see how well each boat sails and how easy it is to move around on deck and in the cockpit. This is when you do your homework, but I promise this will be the most enjoyable homework you've ever done, and will help you find a boat you'll be happy with.

Chapter Two
Rigging the Boat

One of the potentially discouraging things about owning a trailerable sailboat (if you keep it on the trailer instead of slipped at a marina, moored or anchored all the time) is the fact that it must be rigged and de-rigged each time you sail. When you're new to the process, this can seem like a lot of work to go through just for the enjoyment of sailing – like having to assemble a bicycle before every ride. Because this factor often keeps boats sitting at home instead of being out on the water, we need to find ways to minimize the hassles of setting up and taking down the rig.

Friends of ours, Jim and Jayne, bought a 26-foot trailerable sailboat and asked if I'd help them learn the ropes—literally. They had never sailed anything bigger than a beach dinghy, and now that they were getting older they wanted to enjoy cruising without all the athleticism required to sail a little boat. But this wasn't the kind of boat you carry on a cartop rack and rig in two minutes. So they needed guidance about getting the vessel on and off the trailer, as well as rigging it up.

When the boat was sold to our friends, the previous owner had prepared it for transport by darn near permanently lashing and taping every linear inch of rigging to the mast. Well, everything held together during transport all right, but when we got to the marina parking lot and started the rigging process, it took us half an hour just to undo the package.

Midway through the process of untying knots, undoing all the lines tightly wrapped around the mast, and stripping tape from lifelines, shrouds, stanchions spreaders and such, Jim asked me if the set-up procedure was always this hard.

"Absolutely not!" I declared. "This is the worst mess I've ever had to work with, and it's all because the prior owner wanted to make it too neat and clean."

The truth of the matter is, if you try and make the rigging look too organized and pretty when the boat's ready for towing, you'll only complicate your life. In order to keep the set-up and take-down easy and efficient, come to grips with the fact that it's okay for the de-rigged boat to have a mess of "spaghetti" on top, as long as it's well secured.

Keep in mind your boat, on its trailer, will not look like the catalog photos, with a sleek mast devoid of rigging. No, your boat will look like it's been overrun by a gang of worms. But that doesn't mean it won't be secure for trailering. Of course you have to tie the worms down so they don't crawl off the boat while you're driving, but to the uninformed they still look like a bunch of disorganized worms. Don't worry too much about how neat it looks; focus on making everything secure (more on this subject in the section on "take down"). We've towed our boat thousands of miles all over the country to distant waters without a single incident of loose rigging or anything flapping to pieces in the wind while we're going down the road.

With our boat, our goal is to simplify the rigging and de-rigging process to the point that we can set up the boat for sailing or put it back on the trailer and prepare for travel in less than an hour. We have friends who own a boat identical to ours who can do the job in less than 20 minutes. The secret lies in keeping the process uncomplicated by using bungee cords instead of knotted ropes to secure most stuff, eliminating bolts and nuts that require the use of tools, and taking an organized approach to the whole process.

Set-Up

Depending upon the type of boat you have, the set-up procedure varies somewhat, and you should follow the manufacturer's recommendations. Still, certain common points apply to every trailer-able sailboat, along with easy ways to simplify the operation.

During the first check before you begin setting up the rigging, your number one priority should be the space immediately above the boat. I've heard stories about people who raised their mast directly into overhead power lines, with electrifying results. But power lines aren't the only concern. Look for tree limbs, a light post, or anything else that will impede raising the mast.

Next, check the path that leads to the launch ramp. If you're setting up the mast in a parking lot, cast your eyes skyward and trace a line all the way from where you're parked to where the boat will enter the water. Look for every conceivable overhead obstruction. Face it, some launch ramps were designed with fishing boats in mind, not sailboats. This is especially true of pristine mountain lakes, where the trout are legendary, but a sail has never been seen. Under those circumstances, you may have to launch the boat with the mast down and then raise it after you're on the water. This is more easily done if you use mast-raising equipment (a gin pole).

While we're on the subject of checking the path between the parking lot and the launch ramp, I should tell about the fellow who did everything right — almost. Before raising the mast, I watched him look overhead. He even studied the most direct path between his parking spot and the ramp with sufficient care. Assured all was well, he went ahead and raised the mast. When everything was ready to go, he hopped back in his truck and — I kid you not — rather than backing down the ramp, he drove forward and did a loop around the whole parking lot to line up with the ramp. I can only guess he did this because he wasn't confident of his ability to back the trailer from the angled parking slot. Well, as he toured the lot, he clipped several trees and nearly hung his spreaders on a lamp post. My advice — don't do that.

All of this leads to my next point. When you arrive at the boat launch area, scope it out and choose a user-friendly place to park that will make life easy during the set-up and launch process. Here are the ideals:

- Pick a place where you can back down the ramp when the boat is ready, without any other driving around to get into position.

- Pick a level place, because setting up a mast on a slope (especially a sideways slope) is more difficult and more dangerous.

- Pick a spot protected from the wind (especially a crosswind) if possible, because wind may complicate raising a mast.

After you park, unplug the trailer harness from the tow vehicle to keep the trailer's electrical components from receiving power while submerged during the launch/retrieve process.

Once you're confident it's safe to raise the mast and the path you'll take to the ramp is clear overhead, begin releasing all the bungee cords or ropes or whatever you use to secure the rigging while towing. We prefer loop bungees with a plastic ball in one part of the loop, because they're easy to stretch around the mast to hold the collected shrouds and halyards. We place a bungee about every eight feet along the length of the mast, securing whatever needs tying down. It's fast, easy and we've never had a problem with this system. Becky and I have a little drawstring stuff bag we use for keeping the bungees organized when not in use.

Now, before doing anything else, take a final look at everything that is attached to the mast, and ask yourself: "Am I ready to raise the mast?" I can't tell you the number of times I've put the mast all the way up, then realized I had to bring it back down to do something. I may have to straighten an upper shroud that somehow managed to get out of position, attach the Windex that had been removed so it wouldn't get damaged during the long overland trip, remove the red warning flag tied to the masthead while towing, etc. I guarantee it isn't a matter of "if" but "when" you'll make the same mistakes. Take my word for it, spending a few minutes to study the situation first will save time and effort later on.

Before the mast goes up, do a complete rig inspection, looking for signs of wear or damage to everything from the chainplates to the top of the mast. Yes, it's better to do the inspection when you take the rig down, so you can correct any problems before your next sailing adventure. But it's also a good idea to conduct an inspection before setting out. This is similar to the flight check pilots give their planes before every flight. Look for cracks, corrosion, bends, pin wear, deformed ring dings, frayed wires, oblong chainplate holes that were once round, and every other form of abnormality. If anything looks suspicious, don't go sailing until you correct every problem. It would be heartbreaking to motor back to the ramp with parts of a mast strapped to the deck, damage to the boat, and possible injuries to the crew from a failed rig.

Closely inspect the spreaders and their attachment hardware. Trailerable sailboats typically have spreaders that either fold out of the way during towing or fit into socket-type brackets. Look for signs of bending, cracking or wear at the point where the spreaders contact the brackets. I know from personal experience that if a spreader fails to do its job properly, you can lose the portion of the mast above the lower shrouds. It's not a pretty sight when half a mast falls in the cockpit.

Now you're ready to begin the rigging process. Your boat may be quite different than ours, so for the rest of the set-up operation you'll have to follow the specific instructions in your owner's manual. But here are a few pointers to remember:

Our boat is equipped with a CDI Flexible Furler for the headsails, and I don't like to let the business end of that expensive piece of equipment drag on the ground while we shift the mast into position and raise it. So, I tie a line to the furler drum and suspend it loosely from the lifeline so it can hang over the side of the boat but not quite reach the ground.

Keep a close eye on the shrouds, backstay, etc. as the mast is going up, to ensure those cables don't snag something and hang up the whole process — a backstay that loops itself under the rudder, for example.

If you note unexpected resistance while the mast is going up, stop and figure out what's happening. Don't just push or pull harder. If the stoppage is because of a tangled shroud or stay and it suddenly releases while you're grunting and shoving, you may find yourself going overboard, losing your grip on the mast, or encountering something else to cause equipment damage and bodily injury.

With our MacGregor, we use a mast-raising system that allows one person to easily raise or lower the mast. The system utilizes a pole extending forward from the base of the mast, a line led through a pair of pulleys (one of which is connected to the foredeck and the other to the outermost end of the pole), and the jib halyard connected near the top of the mast. A long line runs to the cockpit, where we use the winch and cleat to control tension as we slowly raise or lower the mast. At any point, even with the mast at a severe angle, we can cleat the line and walk around on deck to straighten out shrouds, etc. When the mast is fully down, the upper portion rests on a crutch for travel. The foot of the mast is moved forward and is connected to the bow pulpit.

One key to quick and easy set-up is to eliminate tools from the process. Our boat had at least half a dozen bolts and nuts that needed to be removed, and some of them had to be shifted to a new location after the mast went up. To make matters worse, we were dealing with two different sizes of bolts, so we had to carry a total of 4 wrenches so we'd have one for each end of two different-sized bolts. That was crazy! To solve the problem, I bought new stainless steel bolts with long enough unthreaded shanks so I could cut off the treaded portion, grind a bullet-nose shape on the cut-off end, and drill a small hole through the shank about half an inch from the end for the use of a spring clip. Now, all we do is remove the spring clip and slide out the bolt. No more fumbling with tools.

And finally, organize the tasks involved in raising the mast so everyone knows exactly what to do first, second and so on. Analyze

One person alone can raise the mast if he or she uses the mast raising equipment offered by many sailboat manufacturers. Here, the mast is being raised by the owner of a Catalina 25, using a two-legged "gin pole" device and the trailer's winch strap to pull the mast up.

the process in minute detail, then set about eliminating uncalled-for steps. Organize all the necessary steps to avoid backtracking. You want to be able to board the boat, walk from one end to the other taking care of business along the way, and then be ready to raise the mast without having to run back and forth to do forgotten tasks. If you have to get up and down, on and off the boat repeatedly, you not only track a lot of dirt onto the deck, but you waste time and energy.

With the rig up, grab your binoculars and study the mast-top rigging connections, just to satisfy yourself nothing got twisted or out of place. From the cabin top, reach out and grab the shrouds and give them a tug to see if they feel properly tensioned. Check the headstay and backstay as well. Now, lie down with your head at the base of the mast and look up the mainsail slot, to see if the mast is straight on a side-to-side axis. All this might seem like a lot of needless work, but it only takes a couple of minutes to verify everything is in order.

Our headsail is on a roller furler, so when the headstay is connected, our headsail is already installed, and we run the jib sheets to the cockpit, take a turn around a winch and cleat them. Next comes the boom installation. We replaced the gooseneck bolt and nut with my modified bolt and spring clip to make this part easier. Our boat didn't come from the factory with a topping lift, so I installed one to support the aft end of the boom, and I make that connection next. We leave the mainsheet attached to the boom while it's stored during road travel. I use the tail of the coil-wrapped mainsheet to tie the aft end of the boom off to one side to a lifeline stanchion, so the boom cannot swing back and forth across the cockpit, possibly causing an injury. We normally leave the mainsail on the boom, tied down and protected by a mainsail cover, so when the boom goes on, the foot of the mainsail is already attached. All we do is slide the sail slugs up the mast slot, follow with a stopper to keep the slugs from escaping at the bottom when the sail is lowered, and attach the tack pin.

Finally, we launch the boat and we're almost ready to go sailing. We'll talk about the actual launch sequence later.

Take-Down

Taking the rig down and preparing the boat for travel on the trailer is mostly a reverse order of the set-up procedure, but several things will help you to avoid problems and make the process easier. The simplicity of your next set-up depends upon the methods you use to prepare the rig for highway travel.

At all times when you're working on the deck, be careful about where you place your hands and feet. Fingers in the wrong place at the wrong time can get pinched off, or at least badly damaged, when something moves. Wear deck shoes. Don't kid yourself into thinking bare feet offer better traction than a pair of siped deck shoes—they don't, especially when the deck is wet. And shoes also protect against injury when you stub a toe against the sharp end of a genoa track, or crack your foot into the anchor locker latch. Going barefoot is the best way to spill blood on the deck and lose your balance when you step on something painful. A trip can send you over the side and onto the unforgiving tarmac. On our trailered boat, my head is about 13 feet above the pavement when I'm working on deck, and that's a long way down.

One thing that helps ensure safety is to clear the deck of every unnecessary thing. Remove the boom and mainsail. If you have roller furling, release the headsail sheets and coil-wrap them into a bundle you then tie to a mid-point around the furled headsail. If you don't have a headsail cover, this will keep the sail from unfurling and will get the sheets out of the way. Stow the winch handles, so they won't snag your pants cuff and trip you. Put away the fenders and docklines. Don't leave anything extra on the deck. It's bad enough having to pick your way through the snarl of shrouds and halyards — you don't need somebody's coffee cup or ball cap adding to the obstacle course.

Be especially cautious while lowering the mast, because this is a heavy and unwieldy object that can cause a lot of brain damage if it knocks you on the noggin. Though it takes more time and may seem like a nuisance, using a gin pole (mast raising equipment) to lower the mast is well worth the effort. If your boat permits its use, this piece of gear turns a two-person job into a singlehanded task, and reduces the chance of having a mast-lowering-related accident.

I happened to see a spectacular example of a mast-lowering accident not long ago. The boat owner was in the process of lowering the mast without the aid of a gin pole, when he lost his footing and fell from the cabin top into the cockpit. The distance wasn't far, but on his way down he managed to bang into the steering pedestal and then ricochet off the cockpit seat before hitting the sole. Besides the damage to himself, the mast didn't fare well either — a ding and a gouge.

Because we have roller furling, we take a minute to loosely suspend the end of the furler off the ground, using a lightweight rope that is tied to the lifeline. This keeps the equipment from banging around on the ground while the mast comes down and is being shifted into its travel position.

Depending upon the kind of boat you have, the spreaders might come in contact with the lifelines when the mast is lowered into travel position. Folding spreaders collapse against the mast, where they can be bungeed in place. Our boat, on the other hand, has rigid spreaders that overlap the lifelines on both sides of the boat when the mast is down, so we had to make some accommodations. We installed a keypin locking halyard shackle at one end of each cabintop lifeline, so we can easily release the tension on the lifeline and allow it to droop out of the way of the spreaders.

Okay, the mast is down, resting nicely on its crutch, and secured fore and aft. Now what you have is a mess of cables and ropes on deck. All this stuff needs to be casually organized and tied down in a simple but secure manner. We coil each rope, then take a couple wraps around the middle with the tail of the rope to divide the coil in two, then run the tail through the upper section and tie everything into a nice bundle. Then we take a bungee, run it through the upper half of this wrapped coil and secure it to the mast. That takes care of all the ropes.

Then we turn our attention to the shrouds and stays. The backstay gets coiled and bungeed to the mast. The forestay is part

While towing the boat with the rig down, a mast crutch is used to support the aft end of the mast. Be sure to secure the mast to the crutch so it can't bounce out while traveling.

It takes only minutes to transform a trailerable sailboat from
towing mode to sailing mode. One person can do the job in
half an hour, after becoming familiar with the procedure.

of the furler system. With the fractional rig of our boat, the furler
drum would extend several feet ahead of the bow if we lashed
everything in a straight line along the mast. So, for the upper half
of the furler's length it's bungeed to the mast, then the lower
portion takes a big, lazy loop that lays across the bow from one
side of the boat to the other. The furler drum is bungeed to the
base of one stanchion, and the rest of the loop is secured to the
opposite stanchion and to the mast where the loop crosses the
boat's centerline. Upper and lower shrouds are brought together
and looped the best we can, then bungeed to the mast.

That's about all there is to it. Everything is secure, even if it
isn't pretty. But the best part is, our rigging will be quick and easy
to prepare for set-up the next time we go sailing.

Chapter Three
Up and Down the Ramp

Sometimes, I hear sailing stories that leave me shaking my head in semi-disbelief. It's only "semi" because after all the stories I've heard and all the crazy things I've done myself, almost nothing surprises me anymore. But recently I heard a new one that brought back the old wide-eyed, jaw-dropping head shake.

This happened to a fellow I know who owns a trailerable sailboat. He and his son decided to launch the boat at a spectacular lake. After securing the boat for travel, they drove half a day to the lake. Then they backed the trailer down into the water. That's when my friend noticed that the boat was floating a little lower than normal. A quick inspection revealed the trailer was floating at the same level, which, of course, was much higher than boat trailers are supposed to float. The reason – Dad forgot to release the tie-downs, and the boat was floating the trailer.

We can laugh, but some of us might want to take inventory of our own sailing escapades before we guffaw too vigorously. There's hardly a sailor I know who hasn't done something equally goofy.

Launching

Having successfully rigged the boat, you'll need to check a few additional items. We begin with the rudders. Ours are retractable, and we use stainless steel pegs to secure them in the "up" position for travel, so they can't accidentally unretract and drag on the pavement. When preparing to launch, we must remove the pins so the rudders can be lowered into the water.

If your boat is water ballasted, make sure the valves are closed so water doesn't fill the ballast tank before you're ready. Filling the ballast tank should be a well-supervised process, so you can stop when necessary. The little head start you gain by allowing the ballast tank to fill while launching the boat is NOT (trust me, I speak from personal experience) worth it.

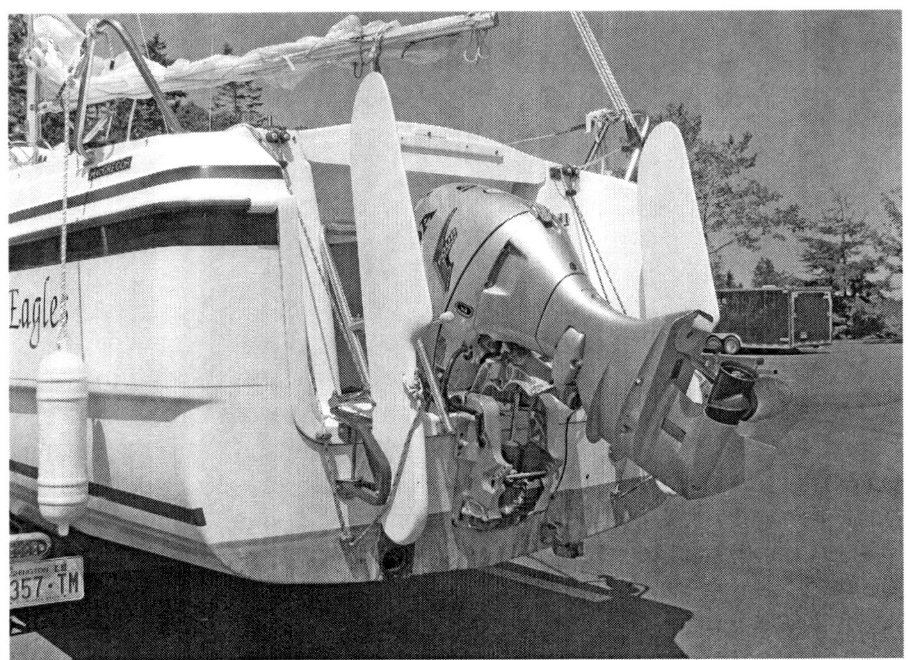

Before moving the boat up or down the ramp, and before towing, raise or remove the rudder(s), and raise the outboard motor to avoid damage from contact with the ground.

Check the motor oil level one last time (call me paranoid). As soon as we pull into the parking lot to begin the rigging process, I lower the motor from its travel position so the oil can settle into the crankcase. I check the oil level after it has had time to settle enough to give myself a true reading on the dipstick. After checking the oil, I raise the motor again, so it doesn't drag on the ground while backing down the launch ramp.

If everything looks good, we make one final walk-around inspection and then Becky walks to the ramp while I climb into the truck. She positions herself so I can always see her in the sideview mirror, and she warns me with hand signals if she sees a problem. I double check for any traffic that sneaked in behind me while I wasn't looking, then begin backing the boat into the ramp lane.

Just a word or two about launch ramps that don't offer the benefit of a floating dock — we've tried 'em, and we learned some hard lessons. Yes, you can launch where there's nothing to tie the boat to, but it's a royal pain ... especially if there's any wind at all. Even a small breeze can blow your boat sideways onto the rocks (or whatever) next to the ramp. And there's nothing like the sound of gelcoat on granite to ruin your day. So, if at all possible, use ramps with some kind of dock where you can secure the boat while you park the truck.

Carefully position the boat trailer next to the dock so you'll be able to reach it to grab the docklines as the boat floats off the trailer.

As you back down the ramp, try to maneuver the trailer close enough to the dock so you can easily reach the bow and stern docklines. Whether you're doing this alone, or have an assistant, somebody will have to reach across to grab the docklines. Position things so that's possible.

As the trailer descends into the water (remember to release the stern tie-downs), the boat will start to float. Stop backing up as soon as the boat begins to float, so you can release the bow winch strap. If you don't stop before the whole boat starts floating freely, the angle of the bow to the bump stop that secures the bow can cause the strap to become tight. Release the winch strap, at least a little. If you have an assistant to take the docklines, you can completely undo the strap and let the boat float free.

When the boat is able to float free of the trailer, walk out on the trailer tongue so you can reach to disconnect the bow strap holding the boat to the trailer.

By attaching lines to both the bow and stern cleats, one person can easily control the boat and move it along the dock.

When the boat floats freely off the trailer, drive forward to pull the trailer out from under the boat. Do this carefully, watching the mirrors constantly for hang-ups. If you see your assistant waving and screaming, stop and see if she's just swatting and cussing the mosquitoes, or there's a problem.

Assuming no issues arise, drive to the parking area (if you're sailing in freshwater) or to the trailer wash-down area and rinse the saltwater off the trailer and the rear of the truck. Even if the truck doesn't get wet during the launch process, saltwater has a magic way of migrating to vulnerable metal and having lunch. Rinse everything thoroughly, if you sail in saltwater.

Hey, congratulations, you're launched!

Retrieving

After your sailing adventure, you'll go through the launching process in reverse. This is what we call the retrieval phase.

Before you take the boat out of the water on the trailer, look up to make sure there will be no conflicts between mast and any overhead obstructions. I know, I know, you already did that when you launched the boat and things shouldn't have changed much (if at all) by the time you pull the boat out of the water. But it's good practice to study every aspect of the launch/retrieve process each time, so go ahead and look up anyway. After all, while you've been away on a leisurely week-long cruise, the marina management might have had a new light pole installed, or run some power wires across the parking lot. You just never know, unless you look up and study the situation.

Plan ahead, so you don't have to drive around looking for a place to park after coming up the ramp. Figure out your parking place in advance and, if necessary, station someone there to hold your space while you go retrieve the boat.

Now you're ready to do whatever you have to do to get the boat out of the water. Some boats are easier to launch and retrieve than others, and you'll have to follow the recommendations of the boat manufacturer to get the job done. This might involve the use of an extended trailer tongue or other methods of getting the trailer down in the water far enough to get the boat on.

I recently helped a fellow launch a fixed-keel sailboat that required us to completely disconnect the trailer from the truck, then ease the trailer down the ramp by using a winch. Not easy. Regardless of what it takes to launch and retrieve your boat, be careful during this stage. Accidents happen. I saw one unfortunate sailor inadvertently submerge his truck while trying to retrieve his boat. Have I mentioned four-wheel-drive is a nice thing to have on a slick ramp? And so is an intimate understanding of the launch/retrieve process.

So there you are on the ramp with the boat in position, and you're ready to haul everything from the water. One last thing—make sure the boat is sitting on the trailer properly. If, in haste, you manage to get the boat a little off kilter on the trailer, damage can be done to either the hull or the trailer. Not only that, but the boat might shift later on, trying to find its correct position, resulting in an accident. Imagine you're up on deck with the weight of a lowering mast in your hands when, all of a sudden, the boat shifts and you lose your footing.

If yours is a water-ballasted boat, open the drain as soon as you start up the ramp. Water weighs about 8.5 pounds per gallon, so it doesn't take much to place a huge burden on the trailer. You want to get rid of all that weight as soon as possible after the boat comes out of the water. If there's no rush to allow others to use the ramp, let the ballast tank drain completely before driving onto the parking area. This will keep the ground around your boat dry and help prevent a mess as you climb up and down on the boat during the de-rigging process.

If your boat is water-ballasted, at the end of the voyage, pull the boat up the ramp just far enough to allow you to drain the water. Don't drain the water on the main parking area, because that creates a mess for everybody else.

After the mast has been lowered and secured, and all the shrouds, stays and lines are organized, it's important to tie boat to trailer at the stern end. I made the mistake once of neglecting to use tie-downs to lash the boat and trailer together, because I was only pulling the boat a couple of miles from the ramp to our house. When I ran into a holiday traffic jam, I decided to cut through a parking lot to a side street to skirt the traffic pile-up. Unfortunately, there was a speed bump across the driveway. Even more unfortunately, I didn't come to a complete stop and ease the trailer over the bump. Even though I moved at a crawl, when the trailer tires hit that bump, the aft end of the boat left the trailer by several inches before crashing back onto the bunks. I watched the horror show in the sideview mirror and cringed as the hull slammed down hard. By the time I realized what was happening, it was already too late. Trust me, it's worth the few minutes it takes to use a set of stout tie-downs to keep the boat tight to the trailer. If your boat doesn't have tie-down eyes bolted to the transom (as ours does not), loop the straps from the trailer around the stern rail and back to the trailer — or run the strap all the way across the cockpit, lashing it to the rear of the trailer on both sides.

Now you're almost ready to go. Plug in the trailer light pigtail to the mating attachment on the tow vehicle, and check the trailer lights for proper operation. Walk around to make sure the clearance lights and tail/stop lights work, and look at everything else about the boat and trailer to make sure everything is secure and ready for travel. Kick the tires, or better yet check them with a tire pressure gauge. The point is to make sure the tires are equally pressurized. Make sure the rudder(s) and outboard motor are secured in the up position, so nothing will drag on the ground. Look it all over carefully.

If possible, rinse boat and trailer with freshwater before heading home. Marinas often have trailer wash-down areas, but primitive launch areas do not. Rinsing is not so critical for boats used on freshwater, but saltwater will quickly start to eat away at metal parts, so it is important to wash the boat and trailer at your earliest opportunity. Occasionally, we run our boat and trailer into a do-it-yourself car wash booth and use the high-pressure wand to give it a thorough cleaning.

A boat used on saltwater needs to have the motor flushed as soon as possible. Flushing with freshwater is a good precaution. Follow the manufacturer's recommendations, of course. For an even more thorough salt removal, we use a product called Salt Away (available at West Marine stores or through their catalog). This is a dedicated salt removal soap fed into the motor's cooling system through a special reservoir that holds a few ounces of the liquid and introduces it into the stream of water flowing through the "earmuff" device normally used for flushing the motor. If the launch area has a wash-down hose, you can flush the motor in just a few extra minutes, so the salt doesn't have time to crystallize inside the cooling system. If not, do this at your earliest opportunity. The motor will love you for it.

Now you're ready to travel.

To preserve the life of your outboard motor, flush it with fresh water after sailing in saltwater. To really get rid of the salt encrustations, use Salt Away and the special attachment to the flushing earmuffs.

Chapter Four
Boat Handling and Sail Trim

I remember waking up one night, about a month before we bought our boat, with a nagging doubt nibbling a tunnel through my brain. Even though I had read everything I could get my hands on about how to handle a sailboat, I had never actually placed my hands on a helm. And in my semi-conscious state, with thoughts wandering shadowy paths of logic (or not), I couldn't for the life of me answer the chicken/egg question: what comes first when tacking and jibing — turning the helm or moving the sails across to the other side and then turning the boat? My head was full of questions like that, when sailing was still a mystery to be solved.

The magic of getting a sailboat to go in any desired direction, using only the power of the wind, is what makes sailing such an enchanting way to travel. Quietly propelled by an invisible force, you move across the globe in silent grace ... but only if you know what you're doing. If you don't know what you're doing, it can be anything but quiet and graceful. So let's get down to the practical aspects of controlling a sailboat.

How Sails Work

In the simplest terms, a sail traveling into the wind works on the same principles as an airplane wing. The curved shape of the sail forces passing air to take a longer path around the leading edge — the same as air passing over the curved upper surface of a wing must travel farther than the air passing beneath the wing. When that happens, a lifting force is created on the side where the air travels farthest. Airplane wings are actually lifted from above, while sails are lifted from in front. So, in essence, a sailboat traveling into the wind is pulled along, rather than pushed. When a sailboat is traveling in the same direction as the wind, however, the sails act like barn doors, catching the wind from behind, and the boat is pushed by the wind.

You won't always be sailing in the same relative direction with respect to the wind. You must understand how to trim the sails by moving them in or out from the centerline of the boat and making a few other adjustments to keep the shape of the sails working most efficiently. I should warn you that sail trim is a complete art/science/religion, and there are sailors who nearly go into convulsions when sails are not trimmed to perfection. Remember, we're cruisers. So put away the blood pressure pills and enjoy the ride.

Anatomy of a Sail

Modern sails are triangular. The top is called the head, which is just logical enough to make it easy to remember. The head of the sail is attached to a halyard; a line used to hoist the sail up the mast or up the headstay (also called a forestay), in the case of a jib, genoa or spinnaker.

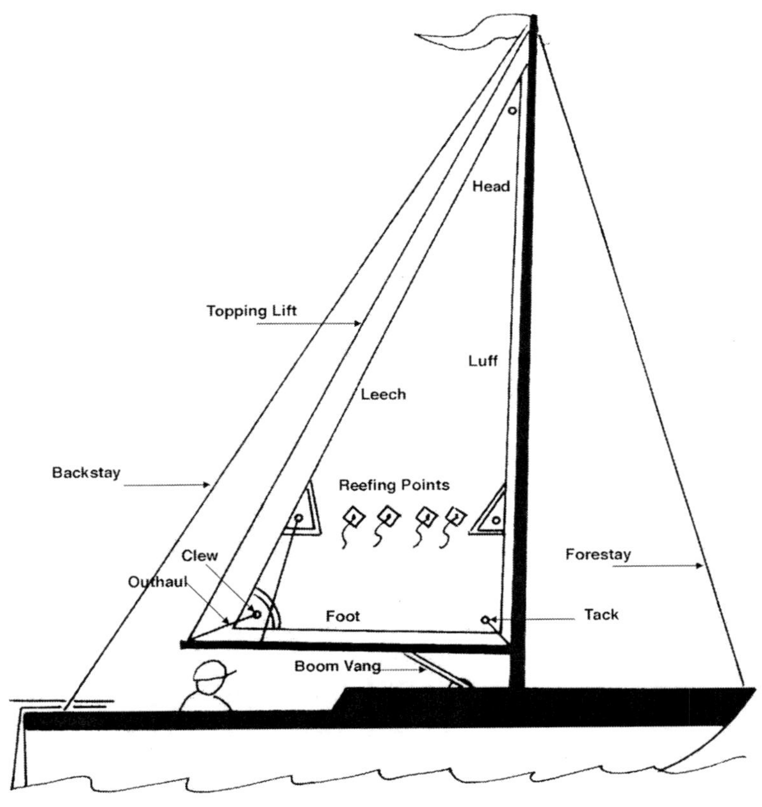

The official names of the parts of a mainsail.

The portion of the sail that runs more or less horizontally across the bottom is called the foot. Most often, the foot of a mainsail is attached to the boom by way of a boltrope inserted in a slot in the upper edge of the boom, or by sail slugs (plastic slides) that go in the slot. Or a mainsail might be totally unattached to the boom along its length (this is called loose footed) and attached only at the aft point of the triangle, which is called the clew. I don't have a clue why it's called that. Of course, the foot of the sail is also attached at the forward point of the triangle, called the tack. Think of the tack as the point where the sail is tacked solidly in one place, either to the lower section of the mast or to the bow of the boat. The tack of the sail doesn't move, but the clew swings back and forth across the boat when trimming the sails.

The forward edge of the sail is called the luff, and the rearward edge is called the leech. I give you these names only because they'll help you picture what's happening to different parts of the sail as I describe how to trim the sails for best performance. The luff, for example, does something called luffing (fluttering or "breathing") when the sail is not properly trimmed.

These parts of the sail are the same for the mainsail and whatever fore sails (also called headsails) you might be using. There's always a head, a tack and a clew; always a foot, a luff and a leech.

Sails are controlled by their sheet—a line attached to the clew of the headsail or the mainsail boom. Easing the sheets allows the sails to move farther out away from the boat's centerline, while tightening the sheets pulls the sails back toward the centerline.

Two other controls on the mainsail are the outhaul and the Cunningham (not all boats have a Cunningham). These lines are used to control how flat the sail is—The Cunningham pulls down on the mainsail luff to add tension and flatten the luff, and the outhaul pulls back on the sail foot to tighten and flatten the sail. The flatter the sail is, the more depowered it is. This is important when the wind pipes up and you want to depower the sail to reduce heel. Some boats also have adjustable backstays that can be tensioned to bend the upper section of the mast backward while moving the midportion of the mast forward to flatten the upper two-thirds of the mainsail. These techniques are part of trimming the sails, but if your boat doesn't feature all of this equipment, don't worry. We'll just deal with the basics here. If you want to delve into the dark arts of sail trim, a whole collection of books will take you into that mystical universe.

Sailing Into the Wind

Each boat has its own characteristics when it comes to sailing into the wind. Some do it well, while others are only mediocre. Racing boats can sail closer to the wind (meaning closer to the direction from which the wind is blowing) than most cruising boats. Makes sense, because racers are in a hurry and don't want to have to tack back and forth (we'll get into this in a minute) any more than necessary to make progress toward a windward destination. No boat can sail directly into the wind. You're doing well if you can sail within 40 degrees of the wind in a cruising boat, but you'll pick up a little speed and the boat will stand up better if you steer a few degrees off the tightest possible angle.

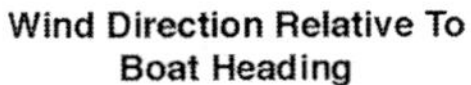

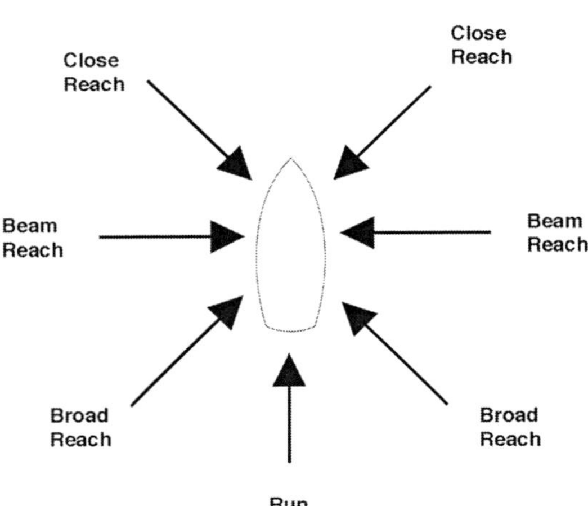

Depending on which direction the wind is approaching the boat,
you will either be on a close reach (also called a beat),
a beam reach, a broad reach or a run.

Sailing as close to the wind as possible is referred to as beating to windward. Depending on wind strength it can be a beat indeed, with the boat heeled to the maximum and water spraying over the bow. The rigging is taut and the boat is under high stress. You might notice the windward rigging is tight as a bar, while the leeward rigging is loose. That tells you just how much strain is on the rigging. Avoid over stressing the boat, or things will break. Important things like the mast. To help reduce stress (on the boat and everyone aboard), reef the main and furl the headsail or replace it with a smaller jib. We'll discuss reefing and furling a little later in this chapter.

When beating to windward, the sails must be trimmed more toward the centerline of the boat, or else the sails will luff and lose power. By observing the sails, you can tell if they are trimmed properly. If the sails are eased out too far, they will begin to luff. As you trim them in, the luffing will diminish and eventually stop, and the sail will become firm. That's where you want to be — just barely into the firm, after the luffing stops. If you trim the sails too tight, you'll lose power, because the airflow won't be creating maximum lift. Ease the sheet to the point where luffing just begins, and then trim in again until it stops. That's the sweet spot.

Turning slightly away from a beat, the boat is on a close reach. The sail trim is eased a little bit farther from the centerline, and you watch the mainsail as you trim it out, looking for the point where it begins to luff, then you trim it back in slightly until the sail is firm. When you trim one sail (the main, for example) you need to match it by trimming the headsail. A significant amount of the performance is created by the slot that forms between the leech of the headsail and the body of the mainsail. If you ease the main and keep the jib in tight, turbulence created by an improper slot between the two sails can cause the airflow to disrupt the mainsail's shape.

High up along the leech of the mainsail there should be a couple of telltales — bits of ribbon that stream backward or get tossed by turbulence as the wind flows off the sail. As you make trim adjustments, watch the telltales and when they stream straight back you've got it in the groove. If they're being tossed by turbulence, the sail is not trimmed properly. The jib or genoa should also have telltales, but they are down low and positioned close to the luff. These telltales indicate smooth or turbulent wind flow across the headsail, and help you determine how to trim for best performance.

Sailing into the wind creates forward lift, and this causes the boat to heel more than on other points of sail. If you are not comfortable with the boat heeling a lot, ease the sails out and turn away from the wind a little bit. That will bring the boat back up on her feet and calm things down.

Sailing Across The Wind

On every point of sail, your ability to make progress is determined by the angle of the sails to the wind. So this leaves you with a choice — you can either trim the sails and maintain course, or you can change course until the wind is playing over the sails exactly right. If you're just out having fun on the lake or the bay, with no destination in mind, go ahead and alter course to keep the sails happy. But if you are trying to reach a particular destination, you must maintain course and trim the sails until they are working properly to carry you to the target.

As you turn to sail across the wind, ease the sails out gradually to maintain the right sail shape and present the sail in the best relationship to the direction of the wind. On a beam reach (with the wind coming directly from the side), the boom should be eased out about midway from the boat's centerline. You'll know if you ease the sails too far, because they'll start to luff. If they do so, trim them back in a ways until they are taut again.

On a beam reach, the boat will move well, but it won't seem as fast because it won't be heeled on its ear, and there won't be spray flying back from the bow. The excitement level is a lot lower, but that's perfectly fine for many cruisers.

Turning farther away from the wind, you end up on what's called a broad reach. At this angle, you're sailing with the wind, but not directly downwind. The boat moves along nicely and there is little if any heel. To trim for this angle of sail, ease the boom out farther, and match the headsail trim. On a broad reach, it might become difficult to keep the headsail fully inflated, because it can be blanketed by the mainsail. You're starting to get into barn door country. The wind coming from behind the boat hits the mainsail first, which can create a wind shadow that steals the air from the headsail. The jib or genoa starts to breathe, falls limp, and then inflates again. If you want to keep both sails fully operational, at some point, you might need to alter your course in relation to the wind, steering a bit back toward a beam reach to keep the headsail happy. It can be tedious. The alternative is to furl the headsail and run under main alone.

Sailing Downwind

With the wind coming from directly behind the boat and the sails eased out as far as they can go, you are on the most dangerous point of sail — for a couple of reasons. This might seem odd, because the boat is standing straight up with no heel and everything seems quiet. In fact, it feels like there's no wind at all. That's because you're running with the wind. Let's take a look at some numbers. If a 12-knot wind is blowing, and you're running downwind and making 7 knots, it feels like there's barely a 5-knot breeze — hardly enough to ruffle your hair. Pay close attention; you might be sailing in a lot more wind than you realize. This can fool you, because everything seems calm.

We got trapped in this situation once as we sailed south in Puget Sound with the wind dead astern. With a big smile on my face, I kept looking up at the mainsail and jib, both appearing full and happy. The water flowed by at a good clip, but the sound of the wind was only a whisper. Then I looked down at the GPS and gasped. We were doing 11 knots. My heart came into my throat, because I suddenly knew we had a lot more wind behind us than I'd imagined — probably more than 20 knots.

Sailing at 11 knots in our little boat is like taking the family sedan on the Indy 500, and I knew we were in trouble. The problem was, at some point, I would have to reduce sail, and although I could furl the headsail (which would help), it's dang near impossible to lower the main while running downwind. I desperately needed to reef the main, but I couldn't just release the halyard to lower the sail, because the wind pressure would pin the sail against the shrouds and keep the main up anyway.

This wouldn't have been so bad — we could have kept running with the wind until I steered us around the back side of a point of land and lost the wind. But as I looked up, I saw a ferry crossing our path about a mile ahead, and we were on a collision course. We needed to bring the boat about and reduce sail, but the waves were big, steep and close together. Between the wind and waves pressing us so hard from behind, I knew we would broach (a special form of capsize) if I tried to turn us around.

I had no good solution. I should have reduced sail twenty minutes earlier, before the wind and waves built to this level, but whining now wouldn't accomplish anything. I felt we were trapped on a runaway train, with only a matter of time until it flew off the track.

I'll tell you how this story turns out when we discuss the art of reefing, in a few minutes. But remember I said this is the most dangerous point of sail for a couple of reasons. In addition to the danger of being unable to lower sails, when you're running with the wind you have the boom eased all the way out, so the barn door is as big as you can possibly make it. The hazard is, if the wind shifts even a little bit, the mainsail can get backwinded, and the boom flies across the boat like a pterodactyl with its tail on fire. This is an accidental jibe. People are killed by this kind of accident every year, as the boom literally bashes their brains in.

I'm never more nervous than when we're running dead downwind, and I never take my eyes off the mainsheet (the control line you use to trim the boom in or out). If I see even a hint of slack in the mainsheet, I immediately steer the boat to keep wind pressure coming from the side of the boat opposite the direction of the boom. In essence, I turn toward a broad reach, so I know the main isn't going to get backwinded. At the same time, my hand goes to the mainsheet, so I can physically restrain the boom if it does come flying across.

Some sailors use a piece of equipment, called a preventer to keep the boom from shifting from one side of the boat to the other if the main gets backwinded. There are a couple different designs, the simplest being a block and tackle arrangement with one end that attaches to the boom and the other end to a stanchion base somewhere forward of the mast. They work, but they're no substitute for a person at the helm being totally aware of what's happening with the wind and sea conditions. The skipper has a responsibility to be competent to avoid an accidental jibe.

Okay, with all the warnings issued, if you do it right, sailing downwind can be a pure joy. One way to reduce the risk is to drop the mainsail altogether and secure the boom in the center with the mainsheet. Run under jib or genoa alone, or raise a colorful asymmetric spinnaker that doesn't require the complexity of a spinnaker pole. Then sit back and steer the boat to keep the headsail full. The problem of leaving the main up (aside from the danger of an accidental jibe) is that it will blanket the headsail anyway, unless you're running wing and wing.

Wing and wing is when you have the mainsail flying on one side of the boat and the headsail on the other. This is nice to see, but tedious to maintain, because it requires an absolutely constant heading, dead downwind. If the wind shifts to one side or the other by even a few degrees, one of the sails will shift sides, and you definitely don't want it to be the main. So you're constantly tweaking the steering to keep the wind perfectly behind the boat. When we sail wing and wing, I find myself literally holding my breath as we walk this tightrope.

One way to make it easier to sail wing and wing is to use a whisker pole to hold the headsail out to one side, then point the boat so the wind comes from an angle slightly to one side of being dead downwind. This will keep the mainsail relatively safe and keep the jib full at the same time. But you can never fully relax your vigilance to prevent a backwinded main. The risk is just too high.

Tacking

When sailing toward the wind, the wind comes across one side or the other of the bow (because you can't sail directly into the wind). If you alter course enough to cause the wind to come across the opposite side of the bow, that's called tacking. The boom shifts across to the other side, and the headsail does likewise. Depending on how close to the wind you've been sailing, the boom may be close to the centerline of the boat, or may be eased out a ways. This is important, because when the boom shifts across from one side to the other, there's is risk of someone getting brained.

Tacking might take you from one angle to the wind to an identical angle to the wind on the opposite side. In that case, you don't need to mess with the mainsheet, other than to manage the boom as it comes across and the sail settles into pulling the boat forward on the opposite tack.

The headsail, however, is another story. The sheet must be released at the proper moment, the sail brought to the other side, and the sheet tensioned the right amount on the opposite side of the boat. Each boat will have its own characteristics with regard to ease and speed of tacking. On ours, it's important to have some speed up so we don't tack so slowly that we get caught "in irons." That's when you fail to complete the tack and end up facing directly into the wind with the sails flapping. Here's how we avoid that:

- Plan the tack in advance, so we can get the boat speed up enough to be able to quickly tack.

- Notify everyone onboard we're going to tack so they can move to a safe position.

- Swing the helm across the wind and aim at a point about 90 degrees from your former direction. Aiming at a point that was on our beam before ensures we'll turn the boat far enough to catch the wind nicely 45 degrees off the bow on the new tack.

• As the bow passes through the wind, keep our heads below the boom as it swings across the cockpit.

• Before releasing the jib sheet, we allow the headsail to backwind slightly to help carry the bow across, and then release the sheet from its cleat and take it up on the opposite side and use the winch to tension the sheet the right amount.

When we're working together, tacking is a clean and easy maneuver. Singlehanded, it becomes a bigger chore, because you have to release your grip on the helm to attend to the jib sheet, and the boat can wander a bit in that moment. If you're short handed, one solution is to calmly furl the headsail before tacking, then tack the mainsail across and establish your new course, then unfurl the headsail and tension the sheet.

Jibing

Just as tacking is the act of turning the boat until the wind coming over the bow changes from one side of the boat to the other, jibing is when you turn the boat so the wind coming from astern changes from one side to the other. This is more dangerous than tacking, and requires all your attention and skill to pull it off smoothly. The reason it is more dangerous is, again, because the boom travels a great distance as the mainsail shifts from one side of the boat to the other. Under pressure of the wind, the sail carries the boom across with enough speed and power to seriously injure or kill anyone unfortunate enough to be clobbered by it.

When we jibe, I do one of two things: I either sheet in the main until the sail is at the boat's centerline, then ease it out on the opposite side as the boat jibes; or, if the wind pressure is low enough, I grasp the mainsheet with my gloved hand and ease the boom across and let the sheet out on the opposite side. Tacks can be made quickly, because the boom doesn't move very far, so it doesn't pose much danger, but jibes are made slowly, to allow the mainsail and boom to find their new positions without too much trauma.

Furling and Reefing

So there we were, out of control and bearing down on the ferry crossing Puget Sound from Edmunds to Kingston on that fateful day when we had too much sail up and too much wind behind us. And we were going to hit the ferry like a soft bug squashed on a windshield, unless I figured out what to do. What to do, of course, was to furl the headsail and lower the main.

To furl the headsail was easy. All I had to do was release the jib sheet and let the sail fly forward with the wind. Once the pressure was off and the sail was flapping, I could easily pull on the furling line that rolled up the sail like a window shade. The trick was to do so before the sail beat itself to shreds, which it will do if left flapping too long.

Once the jib was rolled up, the boat slowed a little bit. That might sound like a good thing, but actually it put more wind pressure behind the mainsail because now we weren't running quite as fast with the wind. The main was eased all the way out to one side, with the sail pressed against the shrouds. Even if I released the halyard, the sail, being pinned against the rigging, would not drop. If I turned to leeward to take pressure off the mainsail, it would result in a suicidal jibe. If I turned the other direction, it would risk a broach. We were doomed.

Being doomed is not high on my priority list, so I had to get the mainsail down and I had only one option. With Becky at the helm, I hauled in the mainsheet enough to get the sail off the shrouds. This caused the boat to heel, turn a bit to windward and start spiraling in what is known as a death roll under the influence of each passing wave ... not good! Working fast, I eased the vang so the end of the boom could rise a bit. I released the halyard and started pulling down on the main with all my strength. (The main is pulled down by using reefing lines that pass through cringles — sort of like grommets — at the luff and leech. These lines run through blocks on the fore and aft ends of the boom and then to cleats, allowing the skipper to control both lines at once and pull the sail down evenly.) An inch at a time, the sail crept down. The boat slowed and we watched the ferry pass ahead of us. Fifteen minutes later, we turned behind a point of land and the wind and waves died. Everything was calm again. Another lesson learned.

The number-one rule about reefing and furling is: Do it the moment you first start to think about it. Waiting until your brain prompts you a second time may be too late. Keep your eyes peeled for indications you should reef the main and furl the headsail. Different boats can handle different amounts of wind — for us, when the true wind speed hits 12 knots, it's time to reduce sail. At that speed we start to see whitecaps, a good visual alarm signal. If we see whitecaps forming in the distance, we reduce sail before the gust reaches us. Reef early and often, I say. It will make life much happier, and perhaps even longer.

How you reef your mainsail depends somewhat on your particular boat. For example, the main might have a boltrope along the luff that slides up into a slot at the rear of the mast. Or it might be equipped with sail slugs that go in the slot instead. The main halyard might be secured at a cleat or a winch on the lower part of the mast, or it might be arranged so you can use the halyard from the cockpit. The sail itself might have one or two sets of reef points. If it has two, there must be reef lines run to the luff and leech cringles at both of those levels.

All of these are issues you have to deal with on your own boat. In addition to the reefing lines, I added one other control line to our mainsail; a downhaul attached to the head of the sail and is used to pull the entire sail down all at once by releasing the halyard and hauling down on the down haul. Clever name, huh?

The physical aspects of how you accomplish a reef are perhaps less critical to this discussion than making sure you reef in time. If you don't, the boat will be overpowered and you can end up in a mess. At the least, you'll be fighting to control an over-canvassed boat, and at worst, you will be upside down. Remember, most small boats sail better and faster after reefing than they do when wallowing under too much sail. So go ahead and reef early. What is early to one boat is not to another. The boat manufacturer might be able to provide some guidelines, but you'll quickly discover your own limits and the boat's limitations by going out in the wind and gaining experience.

Slab reefing is what you do to the mainsail. The first step is to bring the boat directly into the wind, to take pressure off the sail. While the sail is luffing, release the halyard enough to allow the sail to be lowered to the first (perhaps only) set of reef points. Secure the halyard and pull down on the reef lines to bring the luff and leech reef cringles down to the boom. Secure the small reefing ties around the boom to create a new foot to the sail. The line through the reef cringle closest to the leech of the sail should be pulled rearward and secured to a cleat, to tension the foot. After all the reef lines have been tied off (square knots, also known as reef knots, are the traditional method), the halyard must be tensioned again to take up any slack or bagginess along the luff. Bear off until the sail catches the wind, and away you go.

To reduce the amount of headsail you have up, if the boat is equipped with a roller furling system, roll up the sail like a window blind. You can furl the headsail while it is still under pressure from the wind, but it is easier if you turn the boat into the wind momentarily to let the headsail luff. We routinely adjust the amount of headsail that is out while sailing; it just requires a bit more effort.

To do a controlled furl, don't just let fly the headsail sheet—slowly release the headsail sheet while simultaneously pulling in the furling line. This keeps the sail from flogging wildly while you roll it up. If your boat is not equipped with roller furling gear, you will have to go forward and lower the headsail by releasing its halyard, pulling the sail down and replacing it with a smaller sail. Non-furling headsails are clipped onto the head stay, and it takes a few minutes to unclip, stow the old sail, dig out the new sail and clip it onto the stay and then raise it with the halyard. Imagine doing that in rough seas, and you'll understand the popularity of roller furling. True, roller furled headsails are not as efficient (from a racing standpoint) as clip-on sails, but they are easier and safer to use, because you can reduce sail without having to leave the cockpit.

Rule: Never leave the cockpit to work with the sails unless you're at least wearing a personal flotation device, and preferably clipped into a harness system that will keep you close to the boat if you fall overboard.

Using the Boom Vang to Trim the Mainsail

If your boat is equipped with a boom vang (a block and tackle device that applies diagonal downward pressure on the aft end of the boom by pulling down toward the base of the mast), you can use that to help trim the sails for better performance.

When pressure applied by the vang is released, the aft end of the boom is allowed to rise until it is restricted by tension of the mainsheet. This permits some twist to be placed in the sail. Twist is good, to a point, but it must be controlled, in order to maintain good sail shape. By tensioning the vang, the aft end of the boom is forced downward, flattening the twist. Getting the right amount of twist in the sail is a matter of adjusting tension on both the boom vang and the mainsheet. Watch the telltales, and experiment with adjustments until they are streaming backward nicely.

Using the Sheet Cars to Trim the Headsail

The primary trim method for the headsail is to use the sheet, to trim the sail in or ease it out. But the sheet runs through a set of cars (blocks that attach to tracks on both sides of the boat), and those cars can be adjusted forward or backward to provide a secondary method of headsail trim.

Moving the cars forward places less tension on the foot of the sail and allows it to "belly" out more. Moving the car back places more tension on the foot of the sail and flattens to lower part of the sail. At the same time, the upper part of the sail gets a bit more twist. This depowers the sail.

So, the rule is, in light air, move the cars forward to provide more power to the sail, and in heavy air move them back to depower the sail. To figure out how to adjust the cars, keep this in mind: if the headsail luffs at the top of the leech, the car is too far back; if the headsail luffs at the bottom of the leech, the car is too far forward.

Don't let any of this worry you too much. Learning the finer points of sail trim will come with time on the water. Work on one thing at a time and then move on to the next. Soon, it will be intuitive and you'll be trimming without even having to think.

Chapter Five
Watching the Weather

Just because you sail a small boat doesn't mean you can't end up in big weather. In fact, the smaller the boat, the bigger the weather will seem. Weather that won't even ruffle the sails of a large, heavy-displacement keelboat can knock us on our ear. So, of all the sailors, we trailerboat sailors must be most tuned into what the weather is doing and what's it's going to do in the near future. And that's okay, because of all the encyclopedic skills sailors must acquire, learning to keep a weather eye is one of the most important.

Cloud patterns and movement often foretell the approach of bad weather. The atmosphere consists of huge air masses that differ from one another in temperature, pressure and humidity. When the varying conditions found in different air masses bump into and intermingle with each other, the weather changes. These changes are indicated by cloud formation, precipitation and wind. Changes in cloud patterns are the earliest and most visible clues to the type of incoming weather. The three primary types of clouds are cumulus, stratus and cirrus, although there are subsets of these. Proper interpretation of the evolution of the clouds let's you know what's coming.

Cumulus clouds are puffy cotton balls in the sky. They may look gorgeous, but they're unstable, and associated with advancing cold fronts or air rising over high ground. The puffy appearance is caused by vertical movement that causes the air to rise to a colder altitude. When that happens, water vapor in the rising air mass condenses and "grows" the cloud upward. A flock of small cumulus clouds dotting the sky like sheep sleeping on a pasture don't pose a threat. When cumulus clouds gather into a menacing mass, or grow vertically into towering monsters, a violent thunderstorm may form. When warm/moist air masses collide with cold air masses along a frontal boundary, cumulus growth goes malignant, spawning downpours, lightning and thunder, heavy wind, hail, and tornadoes.

Stratus clouds are like layers of slate, leaving a gray, overcast, dreary sky. If light penetrates the cloud layer easily, there is not much threat of rain. But if the clouds evolve into dark, low masses, rain should be expected. Stratus clouds don't foretell violent downpours, the way cumulus clouds do; stratus storms produce steady rain that can last for hours or even days. The problem with stratus clouds is, their dark blanket might hide something much more virulent up above. Under these conditions, it's wise to seek a sheltered anchorage or put the boat back on the trailer and call it a day.

Cirrus clouds are the long-range forecasters of an advancing weather front. These clouds are so high in the atmosphere they are made of ice crystals, so they don't cause rain. They do announce the coming of a warm front. If stratus follows cirrus, and if the stratus progresses into a thicker and darker layer, expect rain. The arrival time of the rain depends on the speed of the advancing front.

When you're listening to the weather forecast on the TV or radio, pay particular attention to every mention of a *front*. Cold fronts arrive with a fury and tend to leave just as quickly. But while they're upon you, you'll wish you were anywhere else. Warm fronts arrive and leave more slowly and without so much fireworks, but they can bring days of gray and rain.

The other thing to listen for is the passage of *high and low pressure systems*. High pressure generally brings more stable conditions — but that doesn't necessarily mean warm and pleasant. High pressure is caused by colder air (cold air being heavier than warm air), so you might end up with clear skies and cool temperatures. Low pressure systems are generally more volatile. The warm air is rising, leaving somewhat of a vacuum at ground level that causes the barometer to drop and air to rush in sideways (wind) to fill the void. The passage of both high and low pressure systems usually means a lot of wind. It might not last a long time, but is often violent — at least for small boats. It's always best to wait for a stable weather window.

Clear blue sky doesn't necessarily mean everything is hunky-dory. If a high-pressure system moves in and pushes a low-pressure system out of the way, it will bring clearing skies — but it might also bring strong and gusty wind as the pressure attempts to equalize.

Small sailboats can be knocked down or punished severely under clear, blue sky. If you don't believe it, read on.

The day began as close to perfect as any we had ever seen. The sun was shining, the wind was an ideal 10-knots, and there wasn't a cloud in the sky. I turned on the TV to see what the forecasters had to say, and they predicted good conditions. Based on that, we decided to launch the boat and sail to Discovery Bay for lunch at the Oyster House.

An aerial view of Discovery Bay looks somewhat like a foot and ankle as seen from the side. The mouth of the bay is wider than the toe, and at a mid-point is an ankle golfers would call a dogleg. Discovery Bay was discovered in 1792 by famed British explorer, George Vancouver, who was sailing his vessel Discovery at the time. Hence the name. By the way, did you know George Vancouver entered the navy at age 13 and served under Captain James Cook on his last two voyages, including the one in which Cook was killed on the Big Island of what is now called Hawaii? Fascinating, but this has nothing to do with our story.

The mouth of Discovery Bay is shielded by Protection Island, keeping most of the nasty weather from getting into the bay. Our home port of Sequim Bay lies about five miles west of the west end of Protection Island. So, if we're sailing to Discovery Bay, we are exposed to the weather of the infamous Strait of Juan de Fuca for only a five-mile stretch before we can duck behind Protection Island and then make the turn into Discovery Bay.

On this particular day at the end of October, our plan was to sail from our launch ramp to the Oyster House, then back again later that afternoon. This late in the season, we're accustomed to watching the sun disappear over the horizon at about four-thirty in the afternoon, so we knew we had to keep an eye on our time. Our son Ryan was along for the day, which turned out to be a good thing.

By the time we got the boat rigged and floated, the tide was at the end of its ebb—perfect to carry us out of Sequim Bay with a friendly current. The plan was to have as close to zero current as possible while sailing to Discovery Bay, then ride a flood down to the toe. You know, play the tides and currents—a real nautical kind of thing. And by golly, it was working out!

After lunch, we played around in Discovery Bay for several hours, still under ideal conditions, until it was time to head for home. The afternoon sun started to get low on the western mountains, so we had to hurry. It was twelve miles from the Oyster House to our launch ramp, and our Honda 9.9 could move us along at around 6 knots wide open. Doing the math, we knew we had at least a two-hour open-throttle ride home. And even then, we were going to be heading into Sequim Bay after dark. We grasshoppers had played too long. But that wasn't even the beginning of our trouble.

As we headed north toward the mouth of Discovery Bay under full throttle, the water was flat calm and there was only a breath of wind. When we got to the ankle, everything changed. The water was disturbed (not the way I'm rumored to be disturbed, but the way water is rippled by the wind). We continued north, still a couple miles from the mouth of the bay, and the water became more unruly the farther we went.

By the time we reached the mouth of the bay, we were taking two- and three-foot waves on the nose. I wondered aloud where this was coming from, because we had felt little wind all day long, and these were wind-driven waves out of the northeast. A good twenty or thirty miles of open water lie across the portion of the Strait of Juan de Fuca whence came this wind, and more than that if you count the miles of Rosario Strait that could funnel a wind toward our position. In such space, a heavy wind can generate large, powerful waves.

As we made the turn toward the west, Ryan and I still hadn't seen anything to worry about. Becky, however, was alarmed. She'd crawled up into the forepeak sleeping area with a book, and was taking the brunt of the rising and plunging bow. A three-foot wave gave her a ten-foot ride, and she started to inquire about what was happening. Inquiring loudly, as I recall.

I encouraged her to put down the book so her stomach wouldn't turn itself inside-out, and move to the berth beneath the cockpit where there would be far less motion. Heeding the advice of the skipper, she did her best to struggle to her feet, but every time she took a step, the bow went into freefall mode and she had to hang on for her life.

"Crawl," I called to her. She got down on the cabin floor and crawled toward the back. Then she tucked herself into the cozy berth beneath the cockpit, closed her eyes and started feeling much better. Well, maybe that's a bit hasty to say. And the worst was yet to come.

In the lee of Protection Island, the waves lost their organization. They were still three-footers, but they were confused because they no longer had the wind to keep them marching in order. Now, they came around both ends of the island, met in the middle, argued about who had right of way, then agreed to head for the mainland shore, where they could break and then reflect back out into our path. So we had seas hitting us from every direction and with no regularity at all.

It was uncomfortable, but the boat handled it, so far. The wind was as disorganized as the waves, swirling around from both ends of the island. We fell ever farther behind schedule, because we had reduced throttle to keep from slamming into the waves so hard. Horsepower was adjusted to keep the boat under control and to reduce the abuse as much as possible. The sky grew dark and the seas were building.

It didn't take long for us to leave behind the protection of Protection Island. It was easy to tell when it happened, because suddenly we were slammed by a breaking wave directly on our starboard beam. This was a sneaky wave that crept up on me while my attention was forward and to port, where the mainland shore a half-mile away was covered by the foaming aftermath of waves beating their brains out on the rocks.

Protests came from below, as Becky started asking if we were all going to die. "Not if I can help it," I replied, and turned to starboard to claw our way farther offshore and so we could take the approaching waves at a more boat-friendly angle.

The waves were suddenly furious and huge. We had about seven seconds between waves, and when we fell off into the troughs we looked straight up at the next crest. Estimating my eyeballs were about six feet off the water, as I sat in the cockpit, I can only guess the crests were perhaps twelve feet above the troughs. I was suddenly glad Becky wasn't in the cockpit, because the sight of those waves would have scared her to death.

Ryan and I quickly came up with a plan. I would keep my eyes on what lay ahead, and he would watch the approaching waves and let me know when they were about to reach us and how big they were.

Our direction of travel to the entrance to Sequim Bay put us beam-on to the waves, which is an ugly situation. Boats do much better with their bow into the waves, because that's the way boats are designed and engineered to pass through water. As long as you can keep from getting pooped or broached, even taking waves from the stern is better than taking them on the beam. So as Ryan announced the approaching waves, I worked with the boat to try to take each one the best way I could.

To approach the waves at the most comfortable angle, I had to turn toward Victoria, Canada. But that would only take us farther out into the Strait. Not a good place for us on this night. And it would also take us farther away from the entrance to Sequim Bay. The GPS indicated the entrance was only five miles away, so I held course the best I could, alternately steering offshore to take the biggest waves with a quartering bow, and turning toward shore to surf down the smaller ones. This was like tacking back and forth, struggling to stay far enough offshore for safety, while keeping the entrance ahead of us.

Suddenly, an enormous wave slammed us from the side. The boat pitched sideways, we became airborne and dropped a few feet. We came crashing down on our port side and the spreaders almost touched the water. Luckily, we lifted and came upright on the next swell, thankfully a more benign one. Ryan and I exchanged glances, knowing we'd dodged a bullet.

Becky yelled from below, "Hey, what's going on up there?"

"Sorry, honey," I yelled back. "We got caught by a bad wave. I won't let it happen again."

Every wave was bad now, but I didn't want to take one like that on the beam again, so I increased my zigging and zagging to cross the violent swells at greater angles.

The sky was fully dark now. The wind howled in the rigging, sea spray covered the windows of the cockpit enclosure, making visibility almost zero, and we were constantly laid over on our port side as wave after wave punished us from starboard. Then things got even worse … the engine coughed, then coughed again. Then it died.

I am convinced God helps us, if we're willing to listen. Right then, I was happy that in the morning, as we had prepared the boat for launching, I thought to have the second fuel tank filled at the marina. Normally, the trip to Discovery Bay and back can be done with just the little 3-gallon tank, and we'd have fuel left over. But under such challenging conditions, the outboard sucked gas at an unprecedented rate. The small tank was empty, with miles to go. And we were being eaten alive by this storm.

I spun the wheel to turn the bow directly into the waves. "We're out of gas," I said to Ryan. "I've got to switch the fuel line to the other tank."

Amazingly, the boat lay head-to-waves with little trouble. It was a relief to be just rising and falling from crest to trough, instead of being knocked halfway over all the time. It was a dramatic demonstration of why sailors caught in violent storms in the open ocean will ride on a sea anchor (a parachute let out three-hundred feet or so on a long line attached to a bow cleat). With the bow into the advancing waves, everything gets more comfortable in a hurry.

But I knew without a sea anchor to hold us into the wind and waves, and with no motor to give us steerage, it wouldn't be long before were shoved sideways again. My choices were to either get the motor working again, or raise sails. And in that wind (later verified to be 45 knots with even stronger gusts) and those seas, I chose to work on getting the motor up and running so we could head the last three miles into the safety of our bay. I had to work fast.

In the darkness of the cockpit, I dove under the seat, reached into the fuel tank bin on the port side, grabbed the quick-release connection on the end of the fuel line and unhooked it from the empty tank. I reached across to the full 9-gallon tank in the opposite compartment and made the connection. I jumped to the cockpit seat and turned the ignition key. Nothing. Turned it again. Still nothing.

Ryan caught the problem. "Dad, you forgot to shift into neutral."

I grabbed the shift handle and moved it to neutral, then tried the key again. The motor turned over, but failed to start. By now, the boat started to turn, laying her tender side open to the full punishment of the waves.

Two more waves, fifteen more seconds, and we would be in the trough being hammered again. If I let that happen, we would be completely at the mercy of the angry seas.

I tried the key again; no luck. Then it occurred to me the fuel hose had been sucked completely dry before the motor quit. I had to prime the hose.

A wave hit us hard, rolled us seriously on our side. I dove under the rear seat, reached for the fuel line priming bulb and gave it some quick squeezes until it firmed up. "Try it now," I yelled to Ryan. He turned the ignition key and the Honda roared to life. "Thank you," I whispered to the heavens, jumped up, took the helm and pressed the throttle forward.

The boat responded by moving powerfully forward, and I turned to surf down the wave that was about to swallow us. I glanced at the GPS and noted we were surfing at 11 knots. Boy, if we could keep up this speed, we'd be in the bay in no time, I thought. But then the wave passed beneath us and left us sitting in the trough waiting to be pounded by the next one. It caught us hard, and we broached as I struggled to regain control and steer us into the next swell.

Ryan said, "Hey dad, look at that," and he pointed behind us. There in the distance were two waves that looked like something out of a Hawaiian surfing movie. They were perfect breakers, and they were huge. "Lucky we got out of there when we did," Ryan said.

We had outrun those waves, but not by far. We were indeed lucky. But maybe it wasn't luck at all. Later on, Becky told us that while we were in the cockpit fighting our way into the bay, she was down below praying. "You guys are good," she smiled, "but I think we owe our lives to God."

I will not disagree with her.

The night was full black now. We only had a couple miles to go, but even at that we had our work cut out for us. The entrance to Sequim Bay can be tricky even in full daylight. It's a narrow channel running between shoal to the north and a spit to the south. Get out of the channel even a little bit, and you're aground. On a night like this, going aground would spell disaster.

Marking the channel are two buoys—the first one is lighted, but the second one is not. As we approached, I could see the lighted buoy in the distance. It gave me hope just to to see it, because that meant we were almost home. But the seas were unrelenting, and as we nosed into the channel, we took every wave on the beam. We didn't have the luxury of steering back and forth now. We had to maintain a straight course through a narrow channel. Too far left and we'd end up on the spit, beaten to fragments by the crashing surf. Too far right and we'd run aground on shoals that would drag the bottom of the boat out from under us.

Rain and sea spray spattered the dodger windows, making it hard to see ahead. If I didn't do it right, we might even hit one of the heavy steel buoys. And if we allowed these waves to drive us into one of those buoys, it would destroy the boat. We had to thread the needle, but I could hardly see the eye.

"You keep a watch on those buoys," I told Ryan. "I'm going to keep my eyes on our GPS return track. If you notice we're too close to the buoys, let me know."

In the darkness, the red light on the first buoy was easy to see, but the second, dark buoy was almost impossible to spot. Our Garmin GPS, however, had it marked on the screen. And I could easily see the "trail of bread crumbs" we left behind as we sailed out of the bay earlier that day. As we approached the buoys, I pressed the zoom button to increase the detail, and steered to keep the boat right on that track.

We passed the buoys cleanly, leaving them to starboard. I looked to the left at the spit, and noticed it was overrun by the surf. A few minutes later, we turned hard left and entered the protection of the bay. Immediately the water was calm, the wind seemed to vanish. This felt like the end of the ride on a roller coaster, when the cars come to a complete stop and you step out and wonder what all the fuss was about.

Ten minutes later, we were tied up at the guest dock. We were too tired to mess with putting the boat back on the trailer and lowering the mast that night. We had passed through five miles of "Oh my gosh, we gonna die!" Now, we wanted to go home, get some dinner and take the rest of the night off.

The next day, as we were bringing our boat back home on its trailer, a neighbor met us and asked if we'd been out the day before. He told us a large cabin cruiser had sunk in that storm — its occupants, in a life raft, were saved by a Navy vessel only a few miles from our position.

This was one of those learning experiences we never want to repeat. As Becky likes to say, "We don't want our learning experiences to kill us." So we have a bit of advice about how to avoid bad weather. Trust me, it's a good thing to avoid.

Advice About Heavy Weather

- If possible, don't go out in it. This stuff is no fun, and honestly, most trailerable sailboats aren't made for heavy weather. Neither are most trailerable sailors, or their crews. So avoid the bad weather, if you can. Check ALL the weather information sources before you go, and continually monitor the VHF weather channels while you're out on the water. Do not trust your life to a TV weather report alone.

- If you get caught in an unforecasted and totally unexpected bad weather situation, as we did, you have choices to make. One plan is to turn around immediately and seek shelter. (That's what we should have done, in retrospect.) Another is to proceed to your destination—a choice that should be made only if you have reasonable certainty you'll make it safely.

• Always make sure everyone onboard wears their personal flotation devices (PFDs). In bad conditions, other sea survival gear can be employed. This might include harnesses and tethers attached to jacklines or some other secure anchor point on the boat.

• This is a time for everyone not essential to the operation of the boat to go below and take up safe positions where they won't be tossed around and injured. Make sure hatches and ports are closed securely, so water won't get in.

• Monitor VHF channel 16 for weather alerts and other Coast Guard notices. This is also the channel you would use to call for help, if the need arises.

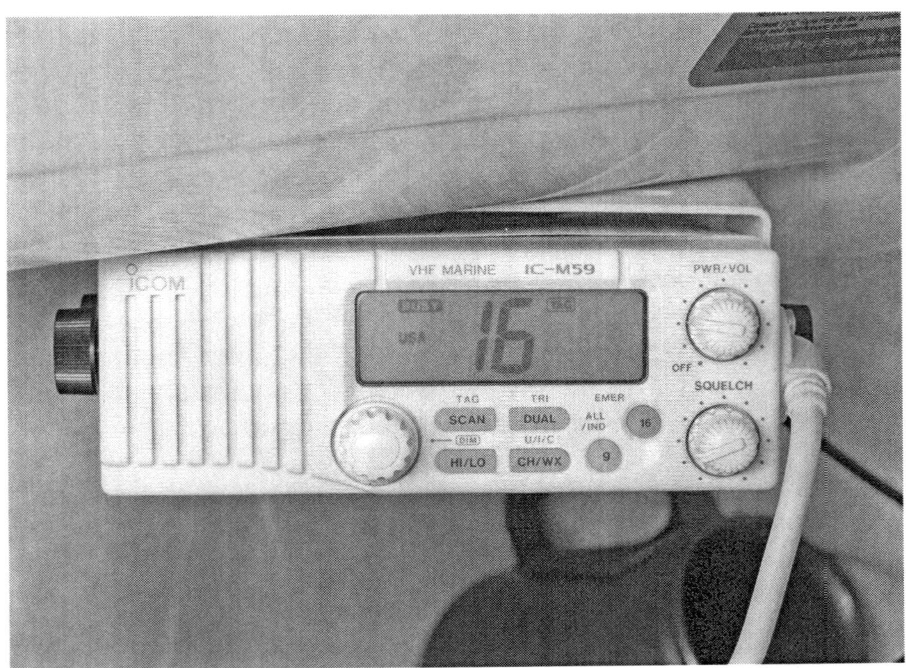

If you have a marine VHF radio onboard, monitor channel 16 continually while underway. This is the channel to use for reporting an emergency and requesting assistance.

• Know your boat's capabilities, and how to handle it in bad weather. Unfortunately, the only way to learn this is by going out in rough conditions, and I've already said you shouldn't do that. That said, you need to learn as much as you safely can each time you're out.

• Take multiple boating courses offered by your local flotilla of the Coast Guard Auxiliary, or by the Power Squadron. Look them up in the phone book, or go to any marine supply store or boat dealer to find out how to get in touch with these organizations.

• Be realistic about your own capabilities, and those of your crew members. In reality, most boats can take more than their occupants can.

• Respect the power of Mother Nature. She is nowhere more powerful than on oceans, lakes and rivers. Her strength and beauty are awesome, and there's no finer way to appreciate all this than on a sailboat—at the right time and in the right conditions.

Chapter Six
Navigation

'Twas a dark and stormy night. I'm not kidding. In all my years, I've never seen a darker or stormier or more confusing night, and it happened at exactly the wrong time. We were trying to bring a boat into the small harbor at Klemtu on Swindle Island in British Columbia. Water poured out of the sky, blowing sideways, washing out every semblance of recognizable landmarks, making it impossible to navigate by eyeball. The swirling raindrops made my head spin, and tricked my brain into feeling the boat was caught in a whirlpool, going round and round. Not only was I dizzy: I was totally lost.

The skipper had been to Klemtu before, but this was my first trip to this remote Indian village, and to me the way into the harbor seemed a mystery. Out of the gloom, misty lights appeared through the fog, and they looked like they were moving rapidly toward our position. For a moment, I thought perhaps it was a building with lights on inside and we were moving toward it. I checked the chart. Nothing; no buildings that could throw so much light. Of course, I wasn't entirely certain of our exact location on the chart. And besides, nautical charts don't show an accurate depiction of every building on shore. It left me confused. I turned to the leather-faced skipper. His weathered hand was steady on the helm, his eyes riveted to the depth sounder and radar. "It's a ferry," he said. "Coming up on our port stern. We'll pull over out of his way, then follow him in."

That night, the realization penetrated my soul about how easy it is to get turned around, and how important it is to keep track of your location at all times. A small boat, such as a trailerable sailboat, is no place to be when you have doubts about your location. Getting off course in a boat isn't like slowly leaving the pavement in a car—you don't just softly run off onto the shoulder; you can hit things that sink the boat. It's absolutely imperative that you know exactly where you are at all times when skippering a boat.

That might sound like a tall order but, actually, small boat navigation is fun and the skills are easy to learn.

Charts

The most important onboard navigation tool is an up-to-date chart of the area you're sailing. Staying up-to-date is important because things change—important things, like navigation buoys, for example. If you depend upon an outdated chart that shows a buoy (these are called aids to navigation, or ATONs for short) in the water, that buoy may or may not actually be there today. Buoys can be blown off station, sink, be destroyed by vessels, or moved to another location by the Coast Guard. By updating your chart with information available weekly from the Local Notice to Mariners website (www.navcen.uscg.gov/lnm/), you can keep track of the status of buoys and other aids to navigation.

The Local Notice to Mariners is divided into several sections. The first contains Special Notices about such things as changes in lock schedules, temporary shutdown of DGPS, military live fire exercises, etc. Section II lists all reported and corrected discrepancies related to ATONs, such as a change in status from what you see on your chart. Section III indicates temporary changes and corrections to the status of ATONs. And on and on it goes, until you reach the section that deals with corrections to the Light List. This list contains information about lighthouses and lighted buoys. After that is information about upcoming dredging operations, boat races and other marine events. All this free information is valuable to the coastal sailor, to keep you safe. But be aware that unless you check the website every week and continually update your charts, you may miss something. Only the latest updates are listed each week, not everything dating back to when your chart was printed. It's best to buy new charts and update them routinely.

Look for charts of your sailing area at your local marine supply store, or by going on the Internet and logging into http://nauticalcharts.noaa.gov/ and following the instructions for locating and ordering the charts you need. Some inland waters such as lakes and rivers are not covered by highly detailed charts. Check with local fishing shops to see if they can either provide a map of the water body or at least some local knowledge about hazards to navigation, good anchorages, etc.

Navigation Tools

With chart in hand, the next thing you need is a basic set of navigation tools. This includes a reliable timepiece, a straightedge, a divider, a #2 pencil, and a good eraser. A slightly more elaborate set of nav tools includes a 12-inch parallel rule, a course plotter, and a nautical slide rule that makes it easy to solve time, speed and distance calculations. The extra tools are nice to have, but you can get along without all the fancy stuff if you understand how to use the basic tools and you do the chart work religiously.

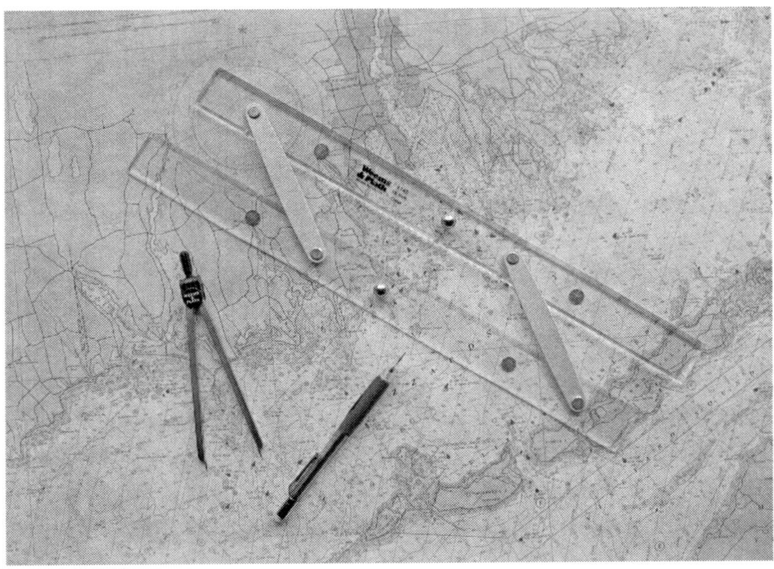

Simple navigation tools enable you to plan your voyage and keep track of where you are as you are underway. To learn how to use these tools and techniques, I recommend that you sign up for a coastal navigation course presented by your local flotilla of the U.S. Coast Guard Auxiliary.

A wristwatch satisfies the requirement for a reliable timepiece. You don't need to go out and buy a dedicated ship's clock, unless you want to. You don't need stopwatch accuracy; keeping track of time in hours and minutes is sufficient.

For a straightedge, I prefer working with a parallel rule (two straightedges hinged to each other in a manner that allows them to expand sideways) that allows me to "walk" angles across the chart from the compass rose (where the image of compass directions is printed on the chart) to my estimated position on the chart. Also, a straightedge is necessary for drawing lines of position and intended course lines on the chart. More about that later.

A divider is used to measure distances on the chart. Along the right and left edges of the chart are hash marks indicating nautical miles and tenths of nautical miles. When you spread the dividers across a distance on the chart, you can then take the dividers to the hash marks and measure the distance. You need to know distances on an intended route so you can plan the time and speed of your voyage. This allows you to know how fast you must travel to reach a destination in a given amount of time. The divider will also measure distances from your last "fix" or from known features on the chart, a lighthouse for example, or a point of land, so you can calculate your position.

The soft #2 pencil is used for writing notations and drawing lines on the chart, and the eraser is for eliminating old plotting information so you don't have to buy a new chart every time you want to sail to a different destination.

A nautical slide rule is used to solve time-speed-distance calculations. If you know any two of the three factors (elapsed time, speed of travel, or distance covered), you can quickly and accurately figure the remaining factor.

A course plotter or protractor incorporates a straightedge and various markings that allow you to transfer course angles from one place to another on the chart. How these tools are used depends upon which specific piece of equipment you purchase. The users manual will cover the fundamentals, but to sharpen your skills with these tools I recommend you enroll in a basic navigation course that is offered by the Coast Guard Auxiliary or the U.S. Power Squadron in your area.

Dead Reckoning

These tools are put to use as you engage in the most fundamental and complete process of navigation, known as dead reckoning. Lest you think dead reckoning is an old fashioned and outdated method, replaced by modern electronic technology, that's an ill informed attitude. The newest and most highly sophisticated electronic equipment can and will fail. When the batteries die (or something else goes wrong), the technology is dead. GPS, radar, depth sounders, and electronic chart plotters are all wonderful. We have some of this equipment on our boat. But even with all of it combined, you still don't have a complete navigation system, because it depends on something else to remain operational.

Dead reckoning, on the other hand, is a total navigation system because it depends on nothing other than the chart, a compass, a pencil, and your observations of time and speed — and your brain, of course. Electronic gear is valuable, but don't elevate it to a status it cannot live up to. Don't rely solely on electronics to keep track of where you are, or one day you'll be disappointed and the consequences of that disappointment may be severe.

Voyage Planning

Dead reckoning involves a couple of phases. The first is voyage planning. This is the phase in which you plot the details of your voyage in advance of the trip. This is when you pull out the charts, decide where you want to go, how fast you want to travel, and deduce how long it should take. You use the straightedge and pencil to draw the intended course lines on the chart, making notations beside the course line to indicate direction and speed of travel. You also indicate your intended progress along that line, in half-hour increments. Say, for example, you plan to begin your voyage at 10:00 a.m. On the chart, you write 10:00 next to the departure point. If you intend to travel at 6 knots, you will be covering one mile every ten minutes. So, you'll travel three miles in half an hour. Measure three miles along your course line and use the pencil to draw a dot on the line, surrounded by a semicircle, and write 10:30 beside it. That's the proper method of notation on nautical charts. Repeat the procedure for every thirty-minute increment.

Unless you intend to travel a straight line from your departure at point A to your destination at point B, the voyage will consist of more than one leg. This is common, because the legs indicate your route around obstacles. When one leg ends and the next begins, mark the chart with the estimated time you will arrive at that turning point. Don't worry if the time notation at a turn isn't right on the half-hour. Go ahead and write the estimated time at the turn and then proceed along the new leg until the half hour is reached, and make the standard thirty-minute notation. Also, along the line for the new leg mark the direction (compass bearing) and speed you intend to travel for that leg.

The whole purpose of doing this pre-voyage plan is to help you study the chart and work out a safe route from departure to destination. It also permits you to estimate time along the route and develop contingency plans — alternate destinations or safe harbors where you can lay over in case the weather turns bad or something goes wrong. The plan must have contingencies for problems, so in addition to studying the chart to identify hazards to navigation, you should look for potential bail-out points, locations for emergency medical care, etc.

Underway Dead Reckoning

With the chart marked with the voyage plan, you're ready to navigate your course. Let's assume you don't actually get underway at 10:00, as planned. Things happen, and you might end up leaving at 10:37, let's say. This means you correct the voyage plan by adding thirty-seven minutes to all of the times noted along the route. Take care of that correction just before leaving the departure point.

Everything else about the voyage plan remains the same. You wrote the compass bearing alongside the course line, so watch your boat's compass and follow that heading. You also wrote the intended speed along the course line, so bring your boat up to that speed. If everything goes perfectly, you will be right on the planned course line and traveling at the appropriate speed. And that means that you will know exactly when to make your turn to the next leg of the route.

Now comes a dose of reality. It's almost impossible to perfectly follow the intended course line. Wind, current, and pilot error all play a role in moving the boat somewhat off the line. The best you can do is try to stay the course until you can somehow check to see how much you strayed. The only way to discover where you are in relation to the intended course is to take a "fix."

Fix your position by making note of visible landmarks, such as a point of land, an immovable ATON such as a lighthouse, or other recognizable object on land that is marked on your chart. For the record, you can also fix your position by turning on the GPS (if you have one that's operational) and reading the latitude and longitude coordinates. But for the sake of this discussion about simple non-electronic navigation technique, fix your position by establishing lines of position to two or more points. Mark them on the chart and note the intersection of those lines. That's where you are.

Line Of Position (LOP) and Fix

To establish a line of position, use a handheld compass to shoot a bearing to a known point on land. Let's say there is a radio tower marked on the chart in a location that should be off to your port (left) side, and you can see a radio tower on land in what appears to be the proper position. Hold the compass in front of you and aim it at the tower, then read the bearing. On the chart, draw a line at the correct compass angle from your estimated position to the tower. That is a line of position, and you are somewhere on that line. But you don't know exactly where on the line you are, so you need to shoot another LOP to an object that is preferably at an angle more than 90-degrees from the first LOP. Let's say you can see a prominent point of land off the starboard side that corresponds with a point on the chart. Repeat the compass procedure to establish a line of position to that point of land, and draw it on the chart. Where the two LOPs intersect is where you are, and this is a fix of your position.

Ideally, this fix falls somewhere on your original course line at a spot that should correspond to the time you have been traveling. If it's close, but off to one side, then you know wind, current or pilot error (or a combination of the three) has shifted your course. At the point where you establish a fix, draw a dot and surround it with a full circle, then write the time of the fix next to the circle. From that point, study your original route plan and determine what you must do to get back on course.

Time, Speed, Distance

Time, speed and distance calculations are every bit as much a part of dead reckoning as marking the course on the chart. In fact, you can't do one without the other. You must be able to figure out distances based on boat speed and time, or you are truly lost.

Calculating the relationship between time, speed and distance is easy to do by using a set of formulas in which D stands for distance in nautical miles, S is speed in knots, and T is time in minutes. The number 60 is factored in to change the time from hours to minutes. By manipulating the formula, if you know two of the three elements, you can discover the third. For example, if we know the distance we want to travel and the speed of the vessel, we can enter those numbers in the formula and calculate for the remaining element — time. In this instance we want to know T, so we write the formula T= 60D/S. If you want to calculate for speed, change the formula to S=60D/T. If you are looking for distance, it is D=ST/60. Always double-check your math, because an error can put you on the rocks.

During the cruise, along with making the course correction,

check the time it took you to arrive at a predetermined point, and compare it with what you originally listed on the plan. If you arrive late, you are traveling more slowly than planned and are probably sailing against a foul current. This implies you'll arrive later than planned at your destination, and reality might cause you to alter your plan so you can reach safe harbor before dark, even if it isn't the harbor you originally intended.

A secondary implication is, you might need to find a place to refuel earlier than planned. Motoring (I know this is a sailboat, but sometimes we end up motoring because of failed wind or foul weather that forces us to drop sail), against the current will eat through your fuel supply at an astonishing rate. So if you seem to be falling behind schedule, you can bet the fuel supply is being used faster than planned. It's far better to stop for fuel early than continue on and run dry.

Rules of the Road

The rules of the road are intended to prevent collisions when you are piloting a boat in the vicinity of other vessels. Actually, it's a lot like driving in traffic, except everything moves more slowly. Fortunately, the rules for piloting a boat are logical and, with a little practice, soon become intuitive. This isn't like moving to a new country and having to learn to drive on the wrong (wrong for us, anyway) side of the road.

The Coast Guard publishes a book called *Navigation Rules* that spells out every nuance of the practical and legal aspects of navigation. I recommend you have this book aboard and familiarize yourself with the contents. Let's distill the basics here. In simplest terms, when meeting another boat head-on you stay to the right, just as you do on the highway. Passing port-to-port is the rule of thumb, though you may have to steer to starboard to make that happen, if you and the other boat are on reciprocal courses. If you're ever in doubt, assume you're on a collision course and alter your course to prevent an accident.

When altering course to prevent a collision, make your move "big" enough to leave no doubt in the mind of the other skipper as to your intentions. Our policy is to show the other vessel the broadside of our boat, even if we need to turn only a bit to avoid a collision. And we make the maneuver early, rather than late. We don't like playing chicken. Not every skipper is paying maximum attention to what's going on around him, so we want to leave absolutely no doubt about our maneuvers. Actually, Rule 8, subparagraph (b) deals with exactly that issue. Get the book and read it.

Rule twelve is a special rule for sailboats: *When two sailing vessels are approaching one another, so as to involve risk of collision, one of them shall keep out of the way of the other as follows:*

> *(1) when each has the wind on a different side, the vessel which has the wind on the port side shall keep out of the way of the other;*
>
> *(2) when both have the wind on the same side, the vessel which is to windward shall keep out of the way of the vessel which is to leeward; and*
>
> *(3) if a vessel with the wind on the port side sees a vessel to windward and cannot determine with certainty whether the other vessel has the wind on the port or on the starboard side, she shall keep out of the way of the other.*

Subparagraph (2) refers to boats traveling in the same direction, because only then would the wind be coming from the same side of both vessels. This is why you sometimes hear skippers yelling "Starboard!" in races, because they're declaring that the other boat is in violation of the right of way.

Rule 13 deals with overtaking another vessel, or being overtaken by another boat. It says *...any vessel overtaking any other shall keep out of the way of the vessel being overtaken.* There is no rule about which side you must take to pass the vessel you're overtaking. You can go left or right, but intuitively, passing on the left is most logical because that's how vehicles on the highway overtake and pass each other. However, Rule 34 gives some instruction about communicating your intentions to the skipper of the boat you're overtaking. This is a good rule to live by, because a boat being overtaken may be totally unaware of the boat coming up from behind, and a sudden maneuver by the boat ahead can result in a collision. So here's the rule: *A power-driven vessel intending to overtake another power-driven vessel shall indicate her intention by the following signals on her whistle: one short blast to mean "I intend to overtake you on your starboard side"; two short blasts to mean "I intend to overtake you on your port side"; and the power-driven vessel about to be overtaken shall, if in agreement, sound a* *similar sound signal. If in doubt she shall sound the danger signal prescribed in paragraph (d).* FYI the danger signal is five short, rapid blasts on the horn or whistle.

You need to understand that anytime a sailboat is under power (using an auxiliary motor), it is considered a power-driven vessel, not a sailboat. The rules about sailboats only apply when the boat operates under sail alone. So, as you read the rules, pay close attention to instructions for power-driven vessels, because they'll probably apply to your boat at least part of the time.

When in a crossing situation, you must yield right of way to a boat approaching to your right, just as you would at a highway intersection.

The boat with the right of way is called the Stand-on vessel, meaning it has the right to maintain course and speed. The boat that yields right of way to the other vessel is called the Give-way vessel, because it's required to alter course and speed, allowing the Stand-on vessel to proceed. When in a crossing situation, the Give-way vessel slows down and steers behind the Stand-on vessel. Give-way vessels are supposed to *"take early and substantial action to keep well clear,"* according to Rule 16.

In spite of every posted rule, the upshot of the whole matter is to do everything you can to prevent a collision, even if you're forced to yield right of way that technically belongs to you. Just be safe.

Chapter Seven
Dropping the Hook

Sometimes staying put is extremely important to the safety of a boat and crew. And when staying in one place is the order of business, nothing will substitute for good ground tackle properly set. By ground tackle, I mean anchors, lines (anchor lines are called rodes), lengths of chain, shackles—all the stuff used to firmly hook the boat to some part of Mother Earth.

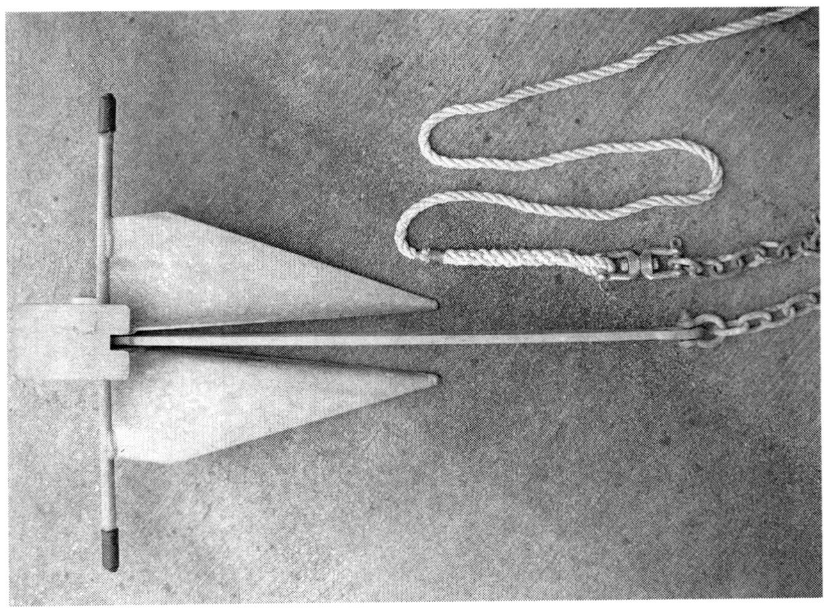

Ground tackle consists of an anchor and rode (either chain or nylon rope, or a combination of both), plus all the attachment hardware such as shackles and swivel connectors.

If you've ever suffered a sudden disconnect from the anchorage in the middle of a dark and stormy night, then you know the feeling of impending doom brought about by a boat suddenly floating free when it's supposed to be tethered. This is when you realize that the boat and everything aboard can be lost to the violence of wind, waves, and a rocky shoreline because a knot failed, a rode broke, or an anchor lost its grip on the bottom.

Properly securing the vessel with ground tackle is more than tossing an anchor over the bow and hoping for the best. In some cases, an anchor may not even be used. Sometimes using nylon lines to tie the boat to trees or rocks ashore is your only choice, because there's precious little bottom to hold to, or it's too deep to reach.

At Lake Powell, one of our favorite destinations, our anchor is usually buried on the beach rather than out in the water, because of the sandstone terrain. In many places the lake bottom is solid rock, with only the thinnest layer of sand to hold an anchor. Anchoring out in the middle isn't even on the menu, but sandy beaches are ideal for beaching the boat and burying a hook. Then the challenge is to keep the boat from swinging side-to-side and ending up on rocks flanking the beaches.

At times like that, three anchors are none too many: One for the bow (assuming we can find a sandy bottom) and another for each corner of the stern. Add a couple of 200-foot lengths of 1/2-inch nylon line, and you can rig a secure web that will tie you to the beach.

Here's how we used our ground tackle to survive the blow on one particularly challenging night. We decided to go stern-to on the beach, so we could step off the boat onto the sand and wouldn't have to swim ashore. We could have gone bow-to, but a bow-to beaching meant a leap from bow to beach, and a difficult climb to get back aboard—or climbing down the stern ladder into waist-deep water and then wading ashore.

As we approached the beach, we dropped a bow anchor and paid out more than 120 feet of rode. This deposited the anchor where we wanted it off shore, while we kept heading toward the beach. Before we beached the boat, we prepared two stern lines to tie the boat to trees and rocks ashore. This method kept us from having to back the boat onto the rocky beach, placing the motor, centerboard and rudder system at risk.

Before getting into shallow water, we raised the centerboard. Then, as the boat nosed onto the sand, we shut down the motor and raised the twin rudders. Then I jumped off with a stern line in hand. I pushed the boat off the beach, while Becky began hauling in the bow anchor line. This turned the boat around, placing the stern to the beach. While Becky hauled in the excess slack in the bow anchor rode, I pulled the stern closer to shore. Each of the two stern lines was let out at about a 45-degree angle and tied to rocks or stout bushes or trees. This kept the stern from wandering. Once Becky had pulled the anchor rode tight and set the anchor firmly, she secured the line to a bow cleat. The first time we did this, we mistakenly thought we were done.

Late that afternoon, a storm blew in and wind speeds picked up to 35 knots. Waves screamed down on our tiny cove, and the boat bobbed and weaved like a pro boxer. We decided to set two additional lines, each attached to a bow cleat and leading at a 45-degree angle back to shore. This is where additional anchors come in handy. Unfortunately, we were a bit short of extra anchors, so we had to bury deadmen (pieces of driftwood and rock we could tie the lines around) in "graves" on the beach to serve as makeshift anchors. These diagonal lines served well to dampen the wild swinging of the bow, and to act as spring lines to keep the bow from being blown ashore in case the bow anchor dragged.

Next morning, unannounced (as these things always happen), the bow anchor dragged. We felt it let go in the heart of the storm, when it was impossible for us to sail forward and reset the anchor. With no effective bow anchor, only the arrangement of diagonal stern and bow lines tied to shore saved the boat. While it is true that we had nothing holding the boat off the beach, at least the diagonal lines kept the bow facing out toward open water. (NOTE: We have since installed a stern-mounted transducer for our depth sounder, so we no longer allow the hull to touch the beach.)

With no tender parts of our boat to be damaged by contact with the soft beach, we backed Three Eagles up to the sand and strung anchor lines diagonally from bow and stern to tie us to trees and rocks. A bow anchor held us from being blown straight backward.

We had to wait until the wind quieted before we could attempt to reset the bow anchor. In a calm moment, we released all the diagonal tie-downs, hauled the useless bow anchor aboard, pushed the boat off and motored out a hundred feet to drop the hook and hope for a more secure set. When the big Danforth caught the bottom, I hauled on the rode as hard as I could, then cleated the line and motored in reverse to apply even more pressure. Easing rode out, we backed the boat close to the beach, where I hopped off and secured the diagonal tie-downs once again. Happily, the anchor held, and we learned the more attention we paid to setting the hook, the better we would be able to sleep at night in a blow. We never had a problem with the bow anchor again.

But late one evening, we did suffer a failure of one of the diagonal lines. When the line parted, Becky and I both felt it immediately. It's amazing how a crew can sense the slightest difference in the way a boat rides to anchor. As we were playing cards in the cabin, both of us simultaneously felt something wrong with the motion of the boat. The next thing we knew the boat swung one side toward the beach, unrestrained because of the failed diagonal line. The bow anchor was doing its job, but the boat had more movement than we wanted, moored right up against the beach as we were.

Immediately, with flashlights in hand, we went over the side and started searching for the problem. There it was—a limp length of dockline floating from the bow cleat, and the other length of the line floating on the water near the beach anchor.

I ran for one line while Becky grabbed the other, and we pulled the free ends together. Then I realized what had caused the problem—because we lacked a long enough line to run all the way from the bow cleat to the shore, I had tied two short docklines together. The line had parted at my knot.

Maximum embarrassment!

Sailors aren't supposed to have their knots untie themselves. After this incident, it took a while for me to convince Becky my new knot would be perfectly secure. I learned a great lesson. Never tie a make-do knot when what you need is the real McCoy. Use nothing less than a bowline when that's required.

Even though we solved the problem, the night wind was so violent I decided to sleep in the cockpit so I could check all the lines through the night. The weather radio warned of 50+knot winds in the area. For once, the weather people were right.

Extreme winds buffeted the boat, screaming through the

rigging with such ferocity that the entire vessel shuddered under the pounding. Part of the shuddering was caused by the violent flapping of the headsail cover that set the furled genoa to shaking the forestay so hard the mast began to pulsate with a powerful harmonic vibration.

We had a choice of removing the headsail cover or wrapping the jib halyard around and around the furled sail and cover in a spiral from the top down. Even with the cover removed, I figured the wind would still whip the furled headsail on the stay, so we chose to try and snug things down by wrapping it all up in the halyard. When I was finished, it looked like a blue and white candy cane, with the white halyard spiraling down over the blue sail cover. I tied the halyard tail tightly to the bottom of the mast, applying tension to keep the stay from moving. And that did the trick.

Quieting the boat did a lot to ease the psychological trauma caused by the wind. Never underestimate the stress caused by the noise of a storm.

Moral of the story — securing the ground tackle, and securing the rigging, sometimes requires creative use of anchors, lines, trees, rocks, deadmen, halyards, and whatever else you can find. Don't leave home without more lines and anchors than you think you'll ever use. The night may come when you'll find yourself stringing out every last foot of line and wishing you had more.

Choosing An Anchor

Which anchor is best? Walk any dock and take a poll of the variety of anchors hanging from bow rollers, and you'll see what I mean. There seems to be no real consensus on this subject, but there are some general rules that will help you understand which anchors perform best with different bottom conditions.

Most boaters agree that Danforth (or fluke-type) anchors perform best for mud and sand bottoms, but fail to penetrate thick grass. Plow-type (CQR, Delta, and such) perform well when the bottom is grassy, but don't hold quite so well in the mud and sand. Bruce-style anchors are favored for rocky (or coral) bottoms, and tend to reset themselves when they pull free for whatever reason.

That's the short version — a book could be written about all the pros and cons of each type of anchor. For our boat and our primary sailing area (Puget Sound and the San Juan Islands), we have two Danforths — one overly large and one regular size for the displacement and length of our boat. For a long time, we considered adding a Delta and a Bruce just to cover all our bases, so we wouldn't be caught unprepared no matter where we sailed. Then we discovered the Box Anchor, manufactured by the Slide Anchor Company.

This is a truly weird looking anchor that opens from its collapsed storage position to take the shape of a shallow box without a top or bottom. Along one side of the box is the connection point for the freely-pivoting shank (to which the rode is attached). Because that side of the box will naturally be pulled on by the boat, I'll refer to it as the leading edge. The opposite side of the box is the trailing edge. Both the leading and trailing edges are equipped with upper and lower sets of flukes (a total of four uppers and four lowers) that angle toward the direction of pull.

When the Box Anchor is set, it doesn't matter which side is up, because it has no up or down. And because the shank is free to pivot, it exerts no leverage against the anchor itself, so it doesn't have the tendency to tear the anchor out of the bottom and leave the boat adrift. If a massive change of wind or current swings the boat all the way around in the opposite direction, the anchor will roll over and reset itself. There is no real need to "set" the Box Anchor as with other types of anchors. Let it find the bottom, back the boat away to pay out sufficient scope, and the anchor will set itself at the first hint of a tug on the rode. For us, because of the ease of operation and reliable performance, the Box Anchor has become our primary. But we still carry the Danforths as backups.

Whatever anchors you choose, they should be appropriate for the size of your boat and the typical bottom where you sail. My personal opinion is: more is better when it comes to ground tackle.

Rode (anchor line)

Anchor rode is another important consideration. Again, this partly depends upon where you typically sail. If you're in coral or jagged rock country, nylon line will suffer from each contact with the ragged bottom. Environmental consciousness dictates you should always avoid coral when anchoring (so theoretically your rode should never come in contact with coral), but practicality says a chain is your most prudent choice. If you anchor mostly in more benign places, nylon offers a lot of benefits over chain.

One of the benefits of nylon is its stretch-factor. As the boat moves about under the influence of wind and current, a stretchy rode is less likely to jerk the anchor free of the bottom. On the other hand, the weight of chain forms a belly of sagging rode that leads from boat to anchor offers a form of built-in "stretch." On the other hand (do we have that many hands?), chain rode is awfully heavy when hauling up an anchor, and can be a mucky mess on deck as the links tend to drag up a good bit of the bottom.

So, what do we use on *Three Eagles*? The bigger Danforth sports 50 feet of 1/4-inch galvanized chain, followed by 200 feet of 3/8-inch nylon. The smaller anchor is equipped with 10 feet of chain and 150 feet of nylon. The primary anchor (the Box) has no chain at all, but relies on 200 feet of 3/8-inch nylon rode. The freely-pivoting shank doesn't try to wrench the flukes free of the bottom, so does not require the weight of a chain to help hold the anchor down in "proper" alignment.

With storage below at a premium, and because an anchor might be needed very quickly in an emergency, it's a good idea to hang the anchor on a bracket attached to the bow pulpit.

Our big Danforth hangs from a West Marine anchor bracket on the bow pulpit, with all the rode coiled in the anchor locker built into the bow deck. The backup anchor also rides in the anchor locker, ready for deployment on a moment's notice. The Box, because of its unfortunate configuration (even when collapsed) won't fit in the anchor locker, so we had to construct a special hanger bracket system for the bow pulpit. In addition, we now have four 100-foot 3/8-inch nylon lines for creative mooring situations. These lines are stored below in a cabin storage compartment.

Anchoring needs to be a well-planned operation, and everything must be "done by the numbers." (That's military talk, so just ignore it if you want to.) Calculate the amount of rode needed, according to the depth of the water, plus the distance from the water to the cleat. Then figure in the anticipated weather conditions. The term "scope" refers to the ratio between the depth of the water (plus height to the cleat) and the length of rode needed under varying weather conditions. For example, let's say you're sitting in 12 feet of water, and the distance from the water's surface to the cleat is 5 feet. That's 17 feet all together, so a 5:1 scope would call for 85 feet of rode.

In good weather, a 5:1 scope is fine. Some experts say you can get away with a 3:1 scope, but I'm just not comfortable with that, so we use 5:1 in good conditions. The harder the wind blows, the more scope you need. The reason is, when the wind blows hard, the rode tends to straighten out directly from the cleat to the anchor, and too little scope will cause the angle to be more vertical, which may pull the anchor off the bottom. More scope means a more horizontal tug on the rode, which actually helps the anchor dig in more firmly. With anchors that have rigid shanks, the weight of a heavy chain will help hold the rode down, so the anchor has less tendency to pull loose.

Tides

If you're sailing on saltwater, don't forget to consider the rise and fall of the tide. Depending upon where you sail, if you set your anchor with a 5:1 scope at low tide, the scope may be severely shortened during high tide. In our Pacific Northwest sailing area, we can see tidal changes exceeding 12 feet. So if we dropped anchor in 6 feet of water at low tide, and ran out a 5:1 scope, we'd have 30 feet of rode out. Six hours later, with the water depth below the boat measuring 18 feet, we would have less than a 2:1 scope, and would be prime candidates for dragging anchor.

This math works the other way, too. If we drop anchor in 6 feet of water at high tide, several hours later the boat would be sitting high and dry on mud and rocks. So be cautious about tides.

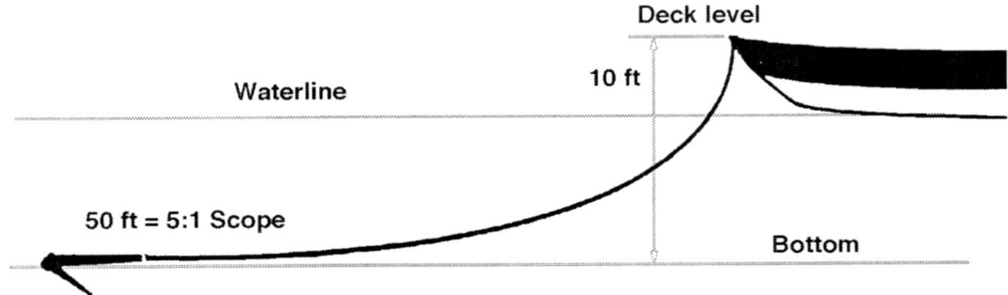

Scope is expressed as a ratio of the distance from your deck level
to the bottom of the anchorage, compared to the length of
anchor line you have out.

Setting the Anchor

To set the anchor, ease it over the side and let it down gently
to the bottom. This will help avoid tangles that can happen if you
just toss the hook and rode over the side with one mighty and
unsailor-like splash. If you've marked the anchor line, say every 10
feet, you can easily see how deep the water is, which will help you
determine how much line to let out to give you the desired scope.
We marked our white nylon rode by stitching through the line with
black thread, over and over again until the spot is easy to see.
We made a single mark at 10 feet, a pair of marks at 20 feet, and
three marks at 30 feet. Then we repeated the markings, figuring
we wouldn't mistake
40 feet for 10
feet just because
it has a single mark.
You may decide
to use some other
system of marking,
such as employing
the nice pre-labeled
plastic tags available
at West Marine
stores.

A nice thing about trailerable sailboats is that they are designed to fit
on a trailer, which automatically gives them a shallow draft configuration that is ideal for anchoring (and sailing) in shallow water.

Photo credit: Com-Pac Yachts

Once the anchor reaches the bottom, play out rode and back the boat up until you have some horizontal distance between the bow and the point where the anchor lies on the bottom. Once you have about a 3:1 scope paid out, apply pressure on the rode to help dig the anchor into the bottom. Keep backing the boat, playing out more rode, and setting the anchor by firm pressure.

Finally, try to hold the boat from moving backward by gripping the rode solidly. Cleat the rode to do this, because it will be too hard to hold the line with your hands alone. When you think the anchor is holding firmly, power up the motor in reverse for about 5 seconds. If the anchor holds fast, you can sleep calmly that night. With the appropriate amount of rode let out and cleated, take a few bearings on nearby landmarks.

It's always a good idea to look around and pick out landmarks that you can "triangulate" on from your anchored position. That way, you can periodically poke your head out of the cabin, check the landmark positions and verify you're still sitting right where you're supposed to be.

Of course, if the wind or current changes, the boat will swing on its rode, and you'll end up in a different position. When that happens, you'll want to make sure the anchor doesn't drag loose because it's being pulled from another direction, so pick out new landmarks and make periodic checks to ensure you're still hooked firmly to the bottom.

Swinging on the anchor rode can move the boat around in a large circle, so you need to make sure you have plenty of swinging room without danger of hitting other boats anchored nearby, or being blown ashore or into rocks. Remember, as the tide falls, the swinging circle will get bigger.

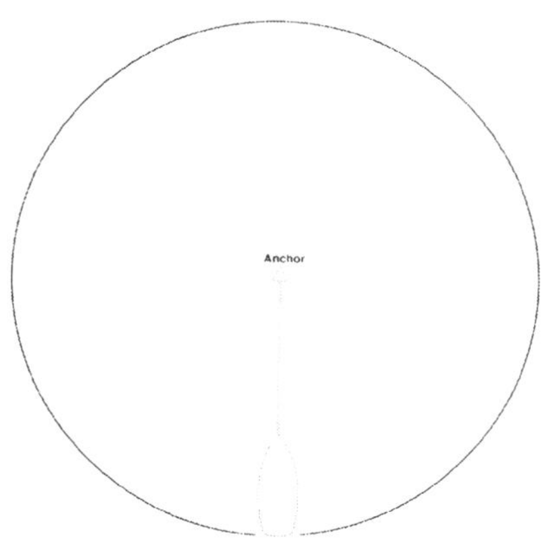

If you use a single anchor, the boat will describe a circle around the anchor as wind shifts and current changes move the boat around on the water.

You may choose to deploy more than one anchor, especially if you're expecting a wind shift or a current change that will cause you to swing around to a new position. A second anchor deployed in a direction that will place it in a perfect position to hold against the new wind or current direction, will give you added security and peace of mind.

There are several methods for setting the second anchor. You may set one off the bow and the other off the stern, with the boat oriented in between them so it's either bow-to or stern-to the current no matter which way it runs. Using that type of anchorage does present a possible problem. A 90-degree wind shift would put the boat sideways to the breeze, with stress on both anchors.

To deploy anchors in this manner, first lower the bow anchor, then back the boat until you've played out twice as much rode as you actually need. This will place you directly over the spot to deploy the second anchor. With that anchor on the bottom, haul the boat forward by pulling on the bow rode (this will actually help dig that anchor into the bottom) while playing out the stern anchor rode until you have just the right amount of rode out both fore and aft. Firmly set both anchors, cleat them off, and enjoy the evening.

The same effect can be accomplished by setting a bow anchor and then running a stern line to a tree on shore. If you choose this method, it's a good idea to run the line around the tree and then back to the boat, so you can cast off the line and drag it around the tree without having to go ashore to untie. Tying to the tree may be accomplished by using a dinghy to haul the line ashore, or by backing the boat up to the tree (assuming there is enough water and perhaps a tree that overhangs the water), looping the rode around the tree, and back to a stern cleat. Then pull the boat forward by hauling in on the bow line, while playing out some stern line until you're a comfortable distance from shore. An excellent anchoring method I prefer to the bow/stern format is to lay out two anchors from the bow, but with a 180-degree angle between the two rodes as they come back to the bow cleats. Essentially, this gives you one anchor 90-degrees off the port bow and another 90-degrees off the starboard bow. Wind or current shifts from the left or right will be easily handled by either one anchor or the other. Dropping anchors in this configuration can be accomplished in the same way as mentioned before, but rather than cleating one anchor to the stern, secure the rodes to separate bow cleats.

Changes in wind or current direction will swing the boat around to the new direction where it will be held by the opposite anchor. A wind or current from the off-direction (not directly in line with the anchors) will place the boat at an angle to, and being held by, both anchors at the same time.

Two-Anchor Technique

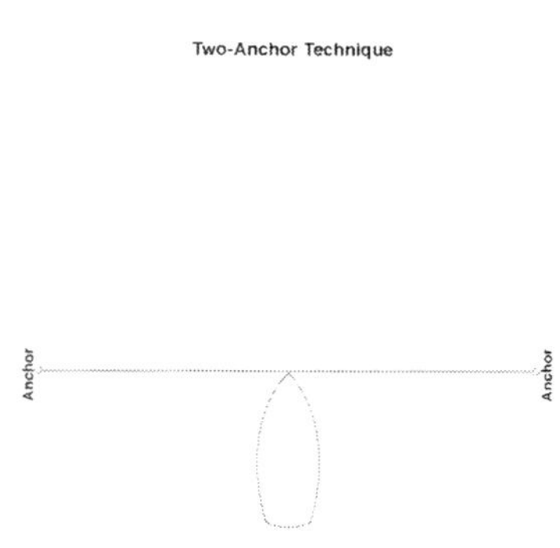

By planting two anchors, 180-degrees apart from each other and with rodes of equal length, and attaching the rodes to the bow, the boat will not move during wind and current shifts. It will only pivot, but will stay in place.

Using a dinghy to row the second anchor out to its position may be easier than trying to maneuver the boat, depending upon wind and current conditions during the anchoring process.

If extra anchors are needed, they and their rodes should be laid out on deck, well in advance of deployment. This is not a part of the overall sailing adventure that can be left as an afterthought. Proper anchoring, after all, may be the only thing that stands between you and a shipwreck.

Try to imagine everything that can possibly go wrong. Ask yourself, "What if part of the ground tackle failed—what would happen, and what would I need to do to solve the problem?"

If you have a plan and execute it well, you'll be prepared to face the dark and stormy night that may seem to last forever.

Chapter Eight
Staying Safe

According to Coast Guard statistics, nearly 80 percent of those who drown in boating accidents were not wearing personal flotation devices (PFDs), even though in many cases there were life jackets on board.

"Many boaters don't wear their life jackets while on the water because they think they will have plenty of time to put them on in an emergency situation," said Rear Admiral Jeffrey J. Hathaway, Director of Operations Policy, U.S. Coast Guard. "The reality is that there is no time to find your life jacket in an unexpected predicament. Boaters should wear their life jackets at all times while underway."

Coast Guard regulations require at least one approved PFD on board for each person on the boat. Some state regulations go a step farther, requiring that children under a certain age must actually be wearing a PFD while on board. Good sense says all of us should wear life jackets while under way. That's because accidents happen at the most unexpected times.

Somebody moves at just the wrong moment, or the wake of a passing boat causes the boat to rock, someone loses balance and goes overboard.

An accidental jibe brings the boom roaring across the cockpit, catches someone in the noggin, and knocks him over the rail.

Or a guy with a full bladder steps to the rail in pursuit of a natural event, the boat shifts and over he goes.

Coast Guard incident case files are full of weird stories about how folks end up in the drink. I am personally familiar with two incidents in our area that occurred in calm weather conditions and resulted in boats being located with their motors still running, but no occupants. In both cases, the bodies were never found. One was a friend of mine.

Cold Shock / Swimming Failure

Those of us who aren't lucky enough to live in the Caribbean sail on fairly cold water, and ending up in *that* kind of water without protection can result in catastrophe. When we talk about being in cold water, most of us think hypothermia is the big killer. Actually, if you fall in chilly water, you probably won't live long enough to die of hypothermia.

The big killer is drowning, and it makes no difference how strong a swimmer you are. When your warm body hits the cold water, a physiological condition called cold shock takes place. Cold shock is the body's reaction to suddenly being immersed in cold water, and it causes instantaneous failure of the ability to breathe correctly. The first reaction is to suddenly gasp for breath, and unless your head is above water when that happens, you'll inhale a bunch of water. That starts the victim choking and induces panic. Cold shock immediately leads to a condition known as swimming failure. The muscles lose coordination and even a strong swimmer will begin slapping at the water, flailing arms and legs, gasping for air, choking, and then swiftly drowning.

The only protection you have against cold shock and swimming failure is to wear a personal flotation device. A good PFD will keep your head above water and keep you from drowning long enough either to be rescued, to rescue yourself, or to slowly die of hypothermia. How well you survive depends somewhat upon the type of PFD you are wearing.

U.S. Coast Guard approved PFDs are ranked in five Types (I through V) and some of these Types are available in three variations — inherently buoyant (primarily foam), inflatable, and hybrid (a combination of inherently buoyant and inflatable).

Personal Flotation Devices must be Coast Guard approved. Look for the certification printed on the product label.

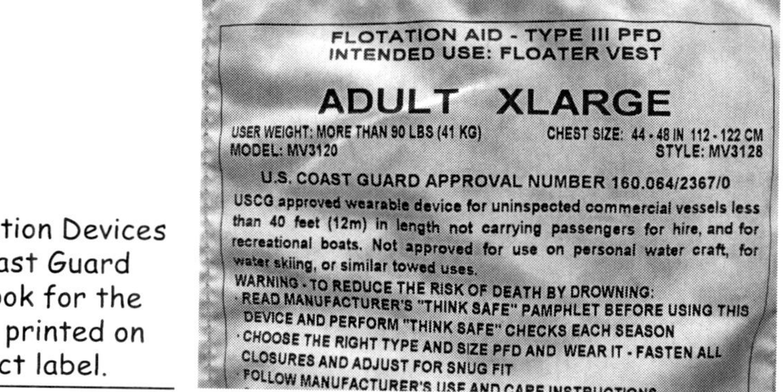

Varieties

Of the three varieties, the most reliable are the inherently buoyant PFDs, because they don't depend upon an inflation bladder that could possibly fail. The wearable ones come in sizes to fit infant, child, youth and adult bodies. And there are throwable styles as well.

Inflatable PFDs come in two versions — manual and automatic. The automatic models activate a few seconds after making contact with the water, without any action on your part. Manual ones require you to pull the "rip cord" to inflate the bladder. You can also pull the rip cord to manually activate an automatic one, if you want to. But if you get conked on the head and end up in the water without all your brain cells operating, you probably won't be able to manually activate the inflation device. So, for my money, the automatic units are the best.

However ... remind me to tell you, someday, about the time Becky decided to wash our automatic inflatables in the bathtub because they were dirty. And while we're on that subject, it's a good idea to learn how to re-arm your inflatable PFDs by yourself. It's easy to do, and a lot cheaper than having a professional service do it for you. It's a simple matter of replacing a CO_2 cartridge, a bobbin (automatic inflatables only) and retaining pin device by following the instructions that come with the PFD.

Hybrid PFDs combine the reliability of foam flotation with the additional buoyancy of an inflation bladder. What you have here is a regular life vest (inherently buoyant) to which an inflatable PFD has been attached. I love the concept ... except for the fact that most folks will tend to avoid wearing the vest because they think it's not comfortable.

Types

As we examine the characteristics of each PFD Type, buoyancy figures for adult sizes will be shown. Youth, child and infant sizes will provide proportionately less buoyancy.

- Type I — Offshore Life Jackets. These are ranked as being effective in all waters, especially open water (offshore) and in conditions where rescue might be delayed. These units provide more positive flotation than any other type and they are designed to turn most unconscious wearers to a face-up position in the water. Inherently buoyant models provide a minimum of 22 pounds of positive flotation (adult size), and the same size inflatable models supply 34 pounds of flotation. Hybrid Type I PFDs are also available.

• Type II — Near Shore Buoyant Vests are intended for calm waters where there is a good chance a rescue can take place quickly. The inherently buoyant models provide 15.5 pounds of flotation (adult size) and will turn *some* unconscious wearers face up, but not quite as well as a Type I. Inflatable models of Type II provide 34 pounds of flotation (adult size) and will turn a wearer face up as effectively as a Type I foam PFD. There are hybrid Type II PFDs, as well, offering 10 pounds of initial buoyancy and 22 pounds when inflated (adult size).

• Type III — These are categorized as Flotation Aids, and are intended for use in calm inland waters where there is a good chance of a speedy rescue. These are designed to allow a person in the water to place himself in a face-up position (not good for unconscious victims). Examples of Type III units are float coats, and vests primarily intended for sports activities such as fishing or canoeing. Adult sizes provide 15.5 pounds of flotation in the inherently buoyant models, and 22.5 pounds in inflatable versions. Inflatables will turn a victim as well as a Type II foam PFD. Hybrids offer 10 pounds of inherent buoyancy and a total of 22 pounds when inflated.

• Type IV — Throwable devices are intended for use in calm, inland waters where there is substantial boat traffic (lots of available help) and an expectation of speedy rescue. These are designed to be thrown to a person in the water, who will then hang on to the flotation device until help arrives. Flotation cushions with handles, ring buoys, and horseshoe buoys are examples of Type IV PFDs. All of these are of the inherently buoyant variety, and there are no inflatable Type IV PFDs.

• Type V — Special Use Devices. This category includes such things as deck suits, work vests, board sailing vests and inflatable vests with safety harnesses. Type V PFDs provide the flotation performance of either a Type I, II or III, as indicated on the product label. Look for instructions that may indicate the PFD must be worn in order to meet the Coast Guard's carriage requirements (this is the requirement that at least one qualified PFD be carried for each person on board). If this is the case, and the Type V unit is not being worn, it won't count toward meeting the minimum carriage requirement.

As a member of the Coast Guard Auxiliary, when I go on patrol I wear a Type V deck suit that not only provides full-length flotation for my body, but also helps protect against the onset of hypothermia. It has an inflatable collar and a full-coverage hood, and the wrists and pant cuffs can be closed tight to prevent cold water from passing freely.

On *Three Eagles* we carry a couple of Type V inflatable harnesses featuring sturdy D rings. These allow us to tether ourselves to the boat when the weather gets rough or when there's a need to go up on deck. If I go over the side, at least I'll stay with the boat rather than being lost in the waves.

The Coast Guard, however, issues cautions about using harnesses with tethers. Their concerns are about shock load injury when a person falls overboard and is suddenly snapped to a stop; and about being dragged to the bottom with a sinking boat to which you're tethered. To address these concerns, harness type PFDs must be properly fitted, with the belt at least 2 inches above the lower ribs, to avoid the shock load injury. And the tether should be less than 6.5 feet long and have a quick-release buckle so you can detach from the tether under load, if you want to.

Selecting the right PFDs for yourself and your crew involves a few more considerations. Proper size is critical. A child who is wearing an adult-sized PFD is not well protected, because he or she can easily slip right out the bottom (unless there are crotch straps). Also, proper size will help delay the onset of hypothermia better than a model that's too big. Before buying, try on the PFD and make sure it fits well. Have someone lift you by the PFD by the shoulders (as might happen during a rescue) to see if it stays in place. If the top of the zipper comes up to your nose, the PFD is too loose.

Color is another area of concern. You might love the attractive blue and green PFD with a fabric pattern in a fish and seaweed motif, but that's not the one you want. If you end up in the water and people are looking for you from their boats and perhaps from helicopters, you don't want to be playing camouflage. You want the brightest yellow, orange or red PFD you can find. The same goes for the kids. They might plead for the cute one with cartoon characters on it, but those small and precious targets need to be as highly visible as possible — just in case.

Ideally, a PFD should have signaling devices on it to help rescuers find the victim. Reflective tape is a beginning, but my PFD also has a shoulder-mounted personal strobe light, a pocket full of small handheld flares, a dye packet, a signal mirror, and a whistle. A small waterproof handheld VHF radio is tethered to one pocket so I can call for help and in another pocket is a small waterproof GPS tethered to the PFD. By using these devices, if I go in the water and am lost to view, I can call the Coast Guard and tell them exactly where to find me. Equipped like that, a PFD becomes a survival and rescue pod, not merely something to keep me afloat until hypothermia sets in and I die a lingering death.

Pre-cruise Briefing

Before casting off the docklines and heading out, there should be a pre-cruise briefing for all passengers who are not already intimately familiar with the boat. It takes only a few minutes to cover the safety issues — where the fire extinguishers are, where the dewatering devices (bailing bucket, bilge pump switch, etc.) are and how to operate them, where the VHF radio is and how to use it to call for help, and what to do in the event of a man-overboard incident. You might need to help each person get into his or her PFD properly. While you're at it, if your boat has a marine head, you might need to give a few minutes of instruction about how to use it.

Periodically check the gauge on your fire extinguisher to make sure it is fully charged. At the same time, turn the unit upside-down a few times to shake loose the powder inside and keep it from clumping.

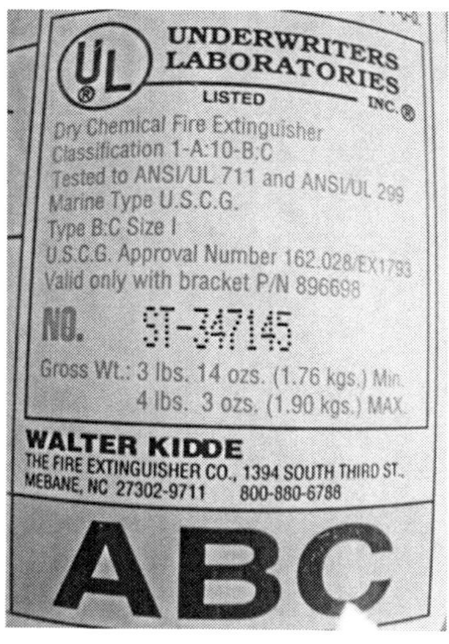

Fire extinguishers must be Coast Guard approved, and you must have enough of them (according to the size of your boat) in order for your vessel to pass a safety inspection. More is better here.

Along with all that, visitors should be briefed on what to expect when the boat is under sail. Many first-time sailors are suddenly stunned when the boat heels, so it's nice to let them know in advance what is going to happen. Depending upon your boat layout, you might need to assign seating, so people don't end up clustering in places that hamper your ability to control the boat. Non-boaters get all excited about the freedom and beauty of being out on the water, and might feel like they are free to wander anywhere on the boat they choose. Rules like, "while under sail, nobody goes up on deck," might help prevent an accident.

You might ask the passengers if they would like to learn how to operate the boat, then assign appropriate duties. Explain what happens during a tack or jibe, and let the passengers handle the sheets or steer the boat. It's best to do this in an area where little damage can be done if the boat doesn't make the turn just right, not in a crowded waterway.

The more your passengers can be involved in the sailing process, the more fun they will have. And they'll come away from the experience with some first-hand knowledge and greater enthusiasm for sailing.

In the end, being safe doesn't mean you can't have fun. It just means you'll live long enough to have fun more than once.

Chapter Nine

Anyone Can Get Seasick ... Remedies That Help
(A Note From Becky)

We have a friend who for more than thirty years has worked the cod, halibut and salmon waters of Southeast Alaska. Rich asked him if he ever gets seasick.

"Heck yeah," Garth said.

We were amazed. How can it be that a guy who has spent his whole life on the sea still gets seasick? Shouldn't he have gotten over that landlubber's weakness by now?

I did a little research and discovered that seasickness isn't a "weakness" and doesn't afflict only those who are new to boating. Anyone can get seasick, depending upon the situation—the individual's health, susceptibility, fatigue, eating habits, state of mind, etc. Seasickness should be called motion sickness, because it isn't restricted to sea travel alone. Being a passenger in a car or an airplane can cause the same problem.

Another interesting thing is that people who normally have an iron stomach can suddenly get sick, if the conditions are right (maybe I should say wrong). Rich never gets seasick ... well, almost never. He's been in extreme conditions for days on end. Once, while helping Garth bring his commercial fishing boat home from Alaska, the guys hit some nasty weather. They were fighting rough seas that broke over the wheelhouse 12 feet above the waterline, plunging the vessel into bottomless troughs and then launching it over the crest of the next wave and free falling into the next trough. A dizzying ride, but not bad enough to make Rich sick. He felt invulnerable to the malady of seasickness.

Then, oddly enough, on a simple little boating trip with friends off the coast of Washington, it happened. The rollers were just so, and his stomach flip-flopped and soon he was bent over the rail. One other time (when our boat was dismasted), the emotional trauma, his exhaustion and the seas conspired to turn his stomach inside out.

Anybody can get seasick. I admit I've had some experience with the nautical nausea myself. Normally, it's not a factor for me, but when the seas churn like a Maytag on steroids, I confess I can get woozy and I'll keep a pail handy (though I've never had to use it—yet).

The trouble with seasickness is, it can reach serious proportions. We've heard stories of people needing rescue, and abandoning ship, because they were too sick to carry on. It wasn't that the boat was sinking or in any kind of real peril—the skipper and crew were too sick and exhausted to continue. If you're sick long enough, you can become seriously dehydrated and completely debilitated.

So, what do you do if you want to go out sailing, but you're prone to motion sickness? Or, what if you're not normally queasy, but feel an occasional bout coming on?

You can take several steps to help prevent seasickness. One is to be well rested before starting the voyage. Then make sure you don't get overly tired or stressed during the trip. Alternate shifts at the helm to prevent fatigue, especially during rough weather. Fatigue definitely makes you more prone to seasickness. Another precaution is to watch what you eat. Avoid rich, fatty food. Crackers or other carbs seem to help me, if I'm feeling a tad on the line.

Don't start the trip if you're already feeling out of sorts. It's better to postpone the vacation than spend it bent over the rail. Anxiety is just as bad as a bug when it comes to getting seasick, so if you're in the midst of a worrisome time, you'll be more vulnerable. One odd thing I've noticed is if I need to make a serious potty stop and don't do so in a timely manner, I'll get nauseous if the water gets choppy. But if the bathroom duties are out of the way, it takes a lot more rocking and rolling to make me feel out of sorts.

If someone starts to become sick during a voyage, put the queasy person at the helm. Driving the boat helps focus the eyes and the brain on the same task, which is the heart of overcoming seasickness. Another good option is to lie down as near to the center and as low in the cabin as possible, where the motion is the least. Close your eyes and pretend you're a baby in a crib and let the boat rock you to sleep.

One of the worst things a seasick person can do is read. Been there, done that! Focusing on a steady page while the eyes are bouncing around and getting confused doesn't work. As a matter of fact, even if you weren't seasick before, reading a book below in the forepeak on a slightly rolling ocean can get you there in a hurry.

Another bad idea is to go below and start cooking. The aromas filling the air may cause you to feel even worse. You may lose your lunch before you even get it down.

Some folks respond well to certain over the counter motion sickness medications. But if you wait until you're already violently sick, taking the pills won't help. You have to take them before the onset of the misery or shortly thereafter. They won't do you any good if you're already vomiting.

A friend of ours always carries a bottle of *Meclizine* on her boat. Shirley purchases it over-the-counter at the local drug store, and finds it helpful for those days when the water is a bit choppy, and she knows she may be prone to feeling woozy. She has a plan of action, so nothing keeps her off the water. There are other medications that can be taken for seasickness. Talk with your doctor so he can advise what's best for you.

I prefer to take the natural route whenever possible and take herbal remedies for motion sickness. I've used a product with some success by Nature's Way. It's a concoction of ginger root and peppermint in capsule form. Ginger is one of those longtime remedies for motion sickness. We even keep ginger snaps aboard... after all you just never know when you might want to take preventative measures for seasickness, by downing a few cookies.

When we bought *Three Eagles*, I'd never been on a sailboat before, and worried I might be prone to seasickness, because motion sickness was a problem for me when I was a kid. In addition to the herbal solutions I brought on board, I also found and purchased wrist bands that are supposed to help with seasickness. They have a small piece of rounded plastic that fits over a pressure point on the wrist.

Normally I'm not troubled by the motion of the boat on the water; I find it soothing. However, a few times I've needed some help. On one sailing excursion, the boat was bobbing up and down at quick intervals. Maybe I was a little tired that day, or for some other reason I wasn't up to par. I began to feel queasy and, after about 15 minutes, I decided to try the ginger capsules. Although they didn't completely relieve the feeling of nausea, I found I wasn't getting progressively worse. I suspect if I'd taken them sooner, I'd have been fine. On another voyage, I ate a few ginger snaps, which were decidedly more tasty, and I felt better right away. Comfort food, right?

On my worst trip, we were in rough seas crossing the Strait of Juan de Fuca, and I waited too long before taking something. This time, I reached for the wrist straps, and even though I was feeling nauseated, by the time I put them on, they actually helped reduce the sick feeling, and I did fairly well in spite of the rough ride. I'm a believer in those wrist bands!

We try to avoid rough seas, but sometimes we've been caught for a few hours reaching calmer water. During one memorable trip, the seas kicked up and Rich put me at the helm because he could see I was getting a little green around the gills. He knew piloting *Three Eagles* was the best chance I'd have of keeping my lunch down.

I was so intent on driving the boat, I forgot to take something for seasickness. We did everything else right, alternating taking the helm back and forth, so neither of us became exhausted. We each took turns "spotting" for the other, to make sure we didn't run into deadheads or beds of kelp. By the time we reached our dock, I was dizzy and nauseated. Didn't lose my lunch, but nonetheless I felt awful.

Now, the moment I feel an uncomfortable queasiness coming on, I take something for it. I don't wait to get a full-blown case of seasickness. After all, when you're out on the boat, you want to spend your time looking over the rail to admire the starfish, not yelling, "Ralph!"

Chapter Ten
Provisioning and Organizing

Trailerable sailboats have one characteristic in common — they're small inside. Even the 26-footer we bought after extensive research to find the most boat for the money, is small inside. So small Rich can't stand up straight except in the companionway with the hatch pushed forward. And yet we love living aboard for weeks at a time. How is that possible?

The answer has a lot to do with organization and selective provisioning. We can't bring everything from home, so we must be choosy about what we take on our trips. Up to a point, the less you have onboard, the simpler life is. However, we aren't big fans of a monastic lifestyle. With a little tricky organizing, we've discovered ways to take enough stuff to make life comfortable, without cluttering the living space.

We can't stand to live on a boat that looks as if it's been ransacked by a hoard of marauding barbarians. To maintain our sanity we must have a place for everything and keep everything in its place. Each boat is different in regard to stowage, so you'll have to survey your own boat to discover how to utilize compartments and other spaces.

The things we take on our voyages fall within several distinct categories: clothing, food, water, cookware, dishware, toiletries, towels, bedding, entertainment, and tools — your mileage may vary. The best approach we've found is to keep like items together and stow them in logical places.

- **Clothing** — We each have a soft duffle bag we use for clothing. That way, when I'm due for a change of underwear, I don't have to rifle through Rich's stuff to find what I'm looking for. The soft duffle makes it possible to cram the bag in an odd corner of the boat where nothing else will fit. In the Army, Rich learned to roll stowed clothing so tight they almost bleed, and that allows us to take plenty of clothing in a small bag.

We use a large mesh bag as the dirty clothes hamper, and on long voyages we look for a laundry facility about once each week. To avoid the need to shop for laundry detergent in a strange town or buy the expensive stuff at the local laundromat, we take our own. A small container of highly concentrated detergent goes a long way. The only other thing you need is a roll of quarters for use at laundromats and marina showers.

• **Food Storage**—We use two primary spaces for food storage on our boat. One is the cooler beneath a dinette seat, and the other location is under the settee. Originally, the food storage compartment under the settee was inefficient, because of the small opening to the space. One of the first modifications we made to our boat was to arrange better access to the "pantry" by cutting away some of the fiberglass that served as a platform for the settee cushion, and then installing a hinged lid to cover the opening and support the cushion. This is where we store canned goods, bread, cereal, condiments, tea, and other food items we don't need to keep cold. Soft packaging and small containers are easier to work with than large or rigid packaging. Small items and soft packages can be stowed in all sorts of irregular spaces, making better use of the compartment.

Simple things like coat hooks go a long way toward keeping the interior of the boat orderly. Notice also the hooks and other organizers along the wall that are inexpensive and easy to install.

Repackaging dry bulk foods is helpful. Empty cereal boxes into a tough zip baggie (perhaps even double bagging for extra protection), makes it easier to stow in an awkward nook or cranny. This trick works well for pasta, dried fruit, nuts, cookies, oatmeal, etc. We keep a supply of zip baggies onboard; they're easier to use and store than rigid plastic containers, and they work well for dry goods. We clean and recycle baggies that aren't damaged; they're efficient and cost effective. Baggies have scores of uses and take up almost zero space in the trash bag after their life is over.

Use every cubby hole to stow supplies. Beneath the settee, we store food and related items such as plastic baggies, paper towels, etc.

• **Quick and Easy Meals** — Cup'o Soup, mashed potato cup, and Cup 'o Noodles type products offer easy ways to make a quick meal. You'll find a variety of "just add water" items in grocery stores, ideal for life aboard a small boat. Add a small amount of hot water to the cup, then stir and wait a few minutes before eating.

These foods have a long shelf life, are relatively inexpensive, lightweight, and the containers can be burned or crushed to take up little space in the trash bag. To further decrease the weight load and simplify our trash situation, we sometimes take Mountain House / Marine Cuisine freeze-dried meals (7-year shelf life). The variety is great; you can get everything from lasagna with meat sauce to scrambled eggs and ham, and fixing the meals is super simple — just add the specified amount of boiling water, stir, close the package and wait a few minutes. You can eat the meal right out of the package, which eliminates dishes. Am I lazy, or what?

• One clever way to cook a healthful and filling whole grain breakfast while you sleep is to use a stainless steel thermos with a large mouth. Before retiring to your bunk, boil water and pour it into the thermos at a ratio of 2:1 water to grains. Add the grains and a dash or two of salt. Stir everything, then seal the top of the thermos. Let sit overnight. We enjoy creating our own blends such as wheat, spelt, kasha, oat groats and rye.

After "slow cooking" all night, the grains are ready to eat in the morning. Just add a sprinkling of chopped nuts, raisins, dates, or other dried fruit. Sweeten to taste. Yum! To minimize the work, we premix these grains and put them in 1-cup quantities in zip baggies before leaving home. We do the same with bulk oatmeal, pre-measuring and packaging so it's easy to whip up a hot breakfast without any fuss.

   • **In the Ice Chest**—We use a combination of block and crushed ice. The block lasts longer, but crushed ice chills better. To maximize the life of the ice, plan ahead before you open the lid. Know what you're going after and then get in and out as fast as possible. When you're putting things back in the chest, get the job done all at once as quickly as possible. Keep the ice chest out of direct sunlight. If that's not possible, insulate it by covering it with a reflective Space Blanket or erect some kind of shade.

   Our preference is to minimize foods we must keep in an ice chest, so we reserve space for fresh meats, dairy, eggs, and condiments. To limit the amount of fresh meat, we carry canned beef and chicken, as well as tuna. As a milk substitute, we use soy milk, because it requires no refrigeration until the carton is opened. We can take a month's supply stowed away among our long-term storage and use it one carton at a time when needed. Cheese can be kept unrefrigerated if it's immersed in olive oil in a sealed container. When we prepare meals, we measure ingredients to keep portion sizes totally consumable, so we don't have leftovers to deal with.

   • **Stocking Up**—We plan stops at grocery stores along the way, but on vacations where stores don't exist, we take enough food to see us through, plus a little extra, in case we have to wait out a bad weather pattern. This long-term food storage is kept captive in plastic tubs in the open space beneath the cockpit.

   • **Green Bags**—Our major concern about reprovisioning consists of buying fresh vegetable and fruits. These keep better when stored in Evert Fresh Green Bags (available online at www.greenbags.com). The trick is to eliminate as much moisture as possible from the produce; place a dry paper towel in the bag, then insert the produce and squeeze out the air before sealing the bag. If you store this in a cool, dark place, the produce (even delicate things like lettuce) will last a surprisingly long time. And the bags can be reused.

• **Garbage** — To reduce the garbage problem, we take as much food as possible in soft packaging, rather than cans or bottles. From time to time along the way, where local conditions and laws permit, we start a campfire and burn the combustibles. We even burn the cans, to eliminate food residue and labels, then crush the cans and pack them in small trash bags and transfer them to a large mesh bag hanging from our aft stanchion, until we can dispose of it properly. Keeping the trash outside helps avoid problems with small critters that like to sneak aboard at night in search of a free meal. Mice will use docklines to crawl onto the boat, unless you find a way to stop them. One effective deterrent to mice is to place small pie tins on the docklines to act as a physical barrier. Poke a dockline-sized hole in the center of the pie tin (Note: eat the pie first) and string the line through. When the mouse reaches the pie tin, he has to turn around and look for somebody else's boat to invade.

• **Water** — Storage of freshwater takes several forms on our boat. Beneath the galley sink is a collapsible 5-gallon bladder that feeds the sink. Unfortunately, the sink is too small for much practical application other than washing silverware or hands. Pots and pans have no chance in that sink. A manual pump moves the water from the bladder through a spout, and we use that to draw water into a small basin for washing dishes. The collapsible bladder is nice, because it has a built-in handle and we can carry it to a water source ashore to refill. We don't use this water for drinking or cooking — for those purposes, we carry extra water in other containers.

Under the forward dinette seat, we place plastic tubs holding 1-gallon plastic water containers and a bunch of 16-ounce water bottles. This is the most convenient way for us to quickly grab water for drinking or cooking.

On longer trips, we take 5-gallon cube-shaped plastic water containers. We can handle about 30 gallons this way, placing one container in the forward-most part of the central aisle, with the rest tucked in the space beneath the cockpit. Taking that much fresh water makes it possible for us to boat camp in remote places for weeks without having to worry about running out of water.

When the container in the aisle runs dry, we replace it with another. The easiest way to draw water is to lay the cube-shaped container on its side on the galley counter and open the valve to pour water into a smaller container. Works like a charm. The only caution is that water weighs about 8.5 lbs. per gallon. Be careful to avoid overloading the boat or causing the boat to ride off-kilter on the water by stowing it improperly. Keep the weight as close as possible to the boat's centerline, and balance the load fore and aft.

 • **Cooking Methods** — We use both electric and propane cooking methods on our boat. If we're spending the night at a marina with shore power, we plug in and use electricity to save our propane supply. If we're at anchor or tied to a dock without shore power, we use the propane. The electric cooking appliances consist of a 1-burner hotplate and a small crock pot. Because these appliances are not built-in, with the use of an extension cord, we can move them to the cockpit or cabin top to cook. We aren't stuck cooking inside the cabin, which is a huge benefit on a hot day.

For cooking with propane, we use a compact single-burner stove that can be used on the countertop in the galley or moved to the cockpit for cooking outside. Some boat owners install a small BBQ on the stern railing, adding another dimension to meal preparation. We store both of our stoves in a plastic tub in the space beneath the cockpit, out of the way and yet easy to reach when needed. For safety, we keep only a single propane fuel canister with the stoves, and additional canisters are stored outside near the outboard motor fuel tank.

 • **Dishware** — Nothing is easier than paper plates. Use them, toss them (burn them when possible), and don't worry about washing dishes. But sometimes you need something sturdier than paper. For those occasions, we have four indestructible plastic plates and bowls that serve as a foundation. We keep four of each in case we have guests for dinner and want to set out our finest china. The plates, both paper and plastic, are stored in a wall-mounted

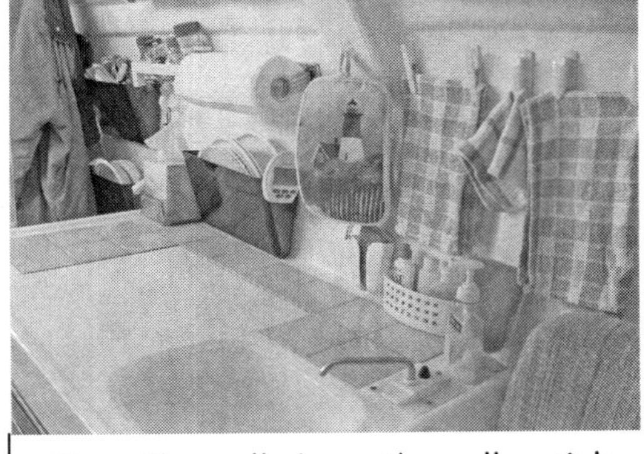

Along the wall above the galley sink and cabinet, we hang hand towels, pot holders, and a roll of paper towels. A small organizer with suction cups holds biodegradable hand soap, dish soap, and a washing sponge. Farther aft is an organizer that holds plastic plates that serve as a foundation beneath paper plates.

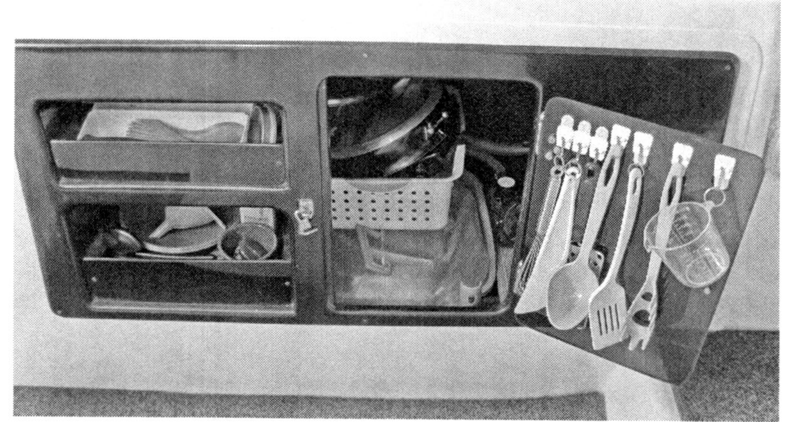

Self-sticking hooks inside the galley cabinet door hold
utensils that now have rings installed in their handles.
I placed shelves inside the cabinet to hold pots
and pans, and silverware is stowed in the cubbies
in the face of the cabinet.

file organizer that we bought at an office supply store. The bowls fit in a cubby in the galley area.

Our boat came with a galley cabinet featuring a couple of silverware cubbies and a door that opens for access to the space below the counter. We needed more storage capacity, so I used the space to install a couple of plywood shelves to hold a frying pan, a small pot, and lids for both. On the inside of the cabinet door, we installed self-sticking hooks to hold a spatula, ladle, whisk, big cooking spoon, and a plastic measuring cup.

We've learned to be creative and make a storage opportunity on every wall. All the "silverware" goes in the front-load cubbies in the face of the cabinet. Included are plastic spoons, forks and butter knives, sporks (spoon on one end, fork on the other), a couple of stainless paring knives and our nifty can opener that removes the lid without leaving sharp edges.

• **Toiletries** — Our head (bathroom) is small, so we can't afford to let it get disorganized. On two walls, we installed special organizers — one is made of fairly hefty canvas and has large pockets that hold heavy or bulky items. The other is a mesh unit with several small pouches for things like toothbrushes in holders, toothpaste, combs and brushes, ponytail wraps, hair gel, a bar of soap in a plastic box, a travel box of Q-tips, and other small items.

On the inside of the head door is a mirror, so anyone who wants to take a peek at how she looks can do it. I never look, 'cause I already know the bad news.

• **Towels** — We hang our bath towels out to dry after showering by using the lifelines and a couple of small but powerful clamps I got at a hardware store. After drying, the towels are rolled up and stowed in a duffel bag until next use. We keep a few extra bath towels in the bag, just because we're paranoid ... I mean just because we like to be prepared. We also have a few extra hand towels and washcloths in the bag. Two hand towels hang above the galley sink — one for drying hands, and the other for drying dishes.

We chose a net organizer to hold rolled up bath towels, but the net can be very useful for all kinds of stowage solutions, including bananas, oranges, apples and such.

• **Bedding** — We've found sleeping bags are the easiest solution to the bedding question. A small comforter with a nautical theme covers the bags when we're not in them. On the wall at the head of our bunks we installed organizers to hold our glasses, a small flashlight, and a notepad and pencil in case we have an important thought while relaxing.

- **Entertainment** — By entertainment, I mean books, magazines and games. We have our favorite games — cribbage, and a few card games like golf and rummy we can play with any old deck. We don't need much space store a deck of cards and a cribbage board, so we found a small spot to tuck those items into next to the dinette where we play the games. The books and magazines are kept where they belong by using office-type wall-mounted file organizers. This kind of low-tech entertainment is ideal for a small sailboat, and we find the break from electronic gizmos is refreshing.

- **Tools** — You never know what's going to break down, so it's a good idea to have a fairly complete set of tools and repair equipment on board. We use a plastic toolbox that lives under the dinette table, only marginally in the way of our feet. With more than two of us aboard, we'd have to make other arrangements. The box holds an assortment of wrenches, pliers, a hacksaw, a bolt cutter (in case we need to cut the rigging if the mast goes overboard), and a screwdriver with a variety of tips. We store a set of jumper cables in a plastic bag near the battery, in case we need help getting the motor started.

- **Miscellaneous Organizers** — For storing supplies like adhesives, tape, and Velcro, we use small plastic tackle boxes with adjustable dividers. Elsewhere in the boat I have a drawstring bag holding small bungee cords and lightweight line. Extra docklines, and a couple hundred feet of anchor line are coiled and reside in a space unusable for anything else below the galley.

In essence, we searched through every empty space and found a way to fill it with gear that rarely gets used but is necessary to have aboard. It's not impossible for water to get aboard and ruin items stored below the floor, so we put everything in some kind of dry storage container — a plastic box, a zip baggie, or a dry sack.

- **Safety Equipment** — A water-tight orange box made by Plano holds all the distress signals — flares and gun, flags, dye markers, signal mirror, horn. A small tray in the top of the box atores our spare flashlight batteries and AA cells for the handheld GPS unit. And for protection, we also keep the binoculars in the safe confines of this box. Because of its importance to safety on the water, we keep the box within easy reach below the companionway entrance. We store extra personal flotation devices for visitors in an open-topped plastic tub adjacent to the flare box. You don't want to have to go far to reach this stuff when needed.

Emergency distress signal equipment, such as flares, should be kept in
a safe, dry location that is easy to reach without having to search
for it. We use a waterproof orange plastic box that is kept at
the foot of the companionway steps.

• **Odds and Ends** — When we started out, we had no place to
hang a jacket. That's the way it is with many boats, and coats
are dropped in any spot that looks empty. Soon you're stumbling
around in a mess. One of our projects was installing a couple of
coat hooks. Next came the paper towel holder, then the spice rack,
and then hooks to hold our hats and sunglasses. Small projects,
every one, but the organizational impact was huge. We no longer
had all these items drifting around the inside of the boat looking
for a place to land.

Inexpensive plastic hooks with self-stick backing are perfect for
the small boat owner, because the hooks install without drilling
holes and sticking screws through the side of the boat. Double-sided
sticky tape is another true friend, and we've used it to add lots
of organizers. We've discovered office supply stores are the best
places to shop for small organizers. We turned to West Marine for
our water bottle (cup) holders that fold up when not in use. These
are located in the cabin beside the dinette and in the cockpit, so
our water bottles don't escape during an exciting tack or jibe.

Provisioning and organizing a small boat is such a purely individual
endeavor that it's impossible for one person to tell another exactly

how it should be accomplished. We love to visit with other boat owners, go aboard, and see what they've done to make their space easy and comfortable to live in. We've come to appreciate the concept that life aboard is more pleasant when the cabin and cockpit are clean and uncluttered. This might sound trite, but "a place for everything and everything in its place" is the best policy. That's what keeps your little ship shipshape.

Chapter Eleven
Stuff for the Boat

A universal law of boat ownership compels skippers to fill every available space with stuff. I've known men who were dedicated non-shoppers during their pre-boat lives, but when a boat showed up in the driveway, they went nuts. Just in case you're wondering, the degree of mental derangement is diagnosed by measuring the stack of boat equipment catalogs on the nightstand. An alternate diagnostic method is to evaluate how much time the skipper spends reading advertisements in a sailing magazine.

When we bought our boat, the dealer gave us excellent advice about buying accessories. Even though he could have fattened his commission by encouraging us to buy all the optional goodies, he said, "Use the boat for a season before you start buying things for it. After you use it for awhile, you'll know what you need and want to add for the type of sailing you're doing."

Good advice. But some items are less expensive when purchased right up front from the factory. We made a careful evaluation of the items on the options list and bought the things

A dinghy is a good piece of safety equipment that is also very con-venient when you anchor out, then row ashore. We stow ours on the foredeck during passages, so dragging the boat doesn't slow us down.

that most interested us. Over the years, we've made other purchases for *Three Eagles* from West Marine and other boating supply outlets. We continue to plan future purchases, as needs arise, always keeping a keen eye on the budget.

Sails

We got the standard main and jib that come stock with the boat. Then we opted for the 150% genoa and the asymmetrical spinnaker (no pole) for times when light air rules the day or we want to make a colorful downwind run on an easy breeze. It would cost more to buy these sails later, so we didn't feel bad about making this purchase from the dealer. We've enjoyed using all three headsails, and our pattern is to use the genoa more than the jib, and the spinnaker only infrequently.

A spinnaker isn't easy to raise or lower. Someone needs to stand on the foredeck sorting out all the mess, and it's easy to get a twist in the sail as it unfurls. This can turn into an adventure, and sometimes we just want to go lazy-sailing without all the gymnastics.

The first time we used the spinnaker, we were lake sailing high in the Rocky Mountains. We positioned the boat so it pointed downwind, and Becky took the helm. Then I secured the spinnaker control lines to cleats on each side of the cockpit and, against Becky's cautionary protests, went up on deck to hoist the chute. She was afraid she wouldn't know what to do when the spinnaker popped open, but I told her to just hold a steady course to keep air in the sail until I could scramble back to

The big, colorful sail is the spinnaker. It's used for downwind sailing in light wind. This sail requires special management when raising and lowering because the fabric is so light that the merest wisp of wind will blow it around and tangle it.

the cockpit.

With a 10-knot breeze behind us, I hoisted away and as the light fabric came out of the bag, it did a double-wrap twist around itself. I grabbed the control lines and tugged this way and that until the spinnaker finally popped open. When it did, the boat took off like it was kicked in the rear. The sudden acceleration threw me off my feet, because I wasn't expecting it. Becky screamed when she saw me go down, thinking I was going to fall overboard and leave her alone on a runaway boat.

Everything worked out — I got back on my feet, scrambled to the cockpit and took the helm. The ride lasted about three minutes before the wind suddenly died. Sailing Rocky Mountain lakes is like that — you chase every puff, only to have it either die or do a 180 on you. But we were satisfied we'd sailed under spinnaker — it was colorful and exciting, and we loved it.

Not long after that, we bought a spinnaker sock — a sleeve that covers the sail and keeps it fully contained even after it has been hoisted. The control lines have already been sorted out, and you're ready for air to hit the fabric. You pull on a line to slide the sleeve off, and the sail pops open. To douse the spinnaker, pull the sleeve back down over the chute, and you're done. Simple as pie. We're far less hesitant about using the spinnaker now, so we consider the sock one of our better purchases. If you're going to have a light-air downwind sail, seriously consider getting a sock for it.

For the jib and genoa, we wanted the roller furling option. After years of sailing, we still feel this is the best way to go (although racing purists make the powerful and correct point that a sail on a roller furler will not have as clean and efficient a shape as a sail clipped on the headstay). For us, safety is the issue, and we're perfectly willing to sacrifice a bit of speed for the sake of safety. With the roller furler, nobody has to go up on the deck while underway to lower a sail or change to another one. When said adjustments are called for, the whole thing can be easily handled from the safety of the cockpit. In a heartbeat, you can reduce sail to compensate for sudden gusty conditions that might put you at risk. For us, roller furling isn't an option; we wouldn't have a sailboat without it.

Unfortunately, the MacGregor factory didn't offer an optional set-up for handling the mainsail halyard. In stock condition, we had to leave the cockpit and go to the mast to raise or lower the main. So one of the first modifications we made was to buy a new, longer halyard, a couple of turning blocks, and a clutch. This allowed us to run the main halyard all the way down the mast, through two blocks, and back to the clutch at the cockpit. Then I added a couple of lines to the reefing points, so I can reach up and grab those lines to reef the main. I also added a downhaul line running to the head of the mainsail, so I can pull the head of the sail all the way down without having to leave the cockpit. None of these modifications were particularly expensive, and we consider it money well spent.

Galley

After talking with other boat owners, we decided not to equip our boat with the optional alcohol stove. At high elevations, alcohol doesn't produce enough heat to do a good job of cooking. Even at sea-level, it's only a marginal fuel. Our stove is a MasterGlow (made by Athena) that operates on Max Burton butane canisters. It cooks just like a gas stove at home, with infinite flame adjustability. This works for us, because we use it on the galley counter when we want to cook inside, but it can also be set up in the cockpit or even on the beach when we want to cook outside. The ultimate convenience.

Sometimes I remove the dodger and bimini and set the stove on the companionway hatch cover, after sliding it all the way back over the companionway entrance. Then I can stand in the cockpit and the stove is the right height for comfortable cooking. In the summer, this keeps the heat and aromas out of the boat. In addition, we have a Toastmaster one-burner electric hotplate that keeps us from burning fuel when we have shore power available.

Cooking inside, or heating the cabin with a propane or butane appliance, creates a potential safety hazard of oxygen depletion and the production of carbon monoxide. Always make sure you have adequate cross ventilation when using any combustion appliance in an enclosed space.

We installed a carbon monoxide detector and alarm to alert us before the situation becomes hazardous. Only one time, so far, has the alarm sounded; when we were cooking on a small backpacking stove known as the JetBoil. This highly efficient stove puts out so much heat it can boil a cup of water in a blink, but the vigorous combustion made our CO alarm go nuts—thankfully. Every boat should have this type of detector and alarm.

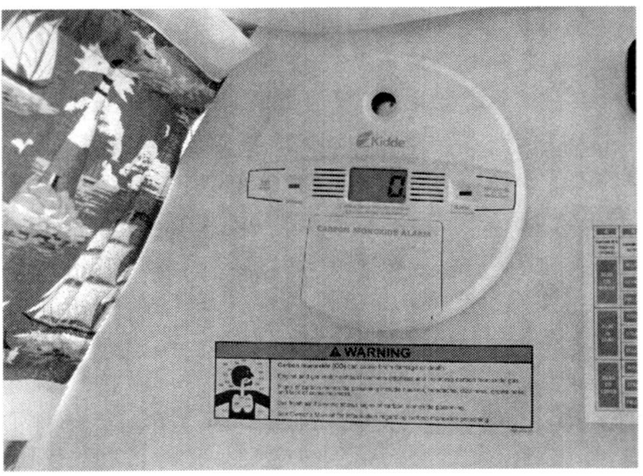

An essential safety device is a carbon monoxide detector/alarm. Carbon monoxide is deadly and undetectable by human senses. Cooking, operating a heater, a lantern, or running the motor can create dangerous levels of carbon monoxide.

Cabin

For the cabin, we added a gimbaled oil lamp attached to the mast compression post in the middle of the interior. Having the lamp there gives us warm, even light all around the cabin. So far, we've never had an accident with the lamp, knocking it out of its perch or breaking the glass. It works perfectly, and we have a nice light for a romantic dinner or when we kick back and relax at the end of the day and don't want the brighter glare of incandescent lights. The oil lamp isn't bright enough for easy reading (we have other specialized lights for that), but it's enough for playing games at the table. We love our oil lamp, and even though it was expensive, we'd make that purchase again.

As a surprise for my birthday, Becky bought a nice Weems and Plath weather station that fits perfectly on the wall separating the head from the main cabin. The station is a simple design, with three dials in one 3-inch round instrument. The barometer

In our boat, a brass oil lamp is attached to the mast compression post next to the dinette, so we can enjoy romantic "candle light" dinners or play games after dark. Warning: Becky is ruthless at cribbage.

is the primary gauge, with smaller hygrometer and thermometer gauges inset in the main dial. This addition is not only handsome, but functional for adding information to the mix of other input for local weather forecasting.

Next to the weather station, we added a cheap digital clock. Isn't it amazing, the one essential instrument that eluded mariners for so many centuries — an accurate timepiece — is now available for pocket change at WalMart.

For reading at night, we started out using tiny clip-on LED reading lights. The cabin's overhead lights shine right in your eyes when you're lying down, so these little lights are much better. They put out a bright, white light, run forever on a battery, and the bulbs are nearly indestructible. Our flashlights are also LED. You can't beat 'em. Recently, I installed inexpensive 4-AA cell-powered one-touch lights (push-on, push-off) at the head of our bunks, for reading, and another one in the head for those late night visits. These work great.

The Head

Three Eagles came from the factory with an empty head — no, I don't mean it was brainless, I mean we had no potty in the enclosure known as the head. In nautical terms, both the room and the appliance that goes in it are known as the head. In our case, we got to decide what kind of head to put in the head.

Our first head was an electric porta potty. The only thing different between a standard unit and our electric one is the flush is activated by pressing a button that turns on a small battery-powered (4 C-cells) electric pump to move flushing water from the freshwater tank into the toilet bowl. During the flush process, we open a slide valve to allow the contents of the bowl to drop into the dark confines of the holding tank. This system served us for more than ten years.

This type of porta potty uses chemicals to break down the contents of the holding tank and eliminate odors. The chemicals are available at marine supply stores, RV supply stores, and even WalMart in the RV section of the automotive department. They're not particularly expensive, and we carry a supply of chemicals on our trips so we never face the day when we run out (heaven forbid). My one issue with a wet-holding-tank-type of porta potty is that it fills up remarkably fast and requires frequent trips to the dump station.

Not every trailerable sailboat has space for a separate potty enclosure. Some tuck the unit under the forward bunk and pull it out into the middle of the cabin when necessary for use. For those who do have a dedicated head enclosure, an alternative to the wet porta potty makes a lot of sense: the composting toilet. Two units currently on the market are the Air Head (www.airheadtoilet.com) and Nature's Head (www.natureshead.net). They work on identical principles. Only a couple of small design differences set them apart.

These composting toilets operate on the principle of separating the liquids from the solids. Urine is collected in a separate container that can be easily removed for dumping. The solids are collected in the main holding bin filled to a certain level with peat moss. After the solids fall into the peat moss, a crank handle is turned a few times to mix everything together, then it is left to compost. A small fan moves air through the compost bin to promote the digestion of the waste material. After composting, the solids gradually evolve into soil that can be placed in a plastic trash bag then discarded in a dumpster or spread as compost on a flower garden. I know, I know. I thought the same thing at first. But this works, and the compost is safe for this type of disposal.

Actually, the longer you leave the solids in the composting bin, the better the whole process works. Some folks with these toilets empty them only once, at the end of the sailing season (your mileage may vary). Or they let it continue composting over the winter and empty it in the spring before their first outing. All that's required to start afresh is to dump the old compost and refill the bin with the appropriate amount of peat moss, and you're ready to go again...so to speak.

If there is one drawback to composting toilets, it's that they are expensive, costing just under $1000. But the benefits are overwhelming; no foul odor, no chemicals, no need to carry a heavy holding tank to a dump station every few days, and they are virtually bombproof. Last year, we upgraded to the Nature's Head, and we love it. Well, as much as you can love a toilet.

On Deck

We started life with two fenders, thinking we'd just move them from port to starboard or back again as the docking situation dictated. Well, that lasted about one season. Then we realized it was much easier to have fenders already hung on both sides of the boat so we could happily slide up to a dock from any direction. So we bought two more fenders, lines and hangers that clip to the lifelines. We realized later that we still needed more fenders, so we bought two more. That gives *Three Eagles* good protection with three fenders on each side. This is ideal, especially when the wind bumps the boat around against a dock.

What do we do with all those fenders while we're sailing? Originally, we thought about getting some kind of fender holders, like the ones you see on big fancy yachts. But our boat is too small for such hardware. We lay the fenders on their sides inboard of the stanchions. They rarely tumble off the cabin roof, even in rough going.

We did the same dance with the docklines, started with two and then added two more when we got tired of having to switch them from one side to the other at the last minute because our "favorite" side of the dock was unavailable. We use a 25-footer on each side at the bow, and a 15-footer on each stern cleat. The tails of the stern lines are led around the stanchions and then just rest inside the cockpit, where we can grab it as we leave the cockpit and step onto the dock.

A convenient way to suspend fenders over the side of the boat is by using strap hangers attached to the lifelines or rails. These can be slid along the lifeline or rail to reposition the fender, or quickly removed and reinstalled when necessary.

Each bow line is led outside the shrouds and everything else on its respective side of the boat and back to the stanchion near the cockpit. We tie the line to that stanchion, using an overhand knot on a bight, leaving a little bit of the bight and tail dangling harmlessly over the side. This arrangement allows us to step off the boat and have instant hands-on control of both the bow and stern docklines. Additional lines are kept below, in case we need to set springlines.

Rubber dockline snubbers are great for reducing the sudden jerking motion as the boat tugs against the line when the wind blows. There are various types of snubbers, suitable for different size docklines.

To help the docklines absorb shock loads more comfortably, we bought and installed some rubber dockline snubbers. The line passes through a hole at one end of the snubber, wraps around the body of the snubber three times, then goes through the hole at the other end. This allows the snubber to stretch and take the most abrupt shock loads before transferring it to the dockline. This arrangement makes life at the dock more comfortable when wind and chop make the boat dance.

Cockpit

The best purchase we ever made for the boat was the full cockpit enclosure. It was EXPENSIVE (about $2500), but worth every penny, because we live and and do most of our sailing in an area where the weather is often cool and rainy.

The enclosure instantly doubled our comfortable cruising season, and immediately doubled the livable space on the boat.

A cockpit enclosure expands the useful space in a boat by including the cockpit as an area that is protected from the weather. Plus, it lengthens the comfortable sailing season, in regions where the climate is cold in Spring and Fall.

Anything that produces these results is a good product. To save money, we ordered all the components and did the installation ourselves – not difficult for anyone who can measure accurately and knows how to use a drill and screwdriver.

Another cool purchase was a little fold-up table we can bring into the cockpit whenever we want to eat there or play a game in the enclosed extra room. We found this table at a hardware store and paid almost nothing for it. When not in use, we collapse it and stow it against the back wall of the head, where it is held in place by a Velcro strap.

After a few years, the factory cockpit cushions were shot and needed to be re-stuffed with a higher density foam rubber. We went to an upholstery shop, tested various durable 3-inch foams and settled on a density that felt comfortable for us. We re-used the original cushion covers, because they were still in good condition, and utilized the old foam rubber as a pattern for cutting the new.

Rather than pay the upholstery shop to cut the foam, we used an electric carving knife to do the job at home in the kitchen. Worked like a charm. In fact, we liked the result so much that we ordered new foam for all the cushions in the cabin as well. The denser foam is much more comfortable. Had we known it would make such a difference, we'd have done this project sooner.

Navigation Tools

Navigation instruments include a bulkhead-mounted compass, a handheld Garmin GPS (I constructed a mount on the steering pedestal) and a Garmin fish finder/ depth sounder. These might not be essential for every trailerable sailboat, but they are for us. We like to take long cruises on inland waters, and the ability to navigate accurately is important. I highly recommend both of these instruments, because using them properly will help keep you out of trouble.

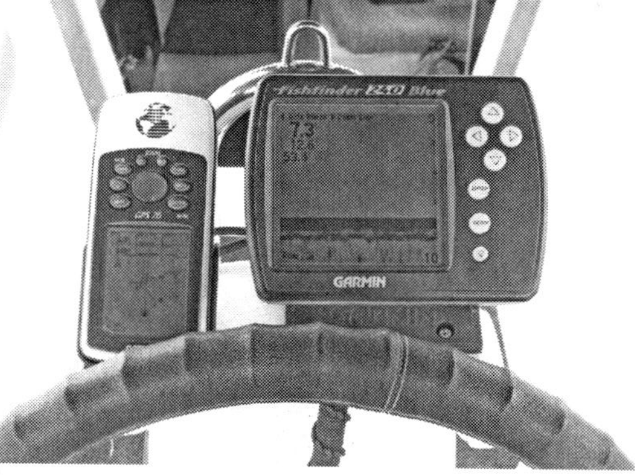

Finding a convenient place to install a depth sounder and GPS might be difficult. I fabricated a platform of plastic sheeting that I attached to the top of the steering pedestal, giving me enough room for the instruments.

Ground Tackle

If you're a racer or day sailor, you can probably get away with a lot less ground tackle than what we consider minimal. We like to cruise to new places and drop anchor in quiet coves. We own three anchors—two of them are Danforth style, and the third is a Box Anchor. We equipped each with adequate chain and nylon rode, appropriate for the areas we sail.

What's Next?

Will there be more purchases? Hey, what a silly question. This is a boat, isn't it? But we carefully evaluate every purchase, not only to make sure we buy the best equipment for the best price, but also to determine whether we need that stuff in the first place.

After all, we don't subscribe to the theory that a boat is a hole in the water where you throw money.

Part Two
Tow Vehicles, Trailers ...
and Other Technical Details

Who Needs This Technical Stuff Anyway?
(A Note From Becky)

"Why do we need a section about tow vehicles, towing, and trailer maintenance in a sailing book?" I asked Rich. That seemed a logical question to me.

"It may not seem necessary to you," he said, "but for the person responsible to keep everything running, it's *really* important."

He's right. The more you do with preventive maintenance, the fewer emergencies you'll have. When something breaks, it's good to have a manual that gives a step-by-step look at how to solve problems.

Mechanical work isn't my forte, or my interest. Oh sure, I'm terrific when it comes to moral support—as in, "Way to go, sweetie pie." I also handle a mean wrench, much as a surgeon's assistant passes the scalpel at precisely the right moment. But taking care of the dirty details is Rich's responsibility. Mind you, I believe women are just as capable in this department. Our former next door neighbor, Kaye, is an inspiration to me. She roofed her house and runs a hardware store. Her husband is a bank manager; he's not the fix-it person. Kaye takes care of all that.

It doesn't matter who takes care of these chores — it just matters that someone does. If that someone is you ... read on.

Chapter Twelve
Choosing the Right Tow Vehicle

The whole reason for owning a trailerable sailboat is so you can sail it anywhere, whether on a local lake or a distant seashore. But in order to do this, trailer sailors need to focus on two important concerns. First is buying the right boat. Then you need to successfully tow it around the country. In this chapter, we concentrate on selecting the proper tow vehicle, because if you can't tow the boat easily, why have a trailerable sailboat in the first place?

Make sure you have a tow vehicle that is rated to pull the load.
To do that, first get an accurate weight of the boat and trailer,
as well as the weight of the tow vehicle. Then check the
tow vehicle specs to make sure it will do the job.

Photo credit: Com-Pac Yachts

With all due respect to vehicle salesmen, you won't easily find one who knows what he's talking about when it comes to towing. What you get when you step onto the showroom floor is a guy trying to move his inventory. The average salesman sells cars and trucks to people who are more interested in image than capability — form rather than function. So he rarely needs to know about esoteric subjects like ring and pinion ratios or payload capacity. Most of the time, you're left on your own to figure it out.

So, my first advice about buying a tow vehicle from a dealer is not to swallow everything the salesman tells you. And if you're buying from a private party, don't believe what that guy tells you, either. If you want to know the truth about a vehicle's towing capacity, you'll need to do independent research. Believe me, it's worth the trouble.

Factory Tow Ratings

A vehicle in the pre-production stages of development goes through a battery of rigorous tests to discover how it will hold up to the stress of towing. Testing involves all the major components, including the engine, transmission, transfer case (if any), the cooling system, gear ratios, brakes, axles, and the frame.

The tests are brutal, conducted in the heat of summer in the desert and at high altitude in the mountains, up and down steep inclines, repeatedly starting and stopping, pulling weights far heavier than the average consumer will ever tow. The purpose of this testing is twofold — to weed out marginal equipment and protect the manufacturer against warranty or liability claims, and to give consumers a vehicle that will tow a given load under normal conditions without mechanical failure.

Some types of vehicles, such as compact cars and minivans, are not to be used for serious towing duty, so they receive a minimal tow capacity rating. Pickup trucks and sport utility vehicles are generally engineered for some level of towing duty (which varies depending upon the combination of equipment such as axle ratio, engine and transmission cooling systems, etc.), so they receive a higher rating. Even with this class of vehicle, you must be careful to get a package that will tow as much as you need.

Using 2008 specifications as an example, a Toyota Tacoma might be limited to towing only 3500 pounds, or can be equipped to tow as much as 6500 pounds. It's all in the equipment selection. A 4.0-liter Ford Explorer may be limited to as little as 3500 pounds of trailer weight, or can be equipped to tow as much as 7130 pounds.

I want to impress upon you that how a vehicle is equipped in the engine, transmission, axle ratio, and towing package departments is of vital importance when you select an appropriate tow vehicle. You must read the towing guide pamphlets provided by the dealership, or research tow ratings for older vehicles for which dealer pamphlets aren't available.

Not everybody wants to run out and buy a new truck just because they're buying a boat. My advice is to check the weight of the boat and trailer you're considering for purchase. Then check the towing capacity of your vehicle. Either make sure the tow vehicle you already own is up to the task, or think about buying a suitable tow vehicle.

Trailerable sailboats range widely in size and weight. Example: a little 15-foot West Wight Potter weighs in at about 825 pounds on her trailer, while a sturdy trailerable Nor'Sea 27 tips the scales at more than 10,000 pounds. Our boat happens to weigh about 3500 pounds on the trailer, so you can see the variety when it comes to towed weight. And don't forget to factor in the weight of water, fuel, and supplies. It's vital to match the tow vehicle to the actual load you'll be towing when the boat is fully equipped and stuffed with supplies.

But remember, the tow rating is biased toward endurance, not necessarily performance. Even though a vehicle carries a tow rating of 7000 pounds, that doesn't mean the driver will be delighted with all aspects of towing performance. The vehicle may be a slug when dragging a load up a steep incline, but the factory says it will tow the rated load without mechanical failure. That's all the tow rating means. It's warranty protection, not a promise of spunky performance.

Vehicle tow ratings are based on a number of factors, including engine, transmission, axle ratio, body style, wheelbase, weight, suspension and so on. The same combination of engine, transmission, and axle ratio in one vehicle might be rated to tow a far different load in another type of vehicle.

For example, a Chevy Suburban and a Chevy 1/2-ton pickup with the same equipment will be rated differently because the Suburban weighs more. All that extra weight is part of what the vehicle has to haul, so it can't be rated to tow the same load because of the extra body weight it's carrying. The drivetrain doesn't know if the weight is on its back or dragging behind it; weight is weight, so to speak. The tow rating must be altered in coordination with all the specifications listed above, and others, such as emissions equipment.

Selecting a tow vehicle can be confusing, due to the number of options from which you can choose. Unless you have a large, heavy boat and trailer, you can normally select either a smaller engine and a lower (higher numerical) axle gear ratio, or a larger engine and a higher (lower numerical) ratio. Both vehicles may be rated to tow the weight, but one will probably deliver better fuel economy, and the other might give better performance while towing.

For example, an older Ford truck with a 351 V8, manual transmission and 4.10 gears and the same truck with a 460 V8 and 3.55 gears may have similar tow ratings, but the difference in fuel economy will be considerable. Yet, the 460 will deliver superior hill climbing and passing performance, and could possibly last longer because, being a more powerful engine, it doesn't have to work as hard at towing the load.

If in doubt, you're almost always better off with a tow vehicle that's a bit more than you expect you'll need. It's a lot easier to back off the throttle and take it easy with a big engine than it is to improve a rig's power and towing capability after buying an inadequate vehicle.

Before making any decisions about buying a tow vehicle, you'll need to know the actual weight of the boat on the trailer. The best course of action is to weigh it at a commercial truck scale when the boat and trailer are loaded with all its cargo and ready for a trip, with the freshwater, fuel and propane tanks (if any) full. This will give you a much better idea about the actual weight than the boat manufacturer's advertised specifications. If actually weighing the boat and trailer is not possible, the best you can do is assume the manufacturer's advertised weight is somewhat close to correct and then calculate the weight that will be added by you as you prepare the boat for travel.

Once you're confident of the boat and trailer weight, visit your local vehicle dealership and ask for the towing and recreational vehicle guides in pamphlet form. These booklets contain all the details you'll need to select a tow vehicle. By using the charts in the pamphlet, you can match your boat and trailer weight to the necessary engine, transmission, axle ratio and other equipment you'll need for safe, enjoyable towing. From a safety and comfort standpoint, tow vehicles with a long wheelbase are generally more comfortable and handle better than short wheelbase vehicles.

GVWR, GAWR, GCWR, etc.

As you search for the right tow vehicle, you'll run into acronyms that may seem mysterious at first. GVWR, GAWR, GCWR—what does it all mean? Actually, these are important factors in choosing an adequate tow vehicle. If you mess up here, you may end up with a vehicle that not only doesn't do the job you hoped for, but will also have a voided warranty because of overloading.

Gross vehicle weight rating (gvwr) is the maximum the vehicle can weigh when it's ready to go, including passengers, fluids and so on.

Gross axle weight rating (gawr) is the maximum an axle can weigh, at the ground. For example, if a truck with a 5000-pound rear axle gawr has an actual weight of 2500 pounds resting on that axle, then you are allowed to carry an additional 2500 pounds on that axle before exceeding the gawr.

Gross combined weight rating (gcwr) is the maximum weight a particular drive train combination is rated to haul. For example, a 10,000-pound gcwr can mean a 10,000-pound vehicle with no trailer, or a 5000-pound vehicle weight plus a 5000-pound boat and trailer combination. No matter how you add it, the total weight of everything combined can't exceed the 10,000-pound gcwr.

Another limitation imposed by the factory is the hitch weight limit. Ordinarily, this won't be much of a problem for trailerable sailboat owners, because the weight of the trailer tongue on the rear of the tow vehicle is fairly light. But be aware of the limitations, because depending upon your vehicle, you may not be able to drop the coupler onto a hitch ball connected to the vehicle's rear bumper. Some late model bumpers aren't meant for hitch duty, and it might be necessary to install a dedicated hitch system. We'll get more into that subject in the chapter where we discuss hitches.

How To Weigh Your Vehicle and Boat

This brings up the question of the proper method for weighing the tow vehicle and the boat/trailer combination, so you know how much weight you're dealing with. You'll want to know three weights:

- The total combined weight of the tow vehicle and the boat on the trailer.

- The weight of just the boat and trailer.

- The tongue weight.

To be most useful, all these weights should be obtained when the tow vehicle and the boat are loaded for a trip. Add the estimated weight of passengers to the total combined weight. This is a little bit like bungee jumping, where trying to fudge about your weight can only have negative consequences.

First, weigh the combination of tow vehicle, boat, and trailer. Then, pull forward so the tow vehicle is off the scales, but you can still lower the trailer's tongue jack on the scales. Lower the tongue jack until it touches the surface of the scale, then uncouple the trailer from the hitch and continue raising the tongue with the jack until it is free of the hitch ball. This will take all the weight off the tow vehicle and put it on the scale. Record the weight, then lower and lock the coupler back on the hitch ball, and away you go.

Subtracting the second weight (boat and trailer only) from the first weight (total combination) will tell you how much the tow vehicle itself weighs.

To discover the tongue weight, position the boat trailer so the tires are off the scale but the trailer tongue is over the scale. Lower the tongue jack, disconnect the trailer from the hitch, and drive the tow vehicle off the scale. After obtaining the tongue weight, hitch the trailer to the tow vehicle and you're ready to go.

It's easy to overload a boat trailer, so pay close attention to the trailer's axle weight rating and the actual traveling weight of the boat and trailer. What's at risk when you overload the trailer are the tires, axles, suspension system, bearings, brakes, and perhaps even the framework itself. Overloading becomes a safety concern, so this issue should receive due consideration.

Tow Vehicle Suspension Upgrades

Naturally, different trailerable sailboats will have different tongue weights. Some are light enough to make the tongue weight a non-issue, especially if you have a substantial tow vehicle. But others may be heavy enough to add a considerable burden on the tow vehicle. When that happens, you may be able to solve the problem by upgrading the rear suspension—assuming the tow vehicle is rated for towing the load. No amount of rear suspension upgrade will compensate for an inadequate tow rating.

Driving around with a heavy tongue load on the back of the tow vehicle can adversely affect suspension and handling characteristics — pressing the rear of the vehicle down while lifting the front end. This throws the vehicle out of balance and results in light steering and poor front brake performance. When this happens, you need more rear spring capacity.

On some vehicles you can install helper springs or progressive overload springs that permanently stiffen the rear suspension. The problem is, that most of us don't want a vehicle with a permanently stiff suspension that's uncomfortable to drive when there's no load on the hitch.

Fortunately, there is another approach to solving the problem — it amounts to nothing less than selective suspension control, allowing you to stiffen the suspension capacity when necessary, and soften it for normal travel without a heavy load. The product I'm referring to is Air Lift — inflatable rubber bellows controlled by the driver to increase or decrease suspension stiffness. I installed this system on my own truck and it has functioned flawlessly for many years. Larger versions of these suspension units are used on heavy vehicles such as busses and motor homes, so they're strong enough for years of service.

Let me stress once again that installing supplemental suspension components, such as air springs, will not increase the factory's recommended load capacities. Gross axle weight rating (GAWR), gross vehicle weight rating (GVWR), payload capacity and such are determined by factory engineers based on many considerations such as brakes, axle strength, frame strength, etc. Increasing spring capacity will not increase load ratings for these other components. Even after installing the Air Lift system, owners still need to be careful not to exceed factory weight ratings.

But, air springs help keep the vehicle level and easier to control when cargo is being hauled and when a heavy tongue load is hung on the hitch. Keeping the vehicle level significantly improves handling and ride quality. One of the things I like best about the Air Lift system is the stock suspension doesn't have to be modified, which makes installation and operation easy, and the ride and handling characteristics are not adversely affected.

Air Lift, and other suspension products are available at auto parts stores.

Transmission Ratings

As a rule, automotive manufacturers give higher tow ratings to vehicles equipped with automatic transmissions, and there are several reasons for this. The problem is, some people tend to burn and destroy clutches under towing conditions, leading to excessive warranty claims. An automatic transmission is easier on the drivetrain because of its smooth power delivery and smooth shifts, neither of which tend to "slam" the drivetrain components. The built-in "slip" and torque multiplication in an automatic help a heavy vehicle get rolling from a dead stop. Finally, some automatics are stronger than manual transmissions because some manual boxes, such as those in light-duty trucks, are designed for light service and economy, not heavy towing.

Of course, heavy-duty manual transmissions are used in big trucks, such as 18-wheelers, but with few exceptions most consumer-level trucks and SUV's have higher tow ratings when equipped with an automatic transmission. If you want to see examples of how much impact transmission choice has on tow rating, look at the charts in the towing booklets you pick up from local dealerships. You'll see different charts for automatic transmission and manual transmission. In some cases, an automatic transmission can mean the difference of several thousand pounds in towing capacity.

Although automatic transmissions offer distinct advantages for towing, they're more vulnerable to heat damage than manual transmissions. Overheating quickly ruins automatic transmissions. At 175 degrees, automatic transmission fluid has an expected life of 100,000 miles. At 195 degrees, that life drops to 30,000 miles. At 275 degrees, the expected life of the fluid is only 3,000 miles, and at 295 degrees, it drops to 1,500 miles. By the time the fluid temperature hits 315 degrees, expect the transmission to die in 750 miles.

Obviously, cooling the transmission fluid is of paramount importance. Even though the vehicle comes from the factory with an integral cooler built into the radiator, this is sometimes inadequate for towing during hot weather or in severe uphill situations. An auxiliary aftermarket transmission cooler is a good idea. You can also purchase special transmission pans with built-in heat exchangers that can help cool the transmission fluid.

Keep an eye on the transmission fluid temperature, so you know when to pull over and let things cool down. Because the warmth of the fluid inside the transmission is the critical temperature, that's where the sending unit should be located. The temperature of the fluid on the way to or returning from the cooler is less important than the temperature inside the transmission pan.

One option is to use a holeless sending unit that goes down the dipstick tube and into the pan. This type of unit is made by Westberg Manufacturing, Inc. But some folks may opt to have a sending unit permanently installed in the transmission pan. This is done by drilling into the pan and brazing a fitting in place that can serve as a drain plug or a port for the sending unit. Have the work done by a professional welding shop, to ensure against leakage.

Auxiliary Transmission

Auxiliary transmissions (some people refer to these as overdrives or underdrives) help solve the problem of towing in hill country and not having the right gear available. Factory transmissions are designed with large spreads between gear ratios, and it's easy to drop a thousand RPM or more shifting up while climbing a hill. That may leave the engine lugging, and soon you're shifting down again to try to restore the engine to a better RPM range. Auxiliary transmissions solve this problem by offering intermediate gears that can be accessed at any time. U.S. Gear and the Gear Vendors units have good reputations. Both deliver intermediate gears where you need them; between 1st and 2nd, between 2nd and 3rd, or between 3rd and 4th.

By the way, towing in overdrive gear isn't recommended, especially if the load is heavy. Towing in overdrive may cause the transmission to constantly seek a more comfortable gear, resulting in overheating the transmission.

Gas Engines vs. Diesel Engines

The debate rages in the minds of some tow vehicle owners about which is better, a gas engine or a diesel engine. Diesel engines cost more than gasoline engines when you purchase the vehicle. So, right from the beginning you find a cost penalty for selecting a diesel powerplant. However, diesel engines are superb for towing and rated for a much longer life than gasoline engines.

A diesel engine requires no tune-ups, in the traditional sense of the word. You have no spark plugs, points, condenser, distributor cap or carburetor to mess with. But this type of engine requires greater attention to certain aspects of maintenance. The oil and oil filter must be changed more frequently, and the fuel filters and water separator must be attended to religiously to help the engine achieve long life.

The cost of diesel fuel fluctuates wildly in comparison with gasoline, Sometimes, diesel fuel costs less in some parts of the country than regular gasoline — although many times diesel fuel is priced even higher than regular gas. There are never any guarantees that the cost of diesel fuel will be an advantage over gasoline. A diesel engine delivers better fuel economy than a gas engine, especially when towing, but it takes a long time to recoup (through lower fuel costs) the initial higher cost of the engine. If you use the vehicle primarily for towing, the cost penalty of buying a diesel is overcome more quickly.

Then there's concern about the fuel itself. Diesel fuel is available in two general grades — #1 and #2. Grade #1 is lighter than #2, and offers less BTU value. Subsequently, fuel economy with #1 is lower than with #2. But the reason it is lighter in weight is to prevent it from jelling when the temperature drops. In cold areas of the country, local suppliers will often blend #1 and #2 in a 50-50 mixture to provide jell-free characteristics while maintaining some fuel economy. Grade #1 is also more expensive, because of the current tax situation regarding low sulfur diesel fuel. There is also such a thing as "winter" diesel fuel. During the cold season, the refinery will blend #2 diesel so it will resist jelling down to 14 degrees above zero F.

As far as water contamination is concerned, diesel engines are vulnerable to this type of problem. The grade of fuel isn't the issue, because condensation can occur in any enclosed fuel tank. What you need is a good water separator and a strict routine for maintaining your filters, both water and oil.

4x4 vs. 4x2 vs. Front-Wheel-Drive

In order of preference for towing duty, four-wheel drive is best, followed by a standard rear-wheel-drive vehicle, and least preferred is a front-wheel-drive vehicle. There are good reasons these vehicle types fall into this lineup. From a practical standpoint, all-wheel-drive can be considered the same as four-wheel-drive; the difference is, it's fully engaged all the time.

Four-wheel-drive is useful for a trailer sailor, because the additional traction may be needed on slick launch ramps. It doesn't take much wet algae, mud or moss on a launch ramp to make the tires slip — a situation that can be inconvenient and dangerous. If you can't control the tow vehicle traction, it may end up in the water with the boat and trailer.

Standard rear-wheel-drive tow vehicles are my second choice. Lacking the additional traction of a 4x4, a rear-wheel-drive vehicle at least has the tongue weight of the boat trailer applying downward pressure on the rear axle and drive wheels.

And that's why front-wheel-drive ranks last—because the tongue weight on the rear of the vehicle will lift weight off the front wheels, reducing traction just when you need it most.

Limited Slip Differential

One of the myths about four-wheel-drive vehicles is that all four wheels are pulling to get you through a place with poor traction. That may or may not be true, depending upon what kind of differentials the vehicle has. Even though the vehicle is a 4x4, you may find yourself with only one wheel on each axle trying to move you forward. That would happen if the vehicle had standard "open" differentials rather than limited-slip, effectively making your 4x4 only a two-wheel-drive.

In a standard "open" differential, the torque is sent to the wheel that has the least amount of traction, while no torque is sent to the wheel that has a good grip on the ground. But a limited-slip differential is designed to overcome this problem by limiting the speed and torque differences between its two outputs. In other words, if one tire tries to spin because it has no solid grip on the ground, the limited-slip differential will send torque to the opposite tire, which might be sitting on a surface providing better traction. The system ensures torque is distributed to both drive wheels, even when one is on a slippery surface. The tire with the traction will receive drive effort, which might be the only thing that pulls you back up a slippery ramp.

Generally, limited slip is only used in the rear axle of a 4x4, because the front tires need to be more disconnected from one another in order to turn tight corners without binding up. Some rock-crawling, nasty-trail-type off roaders want a limited-slip both front and rear, but that isn't necessary (or even desirable) for the rest of us. A limited-slip rear differential is quite sufficient, and provides an honest three-wheel-drive for those of us who own a 4x4, and an honest two-wheel-drive for the rest.

Taking all of this into account, you should be able to determine what vehicle suits your towing needs best. But don't forget you also need a vehicle to carry passengers in comfort. It won't do you any good to have the most mechanically bulletproof hauler if nobody will ride in it without a helmet and kidney belt. By using balance in your purchase of a tow vehicle, you can find one that will do the job well and deliver a comfortable ride at the same time.

Chapter Thirteen
Hitch Equipment

We were westbound on Interstate 90 between Austin and Albert Lea, Minnesota when near disaster struck. Glancing in the sideview mirror, I noticed what was supposed to be trailing obediently behind us was actually attempting a passing maneuver. If anything puts your stomach in your throat, it's the sudden realization that the trailer has come unhitched and at any moment your pride and joy could end up in the ditch.

The hitch system is all that stands between us and calamity, as we tow our trailerable yachts around the country. I refer to it as a "system" because several components are involved in the connective apparatus that keeps the trailer attached to the tow vehicle. And each component needs to be selected carefully, to ensure it doesn't become the weak link in the system.

Although a trailer hitch seems like a simple hunk of steel that shouldn't need much attention, our experience on Interstate 90 proves otherwise. We need to understand hitch equipment, how to select it, inspect it, maintain it, and perform the hitching process properly.

Hitches are rated by the manufacturer according to the maximum amount of weight they are engineered to handle. Class I hitches are rated for towing as much as 2000 pounds. Class II units are for loads up to 3500 pounds. Class III has a rating of 5000 pounds, and Class IV is for loads of up to 10,000 pounds. The weight rating refers to the total weight being towed, including the trailer itself. Choose appropriate hitch hardware to match the weight of your fully loaded boat and trailer. It's best not to cut it too close to the line when dealing with critical equipment like the hitch—it doesn't hurt to invest in materials that are a bit heavier-duty than necessary.

Some Class I hitches are designed to be installed directly to the tow vehicle bumper. This makes the hitch quick and easy to install, but the bumper (especially those on automobiles) may not be strong enough to endure the strain of towing.

A look into the vehicle owner's manual, under the heading of trailer towing, might reveal a disclaimer such as, "Do not use hitches that clamp onto the vehicle's bumper. The bumper is not designed to bear the load." What that means is the bumper isn't strong enough to be a critical link in the towing process. If your tow vehicle owner's manual contains a similar warning, the best solution is to buy a hitch that attaches directly to the vehicle's frame. If a Class I hitch is chosen for light towing duty, buy one that attaches not only to the bumper but also to some sturdy structural points beneath the vehicle itself.

Class II hitches are designed to be bolted to the vehicle frame or crossmembers. This type of hitch might have a permanent ball mount integrated into the hitch itself, or it could have a square tube receiver into which a removable ball mount shank is installed. The receiver will measure either 1-5/8" or 2" square — the smaller is called a mini-hitch. Receiver-type hitches offer the convenient advantage of being able to remove the ball mount when it is not being used. The shank end that slides into the receiver has a hole through it that aligns with holes on opposite sides of the receiver tube. When the hole in the shank is lined up with the hole in the receiver, a hitch pin is inserted and held in place by a spring clip or a lock. Locking hitch pins help prevent the ball mount shank from being removed by unauthorized persons (i.e., being stolen).

Class III and IV hitches have a 5000-pound and 10,000-pound load limit, respectively. These units are designed for bolting directly to the vehicle's frame, and are receiver-type hitches, utilizing 2" square tube for the ball mount.

Hitch bumpers are common on pickup trucks, and serve well within a limited range of trailer weights. One problem with a hitch bumper is that the ball height cannot be adjusted. When the trailer is hitched to the bumper, the tongue might be too high or too low. This can affect towing stability or cause the boat's tail to drag on the ground when passing over uneven surfaces such as driveways or entrances to gas stations, etc. It's often better to install a receiver hitch so you can buy a ball mount that is designed to either raise or lower the ball height the correct amount.

Balls

The choice of hitch ball also needs serious consideration. Balls are available in three sizes: 1-7/8", 2", and 2-5/16" diameter. Naturally, the coupler on the trailer tongue will dictate the required ball size. Most sailboat trailers are equipped with a coupler for a 2" ball, but this is something that you as the boat owner should verify.

Ball diameter isn't the only vital statistic. Some balls have extended bases or undersized shanks (the shaft and threaded portion below the ball). An extended base (to raise the ball height) or an undersized shank will reduce the ball's load rating. Ratings range from 2000 pounds to 10,000 pounds, and it is important that the ball is rated equal to, or higher than, the trailer's GVWR.

Make sure the ball's shank fits the ball mount hole precisely, so there is no slop. Here are a few rules regarding shank size, lock washers and nuts:

• When using a Reese ball mount, if the ball has a 1-inch-diameter threaded shank, use bushing No. 55030 to reduce hole size in the ball mount to 1 inch, and place a lock washer next to the nut.

• If the ball has a 1-1/4-inch-diameter threaded shank and a standard-size (1 inch or more thickness) nut, place a lock washer on top of the ball mount.

• If the ball has a 1-1/4-inch-diameter threaded shank and thin nut (.72 inch thickness), place the lock washer next to the nut.

After installing the lock washer and nut, use a torque wrench to secure the ball to the hitch. On Class I hitches, tighten the nut to 85 lb. ft.; on Class II torque to 105 lb. ft.; and on Class III and IV hitches tighten to 235 lb. ft.

Ball Height Adjustment

Ball height is critical in order to allow both the tow vehicle and the trailer to ride level. To adjust ball height:

• Begin with both the tow vehicle and trailer parked on level ground.

• Using the tongue jack, and a bubble level, adjust the trailer's attitude front-to-rear until it is perfectly horizontal. If the ground itself is not perfectly horizontal to begin with, you need to adjust the trailer's attitude until it matches that of the ground. In other words, you want the trailer to be parallel to the ground.

• Take a vertical measurement from the ground to the highest point inside the trailer tongue's coupler socket. This measurement is referred to as ball height. Ideally, the final height of the ball should be equal to, or slightly higher, than the measurement just taken.

To compensate for the amount of vehicle squat that occurs when the tongue weight is lowered onto the hitch, the ball height can be adjusted slightly higher. Height adjustment is accomplished by either using a ball with a different base extension or by using a ball mount with a different amount of drop (or rise).

The amount of ball height adjustment that is necessary depends upon the type of tow vehicle being used. Trucks with heavy duty springs don't squat much under the burden of a lightweight trailer tongue, so unless the tongue is heavy the ball probably doesn't need to be set any higher than the measured ball height. Light duty pickup trucks with standard springs will squat more, and automobiles squat severely. Adjust the ball upward accordingly.

Once you know the tongue weight (because of your visit to the commercial truck scale, as discussed in the chapter about tow vehicles), you can experiment with your tow vehicle to determine actual squat when that amount of weight is added to the hitch. If, for example, the tongue weight is 350 pounds, and you're using a pickup truck as a tow vehicle, load 350 pounds (a couple of appropriately-sized buddies can serve as ballast for this test) in the back of the bed over the hitch. Take before-and-after measurements to see exactly how much the ball position moves down. As the ball drops, you know you need to raise the ball height to compensate. This might seem picky, but it is best if the trailer rides absolutely horizontal. This is because, under severe braking situations, the trailer will remain under better control and the surge brakes will function best if there is no upward or downward angle at the coupler.

The best way to adjust ball height is to purchase a ball mount with the appropriate amount of rise or drop. Trailer equipment outlets sell ball mounts with varying amounts of drop, to lower the ball position below the receiver. If you need to raise the ball height, turn the ball mount over and what was once a drop-mount now becomes a raised mount. Another option is to buy a ball with an extended base, but be aware that a raised base under the ball reduces the load capacity.

If severe rear suspension squat occurs, you might be able to solve the problem by upgrading the rear suspension. This is, of course, assuming the tow vehicle itself is in every other respect rated for towing the load. An important thing to remember is that no amount of rear suspension upgrade will increase the vehicle's tow rating.

On some vehicles, you can install helper springs or progressive overload springs to permanently stiffen the rear suspension. Another option is installation of an Air Lift system, utilizing air springs to help keep the vehicle level. Keeping the tow vehicle level significantly helps improve handling and ride quality. Air Lift, and other suspension upgrade products, are available at auto parts stores.

Ball Lube

A little dab of ball lube smeared over the surface of the ball before towing helps prevent excessive wear or binding in the coupler. Don't go overboard on quantity here—just enough to coat the ball. A good grade of fibrous wheel bearing grease works well.

Remember our runaway trailer on Interstate 90? Well, it turns the un-lubricated ball had seized in the coupler. With each side-to-side oscillation between the tow vehicle and the trailer, the ball shank nut loosened a little more, because the ball and coupler were bound so tightly they had no freedom of movement. Eventually, the nut and lock washer fell off, and then the ball shank lifted out of the hole in the mount. The only thing that saved the day were the safety chains that were crossed to form a cradle beneath the coupler. And that brings us to our next subject.

Safety Chains

Safety chains must be rated equal to, or higher than, the trailer's GVWR, and they should be installed in such a manner that they run from the tongue (aft of the coupler) to a set of chain loops attached to the hitch receiver. Cross the chains beneath the ball mount to form a cradle that supports the tongue off the ground if the trailer accidentally uncouples from the hitch. Adjust the safety chains so they're loose enough to permit tight cornering without binding, yet tight enough so they don't drag.

Wiring

The wiring that runs from the tow vehicle to the boat trailer is generally attached with a four-prong five-wire harness—each of the wires being a different color. The standard colors are white, yellow, green and brown. Actually, there are two brown wires. At the trailer plug, the two browns combine into one of the four prongs. A a shielded prong (female) is for the white wire (ground) The other three prongs are male, and are designated for one prong to serve each color. The reason there are two brown wires coming out of the plug is that this circuit needs to be split to send the electrical impulses to both taillights. One brown wire is coupled with the yellow wire (port side) and the other brown wire is coupled with the green wire (starboard side) as they lead aft to the trailer lights.

Confusion can arise when trying to decide which color belongs to which function on the tow vehicle, because these four wires handle several functions, including taillights, brake lights, turn signals, side and rear marker lights, and back-up lights. One way to avoid confusion is to use a General T-Connect trailer connector unit that interfaces the tow vehicle wiring harness to a pigtail terminating in a plug at the rear bumper near the hitch. These units are available for all popular trucks and several models of Sport Utility Vehicles.

If, on the other hand, you face the prospect of having to tap into the tow vehicle wiring harness by more primitive means, the job is much easier if you can locate a shop manual that shows the functions of each wire in the harness. If no shop manual is available, here's how to do the job:

• First, locate the tow vehicle's wiring harness near the taillights.

• Use a 12-volt test light or a multimeter as you identify which wires in the harness perform different functions.

• Turn on the taillights by switching on the vehicle's headlights.

• Probe each of the wires in the harness with the test light or multimeter until you find the one that has current. Mark the wire with masking tape on which you have written "tail light."

• Turn off the taillights and switch on the left turn signal.

• Probe each of the wires in the harness with the test light or multimeter until you find the one that has intermittent current. Mark the wire with masking tape on which you have written "left turn ."

• Turn on the right turn signal and repeat the process.

• Activate the back-up light and repeat the process.

- After you identify and label all the wires, use quick connectors to attach a length of 16-gauge automotive primary wire to each source wire in the harness. In order to avoid confusion, these wires should match the colors of the factory wires in the harness, if possible. To these lengths of wire, attach the pigtails from the tow-vehicle half of the plug that mates with the plug on the trailer wiring harness.

- The white wire in the boat trailer harness should be connected to a good electrical ground near the coupler. The trailer itself serves as a ground all the way back from this point to the tail lights, which are individually grounded to the trailer frame.

The green wire and one brown wire combine efforts to power the light functions on the starboard side of the trailer.

The yellow wire and one brown wire power the light functions on the port side of the trailer. One brown wire may already be bonded to the green wire, and the other brown wire may be bonded to the yellow wire as they leave the plug and head toward the rear of the trailer. Each light unit should have its own white wire that attaches to a good electrical ground nearby on the trailer frame.

Maintenance

Routine maintenance for the hitch and all associated hardware is fairly simple. First, periodically inspect the hitch to make sure it's securely attached to the vehicle and nothing is loose. Look for hairline stress cracks around attachment points, or any other indication of metal fatigue or damage. If you find any issues, don't use the hitch until repaired by a professional.

The coupler has moving parts that need to be kept clean, in order for the surge brakes to work properly. Rinse thoroughly after launching in salt water, and clean after road trips to make sure no grime builds up from dust and dirt.

Inspect the coupler to ensure all the moving parts operate freely, with no excessive wear. The lubricating grease recommended for use on the ball will transfer to the inside of the coupler, and grime will eventually accumulate in the greasy environment. Clean the coupler when necessary, to keep things grit-free and operating easily.

Inspect the safety chains and attachment points, to see that everything is in good condition and securely connected.

Assuming the ball height is correct for the tow vehicle and tongue weight in question, hitching up involves the following steps. Lower the trailer's coupler over the ball. Lock the coupler. Insert the safety pin in the coupler. Attach and adjust the safety chains. Attach the cable for the break-away trailer brake switch. Plug in the trailer's electrical cord to the tow vehicle.

This is your ultimate safety device. If the trailer decouples from the tow vehicle, the breakaway switch cable will activate the brake system to stop the trailer. Always use this feature.

Before hitting the road, always check to make sure taillights, brake lights and turn signals work. Next, test the trailer's surge brakes to ensure that they activate when the tow vehicle decelerates. Then you're ready to go.

Chapter Fourteen
Hitching Up Straight

Have you ever observed the mating ritual of trailer boaters? No, not that! I mean the ritual that precedes getting the tow vehicle and the trailer together in a happy engagement. It begins with the driver studying the juxtaposition, visually measuring the angle and distance between the hitch ball and the coupler. It's almost as much fun as watching Tiger line up a putt, walking around, squatting down, staring at every nuance of the job ahead. Once satisfied, the driver hops in the vehicle, backs up a bit, hops out again and repeats step one. This can almost qualify as a cardio exercise, with all the hopping up and down, in and out, back and forth ... not to mention the pulmonary expansion during moments of rustic vocal expression.

In times past, Becky was always a great help, as she waved her arms and shouted directions while I proceeded in reverse gear. But often she was somewhere else, maybe shopping for supplies for our voyage, and I was on my own to bring about the marriage between the ball and the coupler. After years of doing the dance, I searched for a better way to make the whole hitch alignment issue easier, without spending a lot of money.

Commercial products help with this chore, but some of them cost upwards of $100 or more, and I'm kind of a cheapskate who doesn't mind tinkering with a project like this. So, for today's entertainment, I present a couple of low-buck hitch alignment contraptions.

My first solution consists of two 4-foot long sections of 1/2-inch PVC pipe, each fitted with a PVC pipe plug at the bottom. To the cap I attached a strong magnet to form a magnetic base. The concept is to position the magnetic base of one rod on top of the hitch ball and the other one on top of the coupler. The top of the ball has a flat spot that serves as a perfect foundation for the magnet, but the top of the coupler is rounded and needs a large washer placed over the dome to create a flat spot for the magnet.

With the rods in position, the driver puts the tow vehicle in reverse and visually aligns the two rods while backing up. When the rod on top of the ball gets knocked off the ball, it indicates the coupler is now directly over the top of the ball. Mission accomplished.

To make the guides, I went to Home Depot and bought an 8-foot section of 1/2-inch PVC pipe ($1.81), two pipe plugs ($1.36) and a pair of sleeves to attach the plugs to the pipe ($0.42). At a hobby shop, I bought two 1-inch rare-earth magnets that are extremely powerful ($3.98 total) and matching magnet housings with countersunk holes already in place to allow the magnets to be attached to the plastic pipe plugs ($2.78). So, for about $10.35, I had everything I needed for the project.

I attached the magnet housing to the bottom of each pipe plug, using a dab of 3M 5200 and a flathead screw. Then I inserted the magnet into the housing and placed the length of PVC pipe over the plug. Total assembly time was about 15 minutes.

Okay, now for a more elegant method. This one is slightly more complex, but that means the sense of accomplishment is that much sweeter when you succeed. This device is similar to the first one. In fact you can use one of the rods from the first example and stick it to the top of the coupler. But the second upright that goes on the ball mount must have the magnetic base offset to one side. This makes it possible for the vertical rods to come together and touch when the ball is directly below the coupler, rather than knocking the upright from on top of the ball, as in the first example.

In order for the uprights to touch when the coupler and ball are aligned one above the other, the magnetic base holding the second upright must be stuck to the shank of the ball mount just forward of the ball (toward the tow vehicle). The upright must allow room for the coupler to move into position over the ball without disturbing the upright, which is why the two angle pieces are used.

To build the offset guide post, I used 4 feet of 1/2-inch PVC pipe ($0.91), two 45-degree pipe angles ($1.02), a pipe plug ($0.68), a magnet and its housing ($3.38). Less than $6 total.

I attached the magnet housing to the plug, as before, then installed one 45-degree angle, aimed so it points out over the ball. Then a 5-inch section of pipe was installed that reached to the center point above the ball (this measurement will depend on your hitch configuration). Then the other 45-degree angle went on, aimed upward.

The only thing left was to insert the vertical pipe into the top angle piece. I didn't glue the pieces together because they don't need it, and this way I can break them down for compact storage or to change components if I'm using a different hitch configuration. It took about 20 minutes to complete the project.

With the guideposts in position, as the tow vehicle is backed up to the trailer, the two uprights will come together and touch just as the ball is directly beneath the coupler. When they touch, the guide on the coupler will tumble off — an indicator you've made a perfect landing.

I painted one of the uprights black and left the other one white, so I can see their relative positions better through the rearview mirror. As the posts approach each other, the one in the rear disappears behind the one in front.

No matter which method you use, having a simple guide system makes the hitching process easier, and you can expect instant results from the first try.

Chapter Fifteen
Trailer Maintenance

Owners of large yachts can focus all their maintenance efforts on projects like varnish and stuffing boxes and a marine toilet that refuses to swallow. But those of us who are fortunate enough to own a trailerable sailboat don't have to worry about such things. Our pocket yachts probably don't have much of anything that needs varnish, most of us have outboard motors that eliminate concern over leaky stuffing boxes, and our inboard facilities (if any) are simple and reliable. But even with all those advantages, we are by no means totally maintenance-free. One of the major maintenance items in our boating lives is the trailer itself.

One simple truth is that if we don't pay attention to the maintenance needs of the boat trailer, we won't have a trailerable sailboat for long. What we'll have is a boat stuck in one place. Reality is, the boat doesn't dream of sailing in far places and exotic waters — it's the boat owners who do that kind of dreaming. And if we want to have any chance of fulfilling those dreams, we need to make sure the trailer is up to the voyage, so we can get to the launch ramp leading to our cruising venues.

Those who immerse their trailers only in fresh water have plenty to do on the maintenance list, but those who launch in saltwater have even more to be concerned about.

Rinsing

First on the list for us salt-lovers is a thorough rinse-down of the trailer IMMEDIATELY AFTER LAUNCHING OR RETRIEVING the boat. (Oops, sorry. Didn't mean to shout, but this is an important point). Even if your trailer is made of galvanized steel, corrosion is still a serious problem for all the non-galvanized hardware. The longer the saltwater is in contact with the metal of the trailer, the greater the chance of corrosion damage. So, the first order of business must be heading for a freshwater rinse.

It may seem inconvenient to rinse the trailer after launching the boat, because you want to be off doing boat things right at that moment. But if possible, move the boat to a temporary mooring and go back and rinse the trailer. Maybe one of the crew can take care of moving the boat to a rendezvous point, while you rinse the trailer and park the tow vehicle. If you care about the trailer, you'll find a way.

While you have the rinse hose in hand, spend some time rinsing the rear of the tow vehicle, as well as the trailer. Hitch equipment has a way of rusting even though we would swear it never got a drop of saltwater on it.

As you're rinsing the trailer, pay special attention to any area that will catch and trap water. Give it a good drowning, and press your thumb over the end of the hose to increase spray velocity to literally blow the bad stuff out of the trailer framework. Really spend some time in the area of the brakes—flood them thoroughly.

After retrieving the boat, repeat this same procedure, but rinse the boat first, to eliminate any chance that salt residue may migrate from the hull to the trailer. The whole point of this exercise is to leave no trace of saltwater anywhere on the trailer. You will be rewarded for your efforts.

If your trailer is a non-galvanized, painted model, in spite of your best care, the trailer will suffer some paint loss. The best you can do is to make sure rust does not have a chance to get a grip. Do this by touching-up with a rust-inhibiting paint. There are products on the market that chemically "convert" rust into a non-corrosive element, and serve as a primer that will accept paint.

General Inspection

Inspect the entire framework of the trailer, looking for cracks, weld failure, dents, sags, or evidence of other damage or fatigue. Look closely at all fastening hardware, to ensure everything is tight and corrosion isn't getting a foothold. Places likely to show the first signs of trouble include the coupler, the spring hangers and other suspension hardware, the bunk or roller attachment points, and the vertical "goal post" boat guide (if your trailer is equipped with them). These are the places that either carry the load, are constantly in motion, or are subject to a great deal of vibration, resulting in metal fatigue and eventual failure.

The Coupler

It is the job of the coupler to keep the trailer attached to the tow vehicle. Some trailers may have a coupler that's welded to the trailer tongue, while others are fastened with high-grade bolts. Either way, make sure the attachment is secure. The coupler consists of a socket into which the hitch ball nests, and some form of locking mechanism to hold the ball securely in the socket while towing. A small amount of lubrication is needed to ensure the ball can rotate freely inside the socket, and also to allow free operation of the locking mechanism. Take care not to over-do the lubrication, because grease and oil attract dirt. A thin film of fibrous wheel bearing grease on the ball usually does the trick.

Over time, grime and/or corrosion may build up in the coupler socket and mechanism. Before hitching the trailer to the tow vehicle, inspect and clean the socket. You may be able to wipe the socket clean with a rag, but if there's a build-up of petrified grease and dirt, you may need to carefully dig the old stuff out and then spray some degreasing solvent in the socket to help free things up. Operate the locking mechanism a few times, feeling for any resistance or hang-up. If necessary, clean things out with a strong spray of water, followed by a penetrating lubricant such as WD40.

Brakes

Boat trailers are equipped with surge brakes, if they have any brakes at all. Electric trailer brakes, such as are common on RV trailers, are not used on boat trailers, for the obvious reason that submerging electrical components is not a good idea.

Surge brakes operate through an actuator attached to the tongue of the trailer, just aft of the coupler. In fact, the system is integral to both the coupler and the tongue, because a sliding mechanism is necessary to allow the coupler to move fore and aft in relation to the trailer tongue in order to activate the surge brake.

The system is fully hydraulic and includes its own master cylinder beneath a metal covering. As the tow vehicle brakes are applied, the forward momentum of the trailer pushes against the decelerating tow vehicle. The sliding coupler allows the hydraulic actuator to push a piston in the master cylinder, which is connected to the trailer tongue. This action supplies hydraulic pressure to the brakes, and automatically synchronizes the trailer brakes with the tow vehicle braking action.

Obviously, the system has moving parts that can wear out or

become gummed up or corroded. Regular attention to the moving components of the surge brake system will help keep things operating as they should. Keeping everything clean is the best action you can take.

On top of the master cylinder is a cap that should be opened periodically to check the level of the brake fluid. When fluid needs to be added, use only DOT 3 fluid from a container that has *never been opened* before. Brake fluid is hygroscopic, meaning it absorbs moisture right out of the air. So if you have a half empty can of fluid, the air inside the can will contribute moisture to foul the fluid. Don't leave the master cylinder cap off any longer than necessary to check fluid level, and add fluid if necessary.

Now, as to the rest of the brake system, periodic inspection is a good idea. Brake shoes and drums are the two components under the greatest stress. One of the most damaging events in the life of boat trailer brakes is immersion in saltwater. This is one reason why the trailer should be thoroughly rinsed immediately after any exposure to saltwater, with special attention to flooding the brake system. There are brake flush kits on the market to make the flushing process much more effective.

Brake drums have a tendency to collect water in the lower radius, and rust instantly begins its ugly work, pitting the drum. The only way to be aware of component injury is to remove the drum and inspect it and the brake shoes, replacing anything that shows signs of damage. Follow the directions in the owner's manual for your trailer to properly remove and reinstall the brake drums and shoes. Often, the process is no more complicated than removing the hub cover, pulling the cotter pin out of the castle nut, and removing the nut and keyed washer, then pulling off the brake drum. In the process of removing the drum, the outer wheel bearing will also be removed. If you have a wheel bearing grease fitting (Bearing Buddy) on the axle, you must remove it before you can get to the castle nut that holds everything together. Again, look at your equipment owner's manual to see exactly how to take things apart and put them back together.

* * * *

We were twenty-some-odd miles into a trip, with the boat towing happily behind, when a wasp flew in my side window and landed on the seatback right behind my shoulder. He looked hungry and upset, and I decided it was a prudent time to pull over and let him out.

While we were stopped for bug removal, I decided to do a walk-around to make sure everything was okay with the boat trailer. I bent down and felt the sidewall of each tire, then each hub, to check for excess heat. All the tires were cool, and so were three of the four hubs — but one was quite warm.

Before leaving on our trip, I had inspected and repacked all the bearings. I suspected the hub was warm for some reason other than a bad bearing, so I reached in and felt the brake drum. Yeow! It was hot! Not hot enough to smoke, but too hot to continue our trip. So we did a U-turn and hauled the boat back home. There in the relative calm of our driveway, I jacked up the trailer and tried to spin the wheel. It would hardly move, even though all the other wheels turned freely.

I removed the wheel, tapped off the Bearing Buddy and laid it aside on a clean paper towel, then cleaned out all the grease from the hub. In a few minutes time, I had the cotter pin out, the castle nut off, and wiggled the brake drum (while wearing heavy leather gloves to protect my hands from the heat) to remove the keyed washer and the outer bearing. All this stuff went on the paper towel and got covered up by a rag to protect it from contamination.

Drum brakes trap water, making them vulnerable to corrosion, especially if they are ever exposed to saltwater. Even diligent rinsing won't totally prevent the problem. Pull the brakes apart periodically to inspect for rust problems. This one was shot.

The brake drum was reluctant to come off, so I tapped it all around with a hammer — not hard enough to break anything, but hard enough to loosen it. In fact, a steady pile of rust began to accumulate on the ground beneath the drum. Gradually, it loosened enough so I could remove it. The scene was not pretty. The brake shoes had rusted, the return springs were rusted, the retainer pins and springs were rusted. We had a mess.

In an attempt to salvage the rest of our vacation, I removed all the bad parts, then raced down to the parts store with my junk so they could sell me brand new matching components. If the brakes on one side of the trailer were in bad condition, the brakes on the opposite end of the axle were probably no better. I bought two sets of shoes, springs, retainers, etc., so I could change all the components in both brakes. Using solvent and a wire brush wheel on a drill motor, I cleaned up the backing plates, which were in remarkably good condition, then began the re-assembly. Two hours later, I tightened the lug nuts and lowered the trailer from the jack. Vacation time was back on.

A new set of drum brakes will cost some money, but it's an expense that will give you peace of mind and the ability to keep towing your boat.

All this served as a lesson to me. Now, before taking off on any trip with the boat and trailer, I always jack up the trailer and give the wheels a spin and a wiggle to check for brake drag and excess bearing movement. This little procedure beats the heck out of being broken down on the side of the road, or worse yet having the brakes catch fire and burn the sailboat to the ground.

My advice: Inspect your brakes and service the bearings before every trip, then stop after driving for fifteen minutes and feel the spindle. It should run no hotter than ambient temperature, or perhaps a few degrees warmer.

Wheel Bearings

While you have the brakes apart, it's a perfect time to check the wheel bearings. Remove all the old grease and clean the bearings in solvent. Inspect each race for signs of wear, which will show up as a polished area. If the bearings or races show any blue coloration, they have been too hot and must be replaced. If you see no visible evidence of wear or damage, feel the races for any sign of a burr or detectable uneven wear.

After cleaning the bearings, check them in the same manner, looking closely for any pits, discoloration, or uneven wear. If you have any doubts about the bearings, replace them. Before installing new bearings, pack them with marine-grade wheel bearing grease.

You can hand pack the bearings by placing a glob of grease in the palm of one hand and then forcing the edge of the bearing cage down on the grease to take a "bite" out of the glob. This forces grease up into the bearing cage and between each of the rollers. After each bite, turn the cage a few degrees and take another bite, continuing until you have packed the bearing all the way around.

An easier method is to use an inexpensive bearing packer, is a device that fits like a pancake on each side of the cage and allows you to use a grease gun to pack the bearing through a Zerk fitting on one of the pancakes.

After reassembling the bearings and the keyed washer, tighten the castle nut until it seats firmly against the bearings, then back it off about one-quarter turn. Line up the turret slots in the nut with the cotter pin hole, and insert a new pin (don't press your luck by using the old pin).

At this point, you can install the dust cap or Bearing Buddies, if you have them, and then install the wheel. After tightening the wheel lugs, take the tire in both hands (one hand on each side) and try to shake the wheel to feel for excessive bearing wobble. There should be just a little play in the bearing, but not a lot of wobble. It's better to have a bearing a little loose rather than too tight, because if it is too tight, the bearing will heat up easily as you travel. Spin the tire to see if everything rolls easily, without drag in the brakes or friction in the bearings.

Electrical System

The trailer's electrical system is a concern. I've never had good success with so-called sealed taillights that are supposed to be submersible. Mine always found a way to fill with water and the next time electricity went to the light filament, the bulb failed. What a pain!

Eventually I switched over to LED trailer lights, to eliminate the problem. However, when our trailer still wore submersible incandescent trailer lights, I took the liberty of eliminating the sealed housings. Using a Dremel tool with a cutting blade, I entirely removed the clear plastic bubble that was supposed to create a seal over the light bulbs. This was a good idea for two reasons—first, it no longer trapped water; and second, when the light bulb eventually failed (as they all do anyway), I could easily change only the bulb without having to buy a whole new unit.

The swap to LED trailer lights made life a lot easier. It was an easy project whereby I detached the old units and installed new LED pods, then connected the wiring. The LEDs not only are impervious to water infiltration, but they are also a good deal brighter, draw lower power, and do not have filaments to break.

One key to keeping the trailer lights working is to remember to unplug the trailer's umbilical from the tow vehicle before launching the boat. By doing this, no power goes to the lights while they are immersed. After retrieving the boat at the end of the day, and after rinsing everything off, allow the light units to drain and drip dry, while you go about securing the boat. Then, plug the umbilical into the tow vehicle before traveling. This will give your lights their best chance for a long life.

Aside from blowing a bulb, one of the greatest causes of trailer light failure is a poor ground connection. Make sure your ground connections are made to bare metal, not to a heavily painted surface. Naturally, this is going to create a point for potential corrosion, so it will be especially important to pay attention to rinsing this area and applying some rust inhibitor. Once a solid ground connection has been made, the spot can be covered by paint, but it will still bear watching.

Another connection problem is inside the light unit itself. Corrosion will build on the light bulb contact points, eventually disabling the light. Periodically remove all bulbs, inspect them, clean their contacts and the contact points inside the light units, and replace faulty bulbs. Keep a selection of spare bulbs for taillights and running lights in your spare parts bin.

It's a good idea to periodically crawl under the trailer on a creeper and inspect all the wiring, looking for evidence of damage. The wiring harness might be injured during the launch/retrieve process by flotsam that can snag in a wire. This is especially true in lakes where spring runoff from the mountains can carry driftwood downstream and into the lakes. One of our favorite launch ramps in Idaho always seems clogged with floating wood late into the spring – exactly the kind of stuff that will hang up in trailer wiring.

Other damage to the wiring can be caused by road debris (rocks, twigs, etc.) flipping up from a tire as you're traveling down the highway. To help protect the wiring on our trailer against flying objects, we enclosed it in plastic loom material, available at any auto parts store. We also increased the number of tie-down points along the trailer framework, so we could secure the harness to eliminate free-hanging runs of wire that are prone to catching snags.

Bunks / Rollers

Depending on boat design, the trailer will have either bunks or rollers (some trailers have a combination of both) to cushion and support the hull. Bunks are typically made of dimensional lumber (2"x4" or 2"x6") covered with carpeting. Carpeted bunks can be made to work better by applying a quick swipe with a bar of soap just before loading the boat, which helps the hull slide up on the trailer more easily, reducing pressure on the winch.

Two potential problems exist with bunks—first, if the lumber breaks, rots away or sags, it fails to properly support the hull; and second, if there's anything wrong with the carpeting (a pebble in the nap, loose or shredded material, a bolt, screw or staple that has backed out of the wood), the fiberglass will suffer damage. Always inspect the condition of the bunks and the covering material to catch problem areas.

If the entire bunk needs to be replaced, procure the following materials:

- proper sized marine grade lumber
- new carpeting
- galvanized or stainless steel hardware (bolts, nuts, screws)

- a drill motor and the correct size bit(s)
- a high-speed cut-off wheel or hacksaw
- wrenches

Saltwater boats are likely to have rusted bolts that require a high-speed cutoff wheel (either attached to the drill motor or as a dedicated tool such as a Dremel) or a hacksaw to remove. Wear eye protection when doing this job.

Step one: Either unbolt or cut off the old bolts and remove the damaged bunks. Use the old bunks as templates for marking the bolt hole positions in the new bunk lumber. If your bunks have special brackets, use the old bunks to mark the position for the bracket bolt holes.

Step two: Either bolt the bunk lumber directly to the trailer frame or attach the brackets and align them with the trailer and install them in the same position as the old bunks. Be sure the hardware has no chance of working its way to the surface where it can make contact with the hull.

Step three: Install new carpeting. Wrap the carpet over the top side of the bunk and secure it on the underside of the lumber using staples or screws. To reduce the potential hazard to the fiberglass, do not use any hardware on the side of the bunk that faces the hull.

Now for rollers. These little wheels that support the hull are made of rubber or some synthetic material (thermo-plasticized rubber, polyvinyl, polyurethane, etc.) that offers a soft surface for the hull to roll on. Rubber and related synthetics start to crack and break down after being exposed to the sun, heat, cold, smog and UV radiation for a while. Rollers are supposed to roll, but after exposure to saltwater, metal components (shafts, washers, retainer rings, etc.) corrode and stop the rollers from doing their job.

The two types of roller systems are keel support, and side-wobble. No matter which type you have, when rollers stop rolling easily and a little squirt of lubricant doesn't resolve the problem, they should be replaced.

Roller wheels that are worn out or are out-of-round from having a boat sit on them in one position for too long need to be replaced. Likewise, if the wheels have become so old they've begun to split and crack, replace them. An area of concern is the bushing separating the wheel from the shaft. When the bushings wear out, become terminally sticky or wobbly, replace them. When inserting the bushing, a little dab of marine-grade axle grease will help things rotate more easily. Note: Some polyurethane roller wheels do not require the use of bushings.

Sometimes an entire roller assembly will become damaged. If you're dealing with a bent assembly, you might be able to straighten it enough to get you home, but it will never have the same strength or alignment it once had, so it should be replaced with a new assembly identical to the original.

Corrosion can do some downright repulsive things to a roller assembly. Even if the roller wheel itself is still in good condition, you might need to replace the metal parts such as shafts, washers and retainer rings. To remove the retainer rings, use a small pry bar to spread the gripping fingers. Installing new retainer rings is a matter of using large pliers to squeeze the fingers shut.

Trailer Winch

Frequently I inspect the winch and associated cable, rope, or strap, and the snap hook that attaches to the bow eye. A squirt

Make sure your trailer winch rope or strap is in good condition, and replace it if necessary. This is what helps keep your boat from falling off the trailer. Always use a backup system like this chain, to keep the boat on the trailer if any part of the winch fails.

of WD40 on the spring-loaded snap hook will help keep it working freely. And take a good look at the bump-stop, as well. These items are easy to replace, and inexpensive compared to the kind of fiberglass work you'll need if any of this stuff fails at an inappropriate moment (which is exactly when everything fails).

We use a length of chain between the front of the trailer tongue and the bow eye to serve as a backup tie-down, just in case the winch itself, the cable or the hook should ever decide to take an unscheduled vacation.

Tires / Wheels

When it comes to general maintenance, the tires on boat trailers are often overlooked. But if it were not for the tires, there would be no functional trailer. Tires take a beating. The tread has to survive every ugly obstacle the road can lay in its path. The sidewalls are continually flexing under ceaseless vibration and the shock of hitting potholes and expansion strips. Multi-axle trailers impose the added stress of dragging at least some of the tires sideways around sharp corners. It's a tough life.

Trailers need a different type of tires than those used for cars and trucks. That's because car and truck tires wear out fairly quickly because of daily driving, but trailers are used less often, so the tires almost never wear out—they deteriorate from old age. To address this situation, the tire industry formulates trailer tires to be more resistant to UV radiation and other environmental pollutions that promote deterioration of rubber. These tires are marked on the sidewall with the letters ST (for Special Trailer). Even though ST tires are formulated for a long life, after six or seven years they need to be replaced to prevent catastrophic failure because of old age cracks in the rubber.

Cover the tires when the trailer is sitting idle, to protect against harsh UV radiation. There are a couple ways to do this. Pieces of plywood, cut to shield the tires, do the job. Or make a set of UV protective fabric covers to drape over the tires. Some tire chemical treatments protect against deterioration. Never use a tire dressing containing petroleum distillates (check the product label), because it can soften the rubber or cause blistering. I use 303 Aerospace Protectant, an easy to use spray-on, wipe-off product.

Inspect the tires for signs of trouble. Look for irregular wear on the tread, which might indicate imbalance or misalignment of the axle. Check for sidewall damage from bumping against a curb.

Look for signs of cracking in the sidewall rubber — these are an immediate distress signal calling for new tires.

While you're inspecting the tires, check out the wheels. If the tires show sidewall damage, there might also be damage along the rim where the tire bead seats. Look for indications of lost wheel weights, where the paint or the galvanized metal shows the outline of a place where a missing weight was once clamped. Inspect the lug nuts and studs, watching for corrosion. Torque the lug nuts to spec. If you spot any problems, it's better to take corrective action in the comfort of your driveway, rather than beside a distant highway.

Make sure your trailer tires are rated for the load they are carrying. To do this, you need to weigh the boat and trailer when it is fully loaded for travel. Divide the weight by the number of tires. Now, compare that number with the load rating imprinted on the sidewalls. If you're even close to the limit, consider upgrading to the next higher rating. The maximum load rating only applies if the tires are fully inflated to their maximum pressure rating (max cold pressure rating is printed on the sidewall). Keep the air pressure where it belongs, because low air pressure promotes excessive sidewall flex, which in turn increases heat and the chance of tire failure.

Don't be caught without at least one spare tire for the trailer, and a jack and lug wrench so you can change tires easily. It may be possible to use the tow vehicle jack on the trailer, but perhaps not. We carry a small scissors jack for the trailer, because it is just the right size for sliding beneath the spring plate. The hydraulic bottle jack we use for lifting the truck is too tall to fit under the trailer.

Tongue Jack

While we're speaking of jacks, let's not forget the tongue jack. Normally, all you need to do to keep the tongue jack happy is make sure it doesn't get damaged by leaving it extended while you drive over a bump. We did that once. We removed the wheel at the bottom of the jack, then proceeded to drag the lower end of the tube to death across a gravel parking lot. Aargh ... I hate these personal experiences!

Otherwise, keep the jack clean and well rinsed with freshwater after every exposure to saltwater. Depending upon your particular tongue jack, the owner's manual might recommend periodic greasing of the bevel gears.

By tending to routine trailer maintenance before things start rusting and falling apart, you'll save money in the long run and will travel with greater peace of mind. It's always less expensive to replace broken or worn out components while you're at home in friendly territory, rather than being stuck somewhere far from home, at the mercy of a repair shop that notices the out-of-state plates on your trailer.

Trailer Replacement

Trailerable sailboats come from the factory with their own trailer designed to support the hull properly. But it's possible you may need to replace the original trailer at some point. If you buy an older boat, the trailer may be badly deteriorated or corroded. Or perhaps the original owner kept the boat at a marina and had no use for a trailer. Along you come as a new owner, and suddenly you need a trailer.

The best solution is to contact the factory and arrange to purchase a trailer that perfectly fits the hull design. Otherwise, you'll have to work with a trailer manufacturer to design and build a suitable trailer. If possible, show the trailer manufacturer a photo of the original trailer, so the design team can determine the proper configuration of the hull supports. The hull has strong areas, typically where there are bulkheads or other structural members built into the bilge, and the original trailer is built to provide support beneath those points.

For those who occasionally sail in saltwater, the most desirable trailer is made of corrosion resistant galvanized steel. Freshwater sailors can use a less expensive mild steel trailer without too much threat of corrosion, if it's primed and painted with rust inhibiting paint.

Chapter Sixteen
Trailer Upgrade

It was a sight that left an empty feeling in my gut — beside the freeway we spotted a boat resting on its trailer at an ugly angle. We slowed to see if we could help, but no one was around. The tow vehicle was gone, and the boat had been left abandoned, barely out of traffic. The starboard end of the trailer's axle lay in the gravel and dirt. Apparently, the owner had suffered a flat tire and, having no spare, removed the flat and drove off somewhere to have it repaired or replaced.

Seeing that, I suddenly felt vulnerable. Our pocket yacht rides on a trailer made by the factory especially for this boat. Boat and trailer together weigh in at a hair below 3500 pounds when fully loaded and ready for a trip. As luck would have it, the trailer was rated for exactly 3500 pounds. In fact, the single axle was a 3500-pound axle, and the combined weight rating of the two tires was precisely 3500 pounds. We were operating on the edge, and I knew it. All we needed was one major bump in the road, and our trailer would be seriously overloaded. Seeing that lame sailboat with its wounded right leg dragging in the dirt was all I needed to propel me toward a trailer upgrade.

Single-axle trailers labor under the disadvantage of having no "backup" when a tire fails. A dual-axle trailer will at least keep the rig running upright while the driver slows and pulls over to the side of the road to exchange the flat for an ever-ready spare. (You do carry an always-ready spare, don't you?)

But how many times have you seen a trailer (not necessarily a boat trailer) or even a primary vehicle left beside the road with one tire missing? We've seen it a lot — which tells us there are many people running around without a spare tire, betting against a tire failure, then having to suffer the consequences for their lack of preparation when the inevitable flat tire does happen.

Unfortunately, some trailerable sailboat manufacturers do not supply a spare tire as part of the standard equipment package. When we bought our MacGregor, a spare tire did not come with the trailer. We traveled for two years without one. Then we saw that other boat lying wounded and crippled in the dirt, and were reminded it could easily be us.

Immediately upon returning home, we bought two new tires and had them mounted and balanced on new wheels, put them on the trailer and started carrying both of the originals as spares. Before we go any farther, I'd like to convince you that having a spare tire for the boat trailer, as well as for the tow vehicle, is an absolute necessity. Don't go anywhere without spare tires, a jack, and tire-changing tools!

Now, back to the trailer upgrade. As already mentioned, a single-axle trailer operates at a disadvantage. The whole load is supported by one overworked axle that was probably engineered to just barely carry the load, one set of tires barely rated to support the burden, one set of wheel bearings, one set of springs. If any of those components fail, you're in the dirt immediately—or worse yet, in a lane of traffic. Without a second axle to carry half the load all the time, and also to serve as emergency backup in the event of a component failure on its companion axle, you're out of luck and maybe even out of control.

One other consideration for those of us who own water-ballasted boats: when we pull the boat up the ramp at the end of the day, all the water in the ballast tank is supported by an axle and a set of tires not engineered to carry so much weight. The water in our Mac ballast tank weighs roughly 1500 pounds, so now instead of the 3500-pound axle (and tires) supporting a dry weight of 3500 pounds, they are suddenly laboring under a burden of right around 5000 pounds! Until we can drain the ballast tank, the trailer is severely overloaded. And this overload might cause stress on components that will fail somewhere down the road.

All of which is why we decided to upgrade our factory MacGregor trailer by adding a second axle. The original axle was equipped with surge brakes that worked perfectly for the load weight. We wouldn't need the second axle to have brakes; its sole purpose was to add carrying capacity so we weren't right at (or sometimes over) the trailer's weight limit, and to serve a backup function to set our minds at rest while traveling.

Originally, we considered having a brand new trailer built from scratch, but ours was still in pristine condition because of regular maintenance, and it seemed a waste of money to cast it away and start over. Besides, MacGregor had done a good job configuring this trailer, and so the decision swung around to modification rather than replacement. But who could do such a modification?

It didn't take long to find just the right person. All you have to do is talk to people at a local boatyard, and the recommendations will come in. We located a fellow named Kevin who, as luck would have it, built commercial trailers for a living. He understood trailer design, the importance of maintaining a balanced load, and other such things.

Among all the other critical considerations, keeping the proper fore/aft balance is absolutely vital to having a trailer that exhibits good towing habits. If the trailer ends up tail-heavy, you'll suffer continual sway as you tow. If it's excessively tongue-heavy, there'll be too much load on the hitch and on the rear suspension of the tow vehicle, which will effectively unload the front tires and result in steering and braking problems.

As we discussed the work to be done, I didn't let Kevin's experience keep me from mentioning twice that we needed to make sure the centerline between the two axles fell exactly where the centerline of the original single axle was. He knew I knew what was important, and he knew I'd be watching.

Three Eagles was moored at the local marina while we hauled the empty trailer to Kevin's company yard. After analyzing everything, he decided it would be best to install a second axle and suspension system identical to the original. He called MacGregor to see about ordering a perfectly matched second axle. This is a good way to go, if you can, because it ensures the wheel bearings are all identical. You only have to deal with one set of part numbers and carry one set of bearings in your emergency spare parts box. Then, when you're out on a lonely road that leads to Lake Hoochie Coochie, wondering about your wheel bearings, you can rest assured that, if you need them, the set you have in the spare parts box will fit in any position on either of the axles.

Work on the trailer progressed rapidly, after the new axle arrived. Moving the original axle forward made it possible to retain the original brake lines without having to lengthen them. The new axle essentially served as a "tag" axle, and had no other purpose than load-bearing duty. Because of the profile of the trailer's side rails, bending gracefully toward the bow in conformity to the hull shape, it was necessary to add a bit of additional rail to support the forward spring hanger as the axle was shifted ahead. Cross-measurements were carefully taken to ensure the axles would be perfectly aligned. This would minimize tire wear and maximize towing efficiency and control.

When the dust cleared and we had our new trailer, I was a lot more comfortable about towing the boat to distant waters. Now, instead of having a trailer rated to carry 3500 pounds, we have one rated for 7000 pounds. The fact that the boat and trailer only weigh 3500 pounds fully loaded with provisions for several days of cruising gives us a great deal of confidence that our trailer isn't going to groan under the load. We also have the benefit of an extra set of tires and wheels to support the load. Our anxiety about suffering a flat tire has been mostly relieved. The trailer upgrade allows us to feel more comfortable during long trips across country with the boat in tow. And after all, isn't that why we all own trailerable sailboats in the first place?

Chapter Seventeen
Drum Brake to Disc Brake Swap

For boat trailers, whose brake components are routinely submerged in a hostile environment, drum brakes are horribly vulnerable. Water gets inside the drums, coats everything and then sits there, never fully drying out, eternally promoting corrosion. And it's much worse if you ever launch in saltwater. The ultimate solution is to get rid of the drum system and install a disc system designed for use in the marine environment.

Disc brakes offer so many advantages—they're self adjusting, no trouble at all to inspect, self cleaning, and easy to hose off after leaving the launch ramp. Not only that, but they also deliver superior stopping power.

Tie Down Engineering is one source for disc brake systems that are relatively easy to install in place of drums. This is an "un-bolt and bolt-on" kind of swap, with just enough complexity tossed in at the end to keep you from getting bored with the process. The first stage is the un-bolt part.

The tools and equipment for this project include the following:

- Tire blocks to keep the trailer from moving
- A jack
- Jackstands
- Lug wrench to remove the wheels
- Wrenches appropriate to remove the old drum brakes and install the disc brakes
- A rubber mallet for removing and replacing the bearing protectors
- Needle nose pliers for working with the cotter pins
- Rags or paper towels
- Marine bearing grease
- Torque wrench

- New container of DOT 3 brake fluid
- New cotter pins

Step One: Block the trailer tires, then jack up the trailer and place a jack stand under the axle for security. Remove the wheel belonging to the brake you're replacing. On the inner side of the brake backing plate, locate the fitting where the brake line attaches to the wheel cylinder. Remove the brake line from that fitting.

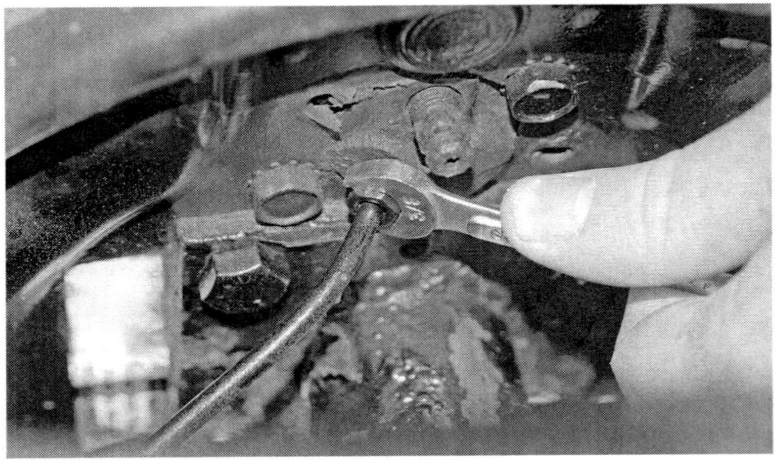

Be careful as you disconnect the brake line at the backing plate, as it might be stuck and need some gentle encouragement to loosen it.

Step Two: Remove the grease cap or bearing protector (i.e. Bearing Buddy), then remove the cotter pin and spindle nut. Finally, pull off the brake drum.

The brake drums might be reluctant to come off, especially if they are worn to the point that a ridge has formed on the inner side that won't easily slide off over the brake shoes.

Step Three: Locate the flange on the end of the axle where four bolts secure the brake backing plate to the axle flange. Remove those bolts. Use wrenches on both the inside and outside of the backing plate to do this; this is why the drum needed to be removed in the first place.

Once the drum is off, you have access to the bolts that hold the backing plate to the axle flange. This photo shows the back side of the axle flange, and you need a wrench on the opposite end of this bolt as well.

Step Four: Now you should be able to slide the backing plate, with all its components, off the spindle. Be careful not to ding the spindle in the process.

Here's the outward side of the backing plate, as you remove the bolts that hold the whole unit to the axle flange.

Step Five: Use rags or paper towels to clean the spindle, getting rid of all the old grease and crud.

The spindle is the part that carries the wheel bearings,
so it will be covered with grease. The grease seals
keep the water out, and the coating of grease
keeps this part from corroding.

Okay, now for the bolt-on part:

Step Six: On the end of the bare axle, attach the Tie Down mounting plate (this is the part that holds the caliper) to the brake flange. NOTE: The mounting plate has holes that permit installation in a vertical or horizontal orientation (plate pointing up or toward rear of trailer). The position you choose depends on the hole positions in your axle flange. The caliper operates whether it is positioned above the rotor or trailing it. To bolt the mounting plate to the flange, use the supplied 7/16" x 1-1/4" zinc hex bolts, lock nuts/ washers, and torque to 40 lb.ft.

Now that all the old parts are gone, begin the brake upgrade by installing the mounting bracket. This component bolts directly to the axle flange, where the old backing plate was removed.

Step Seven: Disc brake systems come in two styles — one has an integral or "one-piece" hub/rotor; the other has separate hub and rotor components. With the separate hub and rotor, it is possible to change rotors without changing hubs, whereas the integral units have the hubs and rotors all together in a single unit. There is not a lot of difference insofar as the installation is concerned, but for our project, we are using the integral hub/rotor.

Our Tie Down hubs came with the bearings and seals already installed and packed with grease. But if they are not, our next step would be to pack and install the rear bearing, followed by the grease seal, then pack and install the front bearing. For boat trailers, the bearing grease of choice is marine grade lithium grease. Slide the hub over the spindle and gently work it all the way back until you feel the grease seal ride up over the raised land where it creates its seal. As you do this, hold pressure on the front bearing set to keep it from falling out of the hub.

The disc brake hub/rotor slides onto the spindle. Inside the hub are inner and outer bearings and grease seals. Slide the hub on carefully, to ease the inner grease seal up and over the raised land where it creates its seal.

Step Eight: With the hub in place, install the spindle washer, followed by the spindle nut. Rotate the rotor while tightening the nut to approximately 50 lb.ft. to seat the bearings. Then loosen the nut just enough to relieve the torque; do not rotate the rotor at this time. Now, finger tighten the nut until it's snug, and back it off just enough to either line up the locking tang washer with a flat side of the nut or to insert a cotter pin. Bend the washer's locking tang tab into place to secure the nut or bend the legs of the cotter pin — whichever applies in your situation.

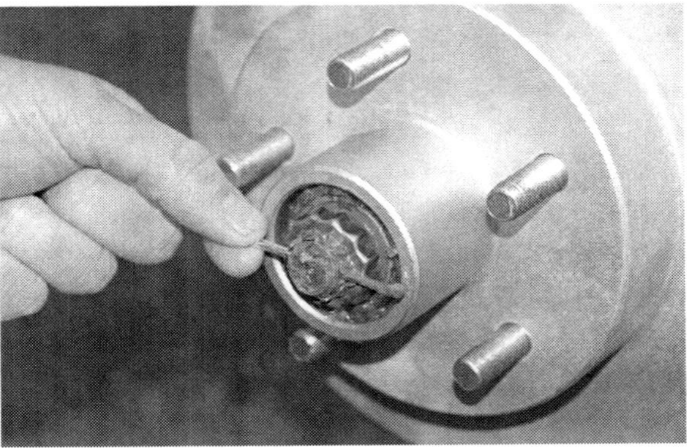

Avoid the temptation to straighten and re-use an old cotter pin. Always use a brand new one — they don't cost much, but the job they do is critical to the safety of your boat trailer, and therefore your boat.

Step Nine: If you're dealing with a separate hub and rotor system, slide the rotor onto the hub, lining up the hub lug studs with the holes in the rotor cap. With either system, the next step is installing the caliper. Install the brake pads to the caliper. The inside pad is spring loaded in the caliper piston. The outside pad is held in place by a pair of metal tabs. Carefully bend the tabs just enough to hold the pad in place (if the tabs are bent too far, the pad will not seat correctly). Test the outside pad to see if it can still wiggle after the tabs are bent.

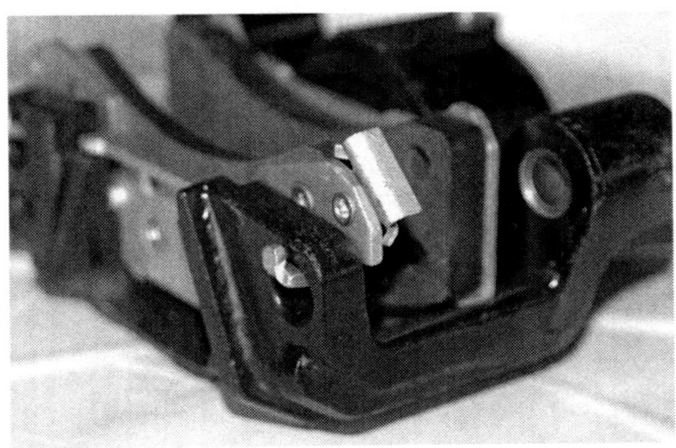

Be judicious when you bend the brake pad tab to hold the pad in place. Too much bending here will render the brakes unable to seat properly.

Step Ten: Place the caliper over the rotor so there's a bleeder valve in the "up" position, or else you won't be able to properly bleed the brakes. The mounting plate fits to the inside of the mating face of the caliper. Line up the bolt holes in the mounting plate and the caliper, then insert the slider pins through the back side of the caliper and into the threaded holes in the mounting plate. Use a 7/16" hex socket to tighten both slider pins to 20 lb.ft. and then check to make sure the rotor spins freely.

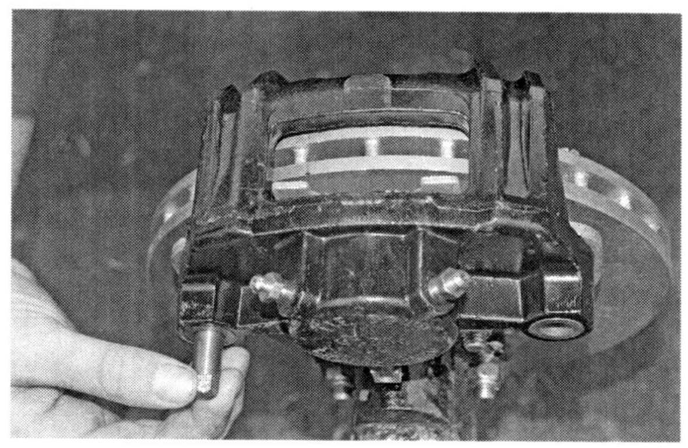

Fit the disc brake caliper over the rotor in the proper orientation, as directed in the installation instructions. Now you're almost home with this project.

Note the slider pins have a coating on the threads. If you ever need to remove the slider pins after initial installation, be sure to clean the threads and apply a fresh coat of permanent Lock Tite® to the threads in the mounting plate, being careful to avoid getting it on the slider pins or bushings.

And now for the little complexity I promised in the beginning. When swapping from drum brakes to disc brakes, it is necessary to install a brake actuator engineered for use with disc brakes. The difference between a disc and drum actuator involves a valve in the master cylinder that permits correct routing of brake fluid. And although there are "free backing" drum brakes, there's no such thing with disc brakes. The disc system must have either a lockout lever or preferably an electrically operated solenoid to interrupt brake pressure whenever the tow vehicle is shifted into reverse gear. When the backup lights are activated, the solenoid stops or redirects the brake fluid to prevent the brakes from operating. This solenoid is part of the new disc-capable actuator, and requires installation of a 5-wire harness in place of the old 4-wire plug, adding the wire from the tow vehicle backup light circuit.

Step Eleven: Now that you have the actuator situation resolved, the final step is to connect the brake line to the fitting on the caliper, and bleed the brakes. Use only DOT 3 brake fluid to fill the brake actuator. Recheck all the connections to make sure there are no leaks, then check again after a test drive of about 25 miles.

After connecting the brake line to the back of the caliper, fill
the master cylinder on the top of the trailer coupler and then
proceed with the brake bleeding process to purge all the
air from the brake line.

Although this might sound like a lot of work, the whole conversion from drums to discs took us only about two hours and required common hand tools. The result? Great braking, lower maintenance, and a system that won't hold the saltwater and corrode into a lump of rust.

Chapter Eighteen
The Fine Art of Towing

Towing In Traffic

One of the most frightening things for a towing novice is to venture out into heavy traffic. It seems there's so much vehicle to keep track of, with a trailer tagging along behind, and the prospect of maneuvering through lanes of traffic can be intimidating. Well, I'm here to tell you nothing short of time on the road will help calm the fearful heart in this situation. But a few simple towing techniques and items of equipment can be used to advantage here.

• Speed — Go easy. No need to keep up with faster traffic, if doing so makes you uncomfortable. On the other hand, do your best not to be an obstruction. One of the most dangerous things on the road is someone traveling slowly, causing other vehicles to make hazardous maneuvers. If you're traveling in the right-hand lane on a freeway and an on-ramp is coming up to bring merging traffic into your lane, adjust your speed and let other vehicles ease into your lane without conflict.

• Be Courteous — This one is closely related to speed. For example, if you're on a 2-lane road and the traffic is stacking up behind you, take the first opportunity to pull off into a wide spot and let the others go on by. Then, when the coast is clear, pull back on the road and continue your trip. If you're entering a highway from a side street, don't pull out until no one is coming for a long enough distance so you can easily get up to speed by the time the next vehicle comes behind you. Small courtesies like these go a long way toward promoting safety on the road.

• Keep Your Distance — Again, a technique closely related to speed. Don't crowd the vehicle ahead, because with the boat and trailer hooked on behind, it will take longer to stop in an emergency. This is especially important if the weather is inclement. Watch the traffic flow around you and anticipate what other drivers might do—then keep an ongoing plan at work as to what you will do if the other guy does something stupid.

• Sideview Mirrors—Your eyes should be constantly scanning the road ahead, your instrument panel (to make sure everything is okay under the hood), and the sideview mirrors. We use sideview mirrors to check traffic behind us; to check that the boat tie-downs are still secure; to check that the mast, furled headsail and all the rigging are still where they should be; and to check on the condition of the tires (it's a real bummer to have a low or flat tire on the trailer and be totally ignorant of the situation).

If your stock mirrors don't stick out far enough from the side of the vehicle, extensions are available for some styles of sideview mirror. In some cases you might need to install a completely separate mirror to allow you to see all the way back down both sides of the boat. Wide-angle accessory mirrors are handy because they substantially increase the view into adjacent lanes.

• Plan Ahead For Maneuvers and Signal Your Intentions Well in Advance—Towing requires advanced planning for any maneuvers. If you need to change lanes, switch on the appropriate turn signal a long way in advance, and then keep your eye on the traffic in the lane you want to move into. When a gap begins to form, it may be an indication the following driver has seen your turn signal and is slowing to make room for you to move over. But keep watching that driver and never assume anything. If the gap materializes, move over into the other lane without keeping the courteous fellow waiting too long—he might get impatient if you languish in indecision.

Cornering

If you're new to towing, there will be a learning period during which you will discover the peculiar characteristics of your particular tow vehicle and trailer combination. How wide must you turn a sharp corner in order to keep the trailer tires from hitting the curb? How fast can you take a corner and still maintain control? What happens when you hit the brakes in a corner? All of this and more are necessary for you to experience, so you can maneuver through traffic, negotiate tight quarters, and cruise a twisty canyon road with confidence.

A trailer will "cut the corner" rather than following perfectly in the tow vehicle's tracks around a bend. The tighter the corner, the more the trailer will cut to the inside. So it's up to the driver to estimate how wide a turn is actually necessary in order to have the trailer track around the curve while still keeping the tires on pavement and in the proper lane. This knowledge only comes with experience, because every trailer and tow vehicle combination performs differently.

Drive into a vacant parking lot early one Saturday morning and put in some time making turns, some tight ones and some wide ones, around the parking curbs. Go slowly at first, and then pick up speed a little bit. Keep a close eye on the trailer wheels, observing how close they come to the curbs with each turn. With a little practice, you'll soon be sweeping through the corners with ease, the trailer obediently following in the intended path.

Backing Up

Here's where life gets interesting. Moving a trailer in reverse can be tricky, for those who have no experience, but there are secrets to success we'll share here. One thing to understand is that the farther the trailer axle is from the hitch point, the more forgiving the trailer will be when backing it up. Long trailers with axles way back toward the rear are much easier to maneuver in reverse than short trailers with the axle relatively close to the hitch point. The former will react slowly to tow vehicle maneuvers, but the latter will react quickly and be unforgiving of driver error, which causes the trailer to jackknife when backing up.

Fortunately, boat trailers are generally long, and designed with the axle positioned farther toward the rear than some other types of trailers, so they're relatively easy to control when backing up.

However, the characteristic that makes them slow to react also makes it necessary to begin maneuvers earlier in the back-up process. The tow vehicle has to move quite a bit before the trailer will respond. Start the maneuver too late, and you might have to abandon the whole process, drive forward and start again. Nothing to get embarrassed about—it happens to even the best drivers. Practice is the only way to make the process easier.

Now for the secret to successful backing with a trailer: *Place your driving hand on the lower arc of the steering wheel*—move your hand to the right if you want the trailer to move to the right, and left if you want the trailer to move to the left. It's that simple! At least, using this method, you won't get confused about which way to turn the steering wheel in order to get the trailer to move in the desired direction.

Use your sideview mirrors to keep track of the rear of the boat, and the trailer tires. If necessary, install sideview mirror extensions, so you can move the mirrors out far enough to allow you to see all the way back to the rear of the boat. When launching or parking the boat, get the dock or parking space lined up in your mirror early, and then keep it in view all the way until it's time to stop. Make small steering adjustments, and move back slowly so things don't get out of control.

If possible, have someone stand behind the boat trailer, off to one side far enough to be out of danger but still visible to the driver via the sideview mirror. This person is the guide, and should use hand signals along with occasionally shouted curses (just kidding) to direct the driver as the backing procedure takes place. It does absolutely no good if the guide is back there waving and yelling instructions at the driver, but is not visible in the sideview mirror on one side of the vehicle or the other. Ideally, the guide should position on the side of the vehicle most useful to the driver—in other words, the side that the driver will be watching because the trailer is easily visible.

For example, if the trailer is angled off toward the passenger side, that's the side the driver will be watching, and that's where the guide should be. Driver and guide should agree in advance on a set of hand signals that indicate "move left," "move right," "keep coming straight back," and "stop." The guide should be somewhat aggressive and precise in the signals, because nothing is more frustrating to a driver than to wonder if the guide is swatting mosquitoes, picking his nose, or actually trying to communicate. Of course, the driver has the ultimate responsibility for the safe maneuvering of the trailer and tow vehicle. If there is confusion or uncertainty, the driver should immediately stop, put the vehicle in "Park," set the parking brake, shut off the ignition and walk back to see what the situation is behind the trailer. Yelling at the guide is not good form.

One final note about backing up boat trailers. If your trailer is equipped with surge brakes, something needs to be done to keep the brakes from locking when the trailer backs up. Surge brakes operate on the principle of a piston system in a master cylinder mounted on the trailer's hitch coupler. When traveling forward, if the brakes of the tow vehicle are applied, the momentum of the trailer will cause the surge brake system to move forward enough to actuate the piston in the master cylinder, thus applying braking effort to the trailer brakes.

The problem lies in backing up the trailer, because traveling in reverse activates the surge brakes as the weight of the trailer resists rearward movement. This is not an issue while backing the trailer downhill, such as for launching the boat, but it is definitely a problem when backing up an inclined driveway or even maneuvering in reverse on relatively level ground. Something must be done to prevent the surge brake from moving enough to activate the piston, or you'll end up shoving the trailer in reverse against locked trailer brakes.

The solution is nothing more technical than to slide a 4-inch-long piece of steel rod through the slot formed between the surge brake housing and the sliding mechanism, to block movement of the system. On some couplers, I've substitued a round file, or two screwdrivers to serve this purpose. As you back up, the surge brake will move only until contact is made with the blocking steel plate, and the piston will be denied enough movement to activate the brakes. Just don't forget to remove the block from the slot before moving the trailer forward again.

Unless your coupler is wired for automatic lockout of the surge brake system when you are backing up, you'll need to use the manual lockout pin to prevent the coupler from activating the brake when you're moving in reverse.

Towing In Wind

Boats have it easy, in comparison with the flat-sided profile of a travel trailer, which can be slammed clear into the next lane by a sudden gust from the side. Wind cuts an easy path around the sleek lines of a hull, reducing the undesirable effect of a stout crosswind. But even though we are less impacted by wind, we do not escape altogether. A sudden gust from abeam can rock the tow vehicle and push the boat and trailer around a bit. You have to be ready for this.

As a good sailor, you'll naturally be observing every sign of wind as you travel — trees blowing, leaves flying, roadside grasses laid over, dust kicking up on a farm field, the persistent tornado that seems to be catching up with you from behind. Use those indicators, just as you would use the sudden advance of whitecaps across the water, to warn you're about to be pummeled by a gust. Slow your rate of travel a bit, firm up your grip on the steering wheel, increase your distance from other vehicles, just in case the gust is more vicious than expected. If a real nasty squall threatens, look for a place to pull off the highway until conditions improve. It's better to heave-to and lose a little time than to be knocked down and lose the whole rig.

Crosswinds aren't the only problem you will encounter — headwinds can also take their toll. Becky and I were traveling south on Interstate 15 in central Utah around Memorial Day a few years ago, with our boat in tow. The 302-powered Ford F-150 we then used as a tow vehicle seemed to be struggling to maintain speed, even though the terrain was fairly level. It wasn't until we stopped for fuel and stepped out of the cab that I realized we'd been pushing into a powerful headwind for more than an hour.

The wind wasn't gusty enough to shake the truck or move the boat around on the highway, but it was strong and steady enough to slow us down considerably. Had we been towing something with a barn-door leading edge (like a travel trailer) rather than a sleek bow, we would have been stopped completely.

Not only did the wind slow us down, but it also raised the concern about our roller-furled headsail secured on the deck for travel. Even though we had a sail cover on the sail itself, the cover could be ripped to ribbons by the constant pounding of the wind. Our stop for fuel expanded into a complete inspection of the boat, trailer, and cargo in the bed of the truck to make sure everything was still secure and able to handle the wind without damage.

Another type of wind can cause trouble for those who are towing — it's called a bow wave, and it's created by 18-wheelers. The large, flat nose on a big commercial truck pushes an enormous amount of wind aside, creating an air version of what mariners refer to as a bow wave.

As the truck approaches you from behind, the high-pressure wave of air attempts to push the rear of your boat sideways. Right behind the bow wave is an area of turbulence alongside the truck, then as the truck passes it creates an area of low pressure. All this combines to do several things: first to blow you sideways away from the truck, then try to suck you back toward the truck into the low-pressure-vacuum. The result can be an unnerving swerve that may cause instability and perhaps even loss of control.

Again, boats are less impacted than are other types of trailers, but the effect can still be felt and you must be prepared for it. Try to anticipate what will happen as you see an 18-wheeler approaching swiftly from the rear, and respond calmly. Knowing the trailer and tow vehicle will move first away from the passing truck, then back toward it, you can be calm as these actions take place. Don't try to prevent the sway by manhandling the steering wheel. Just hold steady, allow everything to move right then back left, and make all your steering corrections small and gentle. The last thing you need is to incite more instability by making radical maneuvers with the wheel.

Wind can be a sailor's friend, in moderation, and at the right times. But when towing, it can be a nuisance or even a hazard. Drive like you sail — with a steady hand on the helm and a keen eye on what's going on around you.

Towing Up and Down Steep Grades

There's a stretch of Interstate 15 east of Baker, California that's infamous for its brutality to vehicles during the heat of summer. Huge black marks on the roadside along the uphill grade mark the places where vehicles have burned to the ground, leaving only charred asphalt to remind other motorists they need to keep an eye on the temperature gauge.

On the downhill grade, other black blotches mark the places where brake fires escalated into full vehicle fires. But no matter where you're towing, it doesn't take the Baker Grade or the desert heat to cause trouble. Towing, itself, causes enough strain on the tow vehicle to merit taking precautions and keeping a close eye on things.

When towing up hills, excess speed and related handling problems generally do not exist. Normally, you'll tack over into the slow lane to allow faster traffic to pass on the left, and just sit back and relax until you reach the summit. But don't get too comfortable, because two areas of concern need your attention. One is engine temperature: the other is automatic transmission temperature. As usual, advanced preparation is the best insurance against a problem.

A well-equipped tow vehicle will have a heavy-duty cooling system, which means an oversized radiator. I've seen some half-ton pickup trucks with ridiculously tiny radiators, so don't assume just because you have a truck it's made to do any serious work in the heat. Take the time to get to know your radiator personally, and if you think an upgrade is justified, swapping in a larger radiator is not difficult.

Make sure the hoses are in good shape. We once had a problem with overheating we eventually traced to a mushy lower hose that collapsed whenever throttle pressure was applied. It caused the water pump to create suction against the lower hose as it pulled coolant from the bottom of the radiator. With the lower hose squeezed shut, the engine instantly overheated. Lower hoses typically have a coil spring inside designed to prevent the hose from collapsing. But I'm here to tell you, when the hose itself becomes soft, even that spring won't save you. Make sure your hoses are in good condition.

Keep the coolant fresh and up to strength. The coolant (antifreeze) should be changed at least every second year, and preferably every year. This is because, over time, a chemical change in the antifreeze results in a corrosive solution that can damage the inside of the cooling system. Another reason for changing the coolant is to eliminate sediment collected in low spots of the system. This will give you a more efficient cooling system, both summer and winter. A 50/50 blend of antifreeze and clean (preferably distilled) water should be used.

Make sure the thermostat is working properly. Cooling system thermostats are designed to remain closed until the specified operating temperature has been reached, at which time the thermostat opens and allows the coolant to flow through the radiator for cooling. If you have any doubts about the operation of your thermostat, there's a way to test it. When the engine is cold, remove the thermostat from its housing and inspect it. If the diaphragm is open, you've got a problem. The heat-sensitive spring that controls the diaphragm should close the gate when the unit is cold. If the diaphragm is closed and you want to know if it will open at the proper temperature, place the thermostat in a pan of water and bring the water to a boil. Place a cooking thermometer in the water along with the thermostat so you can monitor the test. If you have, for example, a 200-degree thermostat, the diaphragm should open at 200 degrees. If it fails the test, replace it.

A thermostat that opens at a lower temperature does not, in and of itself, guarantee the engine will run cooler. Even a fully opened thermostat cannot make up for a plugged radiator or other systemic problems. So, if you're tempted to switch to a cooler thermostat, make sure the entire cooling system is in perfect condition before you make the swap.

Radiator caps are the final component we're concerned with. Most cooling systems are designed to operate at an internal pressure of 14 to 17 psi. As long as the pressure is maintained, the coolant should not boil until the temperature reaches about 260 degrees F. If the cap is not holding pressure, the coolant will boil much sooner, and can leave the radiator dry or low of coolant. If you're losing coolant, but can't find an external leak, suspect the coolant is boiling out. Have the system and the radiator cap pressure tested, and replace or repair any failed equipment you discover.

Okay, now let's talk about the downhill aspect of towing in mountainous country. Several potential problems exist, including excess speed, loss of control, and overheating brakes. Gravity does an incredible job of attracting a tow vehicle and trailer toward the center of the earth, and before you know it you can be traveling so fast you may not be able to slow down or stop.

There's a reason why there are runaway truck ramps on severe hills, and it is because those who engineered the highway understand that, from time to time, the downward momentum will be too great to overcome with brakes alone.

Maintaining slow speed down a hill is far better than attempting to slow a vehicle that's traveling too fast. Over-using the brakes can lead to brake fade or brake fire. When brakes catch fire, the next thing to join the combustion are the tires, and they burn long and hot and often take the whole vehicle with them. Our advice is to select a lower gear and use the engine backpressure to maintain a slow speed. Touch the brakes only when necessary, and let the engine and transmission do most of the work. Going slow and easy will solve every problem related to towing down a steep hill — keeping the vehicle under control and saving the brakes.

Of course, because most boat trailers are equipped with surge brakes that become activated merely by the physical action of holding the trailer back, the trailer brakes may overheat no matter what you do. But there is one recourse — consider alternate routes. We have to admit there are summits we will not cross while towing. One such is Teton Pass in western Wyoming, near where we used to live. If we wanted to sail Jackson Lake, over the pass from our town, we took an alternate route that added an extra two hours to the drive, but eliminated the steep grades on both sides of the pass. The few extra miles and hours involved in choosing an alternate route are well spent in keeping us, the tow vehicle and trailer safe. And ultimately, there is no body of water worth risking our lives and our equipment.

Along the same line as choosing an alternate route is the concept of choosing an alternate schedule. Remember what was said earlier about the infamous Baker Grade? When we bought our MacGregor, we had to cross the merciless son of a simmering asphalt pile to haul the boat from its southern California birthplace to our home in eastern Idaho. To make sure we gave ourselves the best chance of success in getting over the pass and across the Mojave Desert without melting down, we set the alarm clock for 1:00 a.m. and headed across the desert in the cool of the night. By the time the sun was up, we were running along in the more towing-friendly climate of central Utah. We never regretted those few lost hours of sleep.

Trailer Sway

Trailer sway should be recognized as more than just an annoyance. It's actually a safety problem. A trailer that oscillates back and forth can go out of control, pulling the tow vehicle with it, resulting in a serious accident.

One of the most common causes of trailer sway is improper tongue weight. If the tongue weight is too light, the trailer is naturally tail heavy. A tail heavy trailer is prone to sway or fish tail. For best handling, the ideal tongue weight is 10% to 12% of the overall trailer weight. To find out your trailer's tongue weight, tow the boat to a certified public scale and weigh the tongue jack.

Subtract the axle weight from the overall weight, and you have the tongue weight. More weight (in excess of the 12% rule) is okay, up to the limits imposed by the hitch manufacturer and the tow vehicle manufacturer.

You can increase tongue weight by creative loading of cargo, moving more of the supplies toward the tongue and away from the tail. As this is done, the trailer should become more stable. Moving cargo forward of the trailer axle has a doubling effect — lightening the tail by a given amount and increasing weight on the tongue by the same amount — effectively doubling the impact of the weight that was actually moved.

A friend of ours recently swapped from a relatively lightweight 2-stroke outboard to a more powerful and heavier 4-stroke. Trailer sway immediately became a problem because of the heavier tail and correspondingly lighter tongue weight. His only option was shuffling cargo inside the boat to compensate for the imbalance. After he did this, good towing manners were restored.

Freeway Hop

You may have experienced it yourself — you're towing the boat down the interstate and keep getting pounded by an incessant, rhythmic jolt. Worse yet, the jolt is sustained — bam, bam, bam — mile after mile. Among those who tow trailers, the condition is known as (among more unmentionable names) freeway hop. It is uncomfortable and annoying, and it can make you think there's something wrong with your suspension or tires. Unfortunately, it's nothing quite that simple. The problem is poor highway design and construction, employing wide and uneven expansion joints between highway slab sections that create an annoying rocking-horse motion between tow vehicle and trailer.

What can you do to eliminate this annoyance? Nothing we've found will completely neutralize freeway hop, but there are a few things you can do to help reduce the effect.

- First, make sure the tow vehicle has high-quality shock absorbers in good condition. Testing has been done with stiffer and softer shocks, to no avail. The purpose of shock absorbers is to damp suspension action and dissipate energy created by the up and down movement of the suspension system. Stiffness of the shock absorber doesn't seem to affect freeway hop as much as one might think. But it is still important the shocks are in good condition, to quiet the motion and prevent a loss of control as the suspension works up and down over these undulations.

- The problem is exacerbated by loose suspension components that rattle with each jounce across an expansion joint or pot hole, so make sure everything is tight and your suspension system bushings are in good condition.

- Experiment with slightly lower tire pressure. Don't go overboard with this, because tire load capacity decreases as air pressure is reduced. Tires are not intended to be part of the suspension system, even though they effectively soak up the bumps. Altering air pressure may or may not make the ride a little more comfortable. WARNING: Excessively low tire pressure can increase sidewall flex, creating heat that can destroy a tire. Go easy on this. And if you do experiment with lower pressure, be prepared by carrying your own pump or compressed air supply to reinflate the tires to full pressure.

- Experiment with varying speeds of travel. Unfortunately, in our experience this only works if you travel faster, which can be more dangerous from a control standpoint while towing a trailer. But it's worth a try.

- Find another route that doesn't beat you to death. This is kind of like altering course when beating to windward over uncomfortable chop in your sailboat, and it is often the only solution that works. Then let your Congressman know you're displeased with the condition of the highway. This last measure won't improve the ride, but may make you feel better to get it off your chest.

Other Marginal Surfaces

Someday, you will find yourself towing on marginal road surfaces that may negatively affect control and handling of the tow vehicle and trailer. Gravel roads, a severely rutted surface, or a road intentionally grooved (striated) in preparation for resurfacing can toss the tow vehicle and trailer from side to side as the tires interact with the ground. When this situation catches you off guard as you're blissfully driving along at warp speed, it can suddenly furrow your brow, wet your palms (and perhaps other parts of your anatomy and wardrobe), because the trailer might begin to sway wildly.

The only thing you can do to save the day is reduce speed, while trying to hold everything in your lane. Unless it's an emergency, it is best not to jump on the brakes too suddenly, because this could throw everything out of control immediately. Just lighten up on the gas pedal and allow gravity, friction, wind resistance and all that good stuff to gently slow you down. Perhaps a light touch on the brakes would be appropriate, but take it easy.

When you find yourself on icy or snowy roads, the situation can be even more dangerous for a couple of reasons. First, you might be totally unaware of the ice, until suddenly you see taillights ahead of you become headlights and then taillights again — as the vehicle ahead does doughnuts on a glazed road surface. This can put your heart in your throat, as you realize you're on the same kind of surface - pulling a trailer.

Second, this surface is far less forgiving, because once you start to slide, it's all over. The only thing you can do is follow the same procedure — come gently off the throttle (depending upon conditions, even jumping off the throttle too suddenly can cause the drive wheels to lock up because of compression braking), stay away from the brakes, and let speed diminish gradually. Make no sudden maneuvers.

Obviously, the more distance you have between your vehicle and other vehicles on the highway the better off you'll be. Without becoming an obstruction to other traffic, travel slowly on marginal surfaces, and maintain as much distance between yourself and other vehicles as possible. Be watchful of other vehicles, and try to anticipate their actions.

At times like this, it may be wise to seek a safe anchorage until conditions improve. Pulling into a motel and spending an extra night while the ice storm moves on or the road crews do something to improve traction may be the smartest thing.

Interstate Towing Regulations

Regulations regarding towing vary from state to state. Speed limits, combined lengths of tow vehicles and trailers, and weight of trailers requiring brakes are a few of the categories that vary widely. To check for current laws regarding boat towing in every state, log onto the Internet and go to http://www.boatus.com/towing/towlaw.htm. This will give you a state-by-state listing of all the laws pertaining to towing a boat, including speed limits, size limits, and required safety equipment. If you have no access to the Internet, check with the local Department of Motor Vehicles for each state in which you intend to tow your boat.

Part Three
Sail, Sail Away ... Living the Dream

A Collection of Adventures
(A Note From Becky)

There is nothing I'd rather do than spend time with Rich on *Three Eagles*. When we sail away together, we cast off our stress, troubles, deadlines, to-do lists, and hundreds of other pressing issues. That's why sailing off into the sunset together holds so much appeal to me ... it's relaxing, peaceful, and takes me to a place where other concerns disappear. It's just the two of us. With the wind in our sails, we have time for each other. It's sharing, bonding, connecting — it's love. That's what sailing means to me. It doesn't matter where we go — it matters that we do.

* * * *

(A Note From Rich)

Maybe it's a guy thing, but there is something about a horizon that begs to be explored. While Becky and I enjoy returning to places where we've already dropped anchor, I can't deny that the urge to see farther territories quickens my pulse. Part of what I like about a trailerable sailboat is the prospect of heading over horizons in any direction we choose. We've been a lot of places, seen a lot of things, and in the chapters to follow we invite you to join us as we share a few adventures of living the dream.

Chapter Ninteen
The Treasure of Mystery Bay

Everybody loves a mystery, and we're no different. So when we saw the name Mystery Bay on our chart, my attention was immediately piqued. "Let's go there," I said to Becky with a faraway look in my eyes. She's seen that look before and understands there's nothing to be gained by either ignoring it or trying to talk me out of whatever is behind that glassy gaze. So she agreed we should plan a trip to visit the place with the enigmatic name.

On the appointed day, we towed the boat to the marina and raised the mast. It goes quickly with both of us working on it, and before long we were ready to launch. The day was perfect, with a light breeze blowing from the west and us wanting to head east.

Getting to Mystery Bay is tricky. Makes me wonder how long early-day exploring mariners sailed right past the nearly invisible entrance channel leading to Kilisut Harbor (which leads to Mystery Bay) before anyone noticed it. I can tell you this—if we hadn't read the guide book that gave detailed instructions about how to safely navigate the entrance, we probably would never have known it existed.

But finding the entrance is only half the battle. Depending upon the condition of the tide, you might be lured onto sandbars barely covered by water. In fact, on another trip when we sailed to Mystery Bay, we were behind a rigid-keel sailboat that suddenly came to a stop ahead of us. I knew she'd stuck her keel in the soft bottom, and it made me glad we were sailing a boat with a retractable centerboard and kick-up rudders.

After negotiating the circuitous route leading into Kilisut Harbor, we continued southeast to the entrance to Mystery Bay. Inside the bay is a Washington marine state park complete with a dock and a nice selection of mooring buoys. As luck would have it, there was space for us at the dock, so we slipped in and tied up for the night.

This is one of the peaceful places on Planet Earth. There isn't much to do here, except take a walk or kick back and listen to the silence. In a moment of fortuitous inspiration, we decided to wander up the dock to visit the state park facilities (nothing elaborate, let me tell you!) and take a walk along the shell-strewn beach.

Not twenty feet after we stepped on solid ground, we spotted treasure in the bushes growing alongside the grassy area—black nuggets of pure sweetness: ripe blackberries.

"Look, honey, blackberries," I whispered to Becky, paranoid somebody else might hear about the treasure and get to it before we did.

"Let's go back to the boat and get a couple of bowls to collect them in," she whispered back. And we turned around on the spot and walked back down the ramp to the dock as calmly as our racing hearts would allow.

Soon we were back, wading into the thorny bushes, plucking the juicy black fruit into our bowls. So abundant were the berries, it didn't take long for us to fill the containers to the brim, even though we employed our traditional "one for the bowl, one for the mouth" harvesting technique.

Actually, Becky has improved on the method by using a new-math approach that fairly consistently leaves her bowl only half full when mine starts to overflow. I eavesdropped on her muttering to herself as she picked. "One for the bowl," she mumbled, "two for my mouf. Num fo' da bow, two fo' ma mouf. Num, num, num..."

When I burst through the bushes to see what was going on, she looked up with startled eyes and a huge purple grin, like a little kid caught with her hands in the cookie jar. Juice dripped down her chin and her sticky fingers looked like they had been permanently tattooed. "Hi, hon," she mumbled.

"It isn't polite to talk with your mouth full," I reminded her. "Especially when your bowl is still half empty." I pointed to her meager collection efforts.

"Well," she swallowed so she could talk more easily, "I thought we should test these berries to make sure they're worthy of collection."

"And...?" I asked.

"And I'm almost through testing." She grinned.

Later, as we walked back to our boat with two full bowls of blackberries, we stopped to share with other boaters who had come to Mystery Bay without knowing about the treasure that grew nearby, free for the taking.

And that night, our dessert was sweeter than ever, because we captured it with our bare hands. And we had the stains to prove it.

Chapter Twenty
Bioluminescence—When the Sea Blinks

Late, late one September night, Becky and I pushed ourselves away from the cribbage game and went up on deck to brush our teeth and spit. The sky was black, except for the four-thousand or so stars winking at us. The water was peaceful and dark, as if our little corner of the ocean had shut its eyes and gone to sleep. The whole scene begged for reverence, so we found ourselves whispering to keep from disturbing anything.

As a nocturnal scuba diver, I know better than to think the ocean goes to sleep at night. If anything, that's when it all wakes up. The water is alive with activity at night, because that's when so many of the swimming creatures come out from their protective lairs in search of who knows what—food, companionship, a quick game of chase the shrimp, or some other unmentionable activity.

We stared off into the depths of space, then down into the depths of the inky water and enjoyed the warm breeze. It was one of those nights that makes you wonder why the whole world isn't out there sailing.

About then, Becky's toothbrush went to work, and in a minute she was bent over the rail prepared to spit. I have to tell you Becky is one stupendous spitter. I believe she developed her talent while playing touch football in the street with the neighborhood boys when she was about eleven years old. Never one to be outdone by a boy, I'm sure she practiced her "pitooy" pucker so she could spit with the best of them during any lag in the game's action (though she adamantly denies it).

Well, there she was, poised on the starboard rail, puckering like she did way back when. And then she let go. Up, up the foamy pitooy traveled. Out, out away from the boat, which is always a paramount concern at times like this. Then down, down it went toward the black water. And then it hit.

The next thing out of Becky's mouth was anything but a whisper.

"Wow!" she shouted. "Did you see that?"

"What?" I asked innocently. Rare are the times I'm actually innocent, so I have to take full advantage of every opportunity. And this was one.

"My spit exploded when it hit the water."

"What do you mean it exploded?"

"Watch, I'll show you," she said with enthusiasm, always anxious for a chance to spit. She loaded up her mouth with water, rinsed, gargled for effect, then launched her mouthful of leftover Colegate with a trajectory that would make an Olympic long-jumper proud. It hit the surface with a splat and lit up the water for two feet in every direction from ground zero.

"Bioluminescence," I commented.

"Really?" she said with mock fascination at my multi-syllabic vocabulary.

"Uh-huh," I answered, deciding to work with smaller words.

"Tell me about that," she said, taking another swig from the water bottle, then turning to face out away from the boat again.

"Well," I began, "bioluminescence is the light you see from a chemical reaction that happens when the membrane surrounding certain types of plankton is shattered by a disturbance of the water."

She spit and the water lit up again.

"Congratulations," I said, "you've just murdered a million or so little creatures."

She choked, then wiped her lips dry. "Really?" she sounded concerned.

I nodded, and we stood there quietly looking overboard at water dark enough for a funeral. After a moment of respectful silence, I asked, "You want to say anything nice about the recently departed — you know, to comfort the next of kin?"

Her throat moved convulsively and I thought for a moment she was going to cry. But then she took a drink, puckered up and spit.

"Nah," she smiled. "Let's have a wake. We'll celebrate with fireworks on the water."

We didn't get to bed until late that night, because we were up on deck spitting until our tongues were swollen from all the exercise. And that's the mostly true story about the Blakely Island Massacre.

Chapter Twenty-One
Swarmed By Sea Gulls

There was a party going on somewhere. And from the sound of it I was willing to bet it was a bunch of thirteen-year-old girls at a slumber party passing around photos of young, male rock stars, then screaming as only thirteen-year-old girls can. Would have been willing, that is, except that we were a couple miles out on the water, and raw logic told me teenage girls were not likely to be out there having a party.

But the noise had me befuddled. It sounded much like a giddy gaggle of giggling girls. Almost had me scanning the horizon for balloons and confetti. I stopped myself before going that far and made a mental note I shouldn't act like I'm nuts, especially when Becky will notice.

And she would notice. In the more than thirty years of our marriage, she hasn't missed a single time I've acted nuts. Well, there was that one time...but let's not talk about that now.

So we sailed on toward the distant islands. One of the wonderful things about moving under sail is the quiet. Unless the wind is so strong it's shrieking through the rigging, or we're heeling so far over that the crew is protesting in mutinous terms, or stuff is falling off the dinette and crashing to the floor — unless those things are happening, its quiet on the boat. Well, there was the time when Becky stepped into the head for a few moments of, shall we say, contemplation just about thirty seconds before we hit the tide rips. We lost the quiet that time, too. But most of the time, *Three Eagles* is a peaceful place.

On this day, however, there was noise on the water, coming from somewhere ahead, although we saw nothing in our path for miles and miles. But you know how it is with sound traveling across the water. If the wind's blowing just right, you can hear a fellow whisper sweet nothings to his honey from clear across a lake.

The giggling girl noise seemed to grow louder, so I pulled out the binoculars and scanned the water ahead. Then I spotted it, a little bit off to the west of our northerly route. By golly, a party was going on, and some of the gigglers were probably girls, but I couldn't tell because I haven't learned to discern the gender of sea gulls. We came upon a party of sea gulls — a numberless (only because I can't count higher than a bazillion) flock of gulls thrashing about on the water. They took turns flying up a little way and then throwing themselves down on the water in what appeared to be frenzied mass suicide. Kind of reminded me of what I've seen kids do on the dance floor in a thing called a Mosh Pit.

But the sound of gulls splatting against water was lost in the cacophony of the survivors, who were evidently engaged in ritual wailing and mourning for the poor lost souls who'd just broken their necks by hitting the water so hard. Oh, it was an awful sight.

But you know how it is with guys witnessing awful sights like brutal hits in a football game, or a fiery crash at a car race, or... well, let's not go there. Anyway, I couldn't put the binoculars down — but you probably already guessed that. Then a plan emerged. Maybe we could save some of the gulls from self-destruction, if we interrupted this whole mess. So, in my best skipper voice, I gave the command, "Honey, would you please steer us about five degrees more to the left."

"You mean come half a point to port?" she asked.

"Okay," I nodded, "do that."

I made a mental note that one of these days I've gotta bone up on my nautical vocabulary. But right at the moment, we were on a mission to save the sea gulls. Doesn't sound quite as profound as saving the whales, but it was all we had to work with, so we went for it. Becky adjusted the helm, the boat responded, and we glided silently toward the area of destruction.

Amazingly, as we closed the distance, the gulls didn't even look up and see us coming. Yes, we were moving quietly, but we were still a big target and I expected the gulls to forget their mindless act of self-mutilation and come to their senses. I've heard it said that sea gulls are brain dead and do all their thinking with their stomachs, but then I've heard much the same thing about guys watching Monday Night Football. These gulls seemed to fit the description.

The gulls paid us no attention as we sailed right into the middle of them. And that's when we saw what all the fuss was about. They weren't committing suicide after all. They were in a feeding frenzy. In the water below the gulls was a huge herring ball, a whirling mass of the sea gull's favorite snack. When under attack, herring (among some other types of fish) will begin to circle the wagons, swimming around and around, forming a living ball. It's some sort of survival instinct intended to protect the fish in the middle of the ball, so the whole school doesn't get eaten, thus preserving the species. Meanwhile, the gulls were out of their minds with glee as they attacked the perimeter.

And we were right in the middle of it — a National Geographic moment. Did we reach for the camera, to capture this magic moment? Are you kidding? We sat mesmerized, gulls splatting into the water, the herring ball whirling around and around beneath our boat. And then somebody in that gaggle of giggling girls looked up and nudged her neighbor and probably said something like, "Hey, Doris, what's that sailboat doing running over our lunch?"

Some kind of telepathy took over and the entire flock left the water at once. Suddenly, we couldn't see the sky, because it was blotted out by flapping wings and screaming gulls. They were all around us, and they weren't giggling any more. Many of them demonstrated their displeasure the way sea gulls do it best.

If you have ever wondered whether or not sea gulls make intentional bombing runs — yes, they do.

That evening we washed the boat.

Chapter Twenty-Two
Romance vs. The Fear Factor

(A Note From Becky)

Sailboats are romantic. There's nothing like the magical feeling of cruising across a dreamy stretch of water under the quiet power of wind and sails. Makes me want to cuddle and snuggle with my lover. But that wonderful, romantic feeling will be tossed overboard the moment things get too scary.

The definition of "too scary" is an individual thing. When the fun-o-meter (that's my name for it — Rich calls it an inclinometer) hits 20 degrees of heel ... that's plenty! My comfort zone is around 10-15 degrees heeling. At 25 degrees things get noisy onboard, because I start screaming. Screaming kills the romance in a hurry.

So, pay attention, guys — be sensitive to the limits of your sailing partner. Some people like a roller coaster ride, but for others it scares them witless. The fastest way to ruin your partner's enthusiasm for sailing is to take her out, put the rail in the water and listen to her screaming. And you can be sure, you won't find her warming up to you later on in the evening.

I still haven't completely forgiven Rich for scaring the daylights out of me when we were novice sailors. (Well, actually, I have. But I do like all the flowers and sea shells he surprises me with when he's feeling guilty). He knew a lot more about things nautical than I did; how the boat reacts to sail trim, and other such technical things. But he kept it all a big secret from me.

One day when the breeze was full of puffs and gusts —and the boat alternately sailed nicely and then abruptly was knocked over to 25 degrees — I pleaded with him to do something to make the boat stand up straight. He insisted everything was okay and this was fun! The wind was knocking us over and he couldn't do anything about it. After all, only God can control the weather, he implied. "We just have to sail through it," he smiled, keeping a firm hand on the wheel.

That was fine for him — intrepid sailor that he is — but it wasn't fine for me. In a rare moment of compassion (maybe because I'd curled into a fetal position and alternately mumbled a prayer and sucked my thumb), he reached over and uncleated the mainsheet, eased the boom out a few degrees and ... *viola* ... the mainsail was depowered and suddenly up she came. *Three Eagles* sailed upright, and I was no longer threatened by a watery grave. I gave Rich one of those "looks" that prompted a reluctant confession... he knew what to do all along. (Now that I think about it, he's still not completely out of the doghouse for that one. I am currently accepting flowers and sea shells.)

Well, girls, all I can say is, learn everything you can about how the boat handles so your skipper can't keep any secrets from you. And skippers, if you want a little romance at the end of the day's sail, for heaven sake, don't scare the First Mate.

Chapter Twenty-Three
The Day the Sunstar Came to Visit

Crabbing season was in full flower. We knew because the surface of the bay had blossomed with red and white crab pot floats that turned sailing into a slalom sport. For those of you not familiar with the religion of crabbing, I'll explain the fundamentals. First, the object is to catch crabs in some sort of trap. One popular type of trap is the crab pot, a wire mesh box (either square or round) with one-way doors. The crabs can walk in, but can't get back out. What lures them in is stinky bait, often chicken guts or salmon parts.

When we first moved to the Pacific Northwest from the Rocky Mountains, where salmon is an exotic import, we thought people were nuts to use salmon as bait to catch crabs. But, hey, I'm no psychiatrist, so what do I know? Actually, crab hunters only use discarded bits of salmon, not the filets. Whew!

The bait is kept inside a special little mesh container, so the crabs can smell it and almost taste it, but can't actually get to it. It's a form of crustacean torture, leaving the crabs wide-eyed and panting, with tongues hanging out, drooling over what they desperately want but can't have. Kind of like the truck dealer in our town who keeps a beautiful crewcab diesel pickup parked at the edge of his lot, and a price tag so high even the Mars space program couldn't reach it. Excuse me a second, I've gotta go blow my nose—I'm starting to cry.

Where were we? Oh, yes, the baited crab trap is lowered to the bottom of the bay, and a red and white float marks its position so the owner can come back later, grab the float, pull up the trap and harvest the catch. Trying to decide exactly where on the bottom of the bay to lay your trap is the tricky part, a science unto itself, and clearly beyond the scope of this book—primarily because I haven't a clue what to tell you. I'll just say it's some kinda voodoo, and leave it at that.

Our personal approach to catching crabs is hit and miss. Mostly miss. But that's not the point. The point is to go out and have fun, and if you catch anything worth hauling home for dinner, well ... well, I don't know how it feels, because we haven't experienced much of that yet. But we do have a lot of fun trying.

Take, for example, the day we caught a sunstar. Rather than a pot, we use what's called a crab ring. It consists of two metal rings (one smaller than the other), connected to each other by a nylon mesh like that used on fishing nets. Because the rings are the only rigid structure, the whole thing collapses nicely, making it ideal for use on a small boat like ours. The idea with the ring is to attach a bait container to the inside of the bottom, then lower it over the side and ease it down the to sea floor. You turn it loose from your boat, so it doesn't get dragged around while you are adrift. So you use a float, just like the folks with the high-zoot crab pots. The ring lies there on the bottom completely flat, so the crabs are free to walk onto the netting, drool over the bait, and walk off again, having never been trapped at all.

Whenever you're ready — like between rounds of cribbage, or after you've finished your sandwich, or maybe you're just overcome with some kind of delusional confidence there's a crab on the ring — you grab the float, pull up the rope and retrieve the ring. As you pull it up, the top ring is lifted, and the smaller bottom ring drops, forming a closed funnel to keep the crabs that are on the netting from escaping. But you have to pull fast, because those crabs are smart and they've heard about what happens if they take a ride in the stovetop Jacuzzi. They'll try to make a run for it, so you have to raise the ring quickly to keep them from escaping.

Using this system, we've actually caught crabs. But mostly we caught other stuff. Like the sunstar I started telling you about before I got distracted by thoughts of the truck.

Here's what happened. We baited the ring, lowered it over the side and settled down to do something, I can't remember what. A few minutes later we decided it was time to pull up the ring and see what was there. This isn't like fishing with a bobber. You just have to go with your feelings. We felt this was the time to pull up the ring. So we did.

"Hey, I think we've hit the jackpot," I exclaimed, as I strained to pull up an unusually heavy crab ring. "Must be full."

"Oh goody!" Becky jumped up and down in anticipation. She's like that. You should see her when she catches a fish — she does a dance, right there in the boat. If you've ever gone fishing with a grumpy old geezer who makes you wonder who killed all the fun in life, you should go fishing with Becky. She'll restore your understanding of how to have fun. In fact, she'll give you a live demonstration. Just move the bait bucket, so it doesn't get kicked over the side.

When the crab ring hit the surface, we saw not a single crab in it. What made it so heavy was ten pounds of sunstar fish. This is kind of like a starfish on steroids. They get huge, and this one had twenty-one arms (no, I'm not kidding). It covered our crab ring from edge to edge, leaving no room for crabs.

"Oh, that looks like fun," Becky said. "Let's play with it for a minute, before we turn it loose."

This is where my better judgment took a vacation, and I brought the creature into the cockpit and laid it on the bench seat. Well, you might imagine what happened next. I'll preface the narrative by noting that starfish have suckers on the bottoms of their arms. That's how they catch things — they suck onto them, then pull them to pieces, then they eat the pieces. Mother Nature isn't always warm and fuzzy. Well now, knowing that, guess how many suckers a starfish with twenty-one arms has. A bazillion! And they all started sucking at once. They clamped down on the seat like they had never seen gelcoat before, but were enjoying the flavor.

I looked at Becky, she looked at me, then we both looked at the sunstar, and it started wandering around the cockpit. "Okay, I think we've had enough fun," Becky said, backing away from several sunstar arms on a mission of exploration. "Let's throw him back overboard."

"Right," I agreed. Then the fun began. Have you ever tried to pry loose twenty-one arms, each of which is equipped with actively operating suckers? No, probably not. Well, let me tell you, it sounds like more fun than it is.

Every time we de-sucked one arm, the sunstar grinned and sucked harder with twenty others. We were in trouble. "Is this the kind of thing we can call the Coast Guard to come and help with?" Becky asked.

"I don't think so," I grunted, reaching for two arms at once. "They might haul us in for harassing the wildlife."

It took us a long time, but eventually, we figured out how to grab several arms at once and rip them loose from our cockpit. Finally we were able to wrestle the beast back into the water. But there, spread all over the cockpit seats, were acres of slime.

"Yuck," Becky said, "looks like you've got a mess to clean up. I'll go make sandwiches." And she disappeared below. But then her conscience took over, and she reappeared with a bucket and some rags, and we spent the next half-hour scrubbing slime off the gelcoat.

So, what's the lesson in all this? I don't know. If you figure one out, give me a call. I can use all the help I can get.

Chapter Twenty-Four
Jellyfish Heaven

On a warm, sunny late-summer afternoon, we cruised into the quiet waters of Reid Harbor on Stewart Island, looking for a mooring buoy to hook onto for a couple of days. Stewart Island is only inches from Canadian waters — at least it looks that way on the chart. It's a wonderful place, clothed with a typical Pacific Northwest forest with postcard views no matter which direction you look.

When we pulled in, it wasn't quite the end of the season yet in the San Juan Islands, and the long, narrow bay was filled with boats that had already claimed all the State Park buoys, as well as all the space on the floating dock. It's amazing how much dock can be consumed by a single mega-poweryacht, barely leaving any room for a dinghy to land and tie up.

But the afternoon was young, and in the back of my mind I envisioned a couple of the boats casting off and giving us a chance to grab a buoy. So I drove our boat toward the head of the bay where the water is too shallow for most keelboats and found an empty private buoy intended for tethering a skiff. One of the blessings of our trailerable sailboat with shoal draft and kick-up centerboard and rudders is we can float her in 18 inches of water. It was no problem to move into skiff country just to hang around and wait for a State Park buoy to come available.

Wouldn't you know it ... just as I got us secured to the private buoy, I heard the sound of a diesel engine and looked up to see people scurrying around on a large sailboat in the middle of buoy-land. Sensing an opportunity, I whispered to Becky to start our quiet little Honda 9.9 and be ready to make a run for the prize. I untied our mooring line and, as the yacht started moving off, gave Becky the signal. She opened throttle and we were on the empty buoy before the former occupant's wake had even reached the next boat in the mooring area.

The truth is, I would rather moor than anchor, any time. Not that anchoring is bad. One certainly needs to know how to do it properly, but I always sleep better when I'm securely linked to a powerful mooring than when I'm swinging at anchor over a bottom I haven't been able to personally inspect.

Reid Harbor is a long finger of a bay on the southern side of Stewart Island. On the northern side is another popular bay called Prevost, and the two are separated by only a narrow waist of land that can be crossed on foot in a matter of minutes. And there's something else about Reid Harbor — it seems to be favorable water for jellyfish.

After we were tied up and had settled back in the cockpit, under the protective shade of our bimini, we were lazily admiring the surroundings when I spotted stuff floating in the water. I studied it for a minute and realized our boat was surrounded by translucent/white jellyfish that ranged in size from dime to baseball. Hundreds of them ... no, thousands. Gazillions, maybe. Or more ... they were everywhere, slowly undulating in a kind of jellyfish backstroke.

We figured we must have landed in a jellyfish nursery and it had been a busy day in the delivery room. If any of our grandchildren ever ask, "Grandpa, where do jellyfish come from?" I'll have the answer ... Reid Harbor.

Curiosity got the best of us, and we decided to get a closer look at these fascinating marine creatures. All it took was lowering a cup into the water next to one, and it slid into the cup almost as if it had been vacuumed up. This was the first jellyfish to visit the cockpit of our boat, and he (?) looked content to be there. As if he had never left the bay, he just kept on undulating, flexing and relaxing his skirt to move water and perhaps microscopic food through his system. It was an amazing show, and literally within inches of our eyeballs.

Becky said, "Touch him, see if he stings you."

I looked at her and smiled. She's like this sometimes, using her feminine wiles to get me to do "manly" things that don't always turn out quite right. So, being manly, I naturally followed her suggestion and reached a finger into the cup. Then leaping back and doing my best imitation of an electrocuted man, I screamed and she screamed, then I laughed but she didn't. She punched me. She actually punched me, after only a heartbeat before being scared I was electrocuted. But, hey, I deserved it. And she screams so cute — it was worth it.

Actually, the jellyfish felt different than I expected. There was more to it than the eye could see, because the bulk of the body is completely invisible in the water. Rather than just being the lacy skirt we could see, the creature had a substantial lump of quite solid "jelly" to its body. This surprised us, because we'd never been so close to one of these animals.

After a while, we gently returned the jellyfish to the company of his siblings, and considered what a thrill it was to be moored in this small corner of the grand aquarium that is the sea.

Chapter Twenty-Five
The Sky On Fire

Dinner was over, the dishes washed and put away, the stove folded up and stowed, and we had settled down to an evening of cribbage and conversation as the boat gently rocked. Trailerable sailboats rock so easily, and we both love the motion. And the motion rocks me to sleep earlier than I would normally go to bed at home. So after losing another game to Becky, I yawned with deepest sincerity and reached for my toothbrush. "I'm going on deck," I said as I slid the hatch open.

With a cup of water in hand and my toothbrush sticking out of my mouth, I climbed into the cockpit, yawned, stretched and started brushing. Right behind me came Becky. The night was clear and endless, and the stars winked like an eternity of diamond chips on black velvet.

I'm an enthusiastic tooth brusher, and after a minute I looked like a rabid dog with foam escaping down my chin. Becky looked at me and laughed at the sight, but then her gaze went past me and she mumbled a foamy, "Whas at?"

I turned to see what she was looking at. There in the northern sky a broad band of light was dancing. It stretched all the way across from west to east, swimming through the stars and shooting sudden rays this way and that. "Murmff," I foamed, then spit and, in a muffled sort of shout, exclaimed, "Wow, that's gotta be the Northern lights."

Suddenly I wasn't sleepy, I was enthralled. With evening hygiene finished, we sat arm in arm in the cockpit and watched the light show. This wasn't the most spectacular display of the Aurora Borealis—I know that because I've seen photos of better. But it was an awesome sight, an incredible spectacle we'd never have seen if we had stayed home glued to the TV.

From somewhere out in Deep Space, mysterious elements had combined on a collision course with our upper atmosphere, and the result was a colorful, dancing chorus line of electrons performing for us. The sky was alive with light in delicate hues, vibrating to the beat of a Celestial drummer.

That's the beauty of spending time on our sailboat. On sure, we could have had our brains numbed by the end-of-day rehash of the news, or some entirely mindless sit-com. But instead, we were among the fortunate few who happened to be outside, looking at a sky filled with magic.

As I sat there beside the girl of my dreams, watching an amazing display in the sky, feeling the gentle rhythm of our boat on the water, smelling the salt in the air, I knew I was the luckiest guy alive.

Chapter Twenty-Six
Beware the Exploding Porta Potty

Ordinarily, I wouldn't want to talk about the subject we're about to embark upon, but for the purpose of contributing to the more well-rounded nautical education of the reader, here goes.

It was a glorious day, with temperatures right up there in the comfort zone. The sunshine felt so good, in fact, that it just about erased all the negative emotion I felt about the chore I had to take care of — cleaning out the porta potty. But I couldn't put it off any longer, because the 6-gallon-capacity holding tank had only about a teaspoon of room left. And I knew that there was no time to lose, 'cause Becky had that look in her eye.

You know the look — one minute she was innocently laid back reading a book, and then her eyes strayed from the page and she gazed at the ceiling for a long, thoughtful moment. The next thing I knew, she looked straight at me, and I could see a question forming before she even said a word. Knowing I could read her mind did not slow her down, though, and she said the words anyway. "Honey, have you cleaned the porta potty yet?"

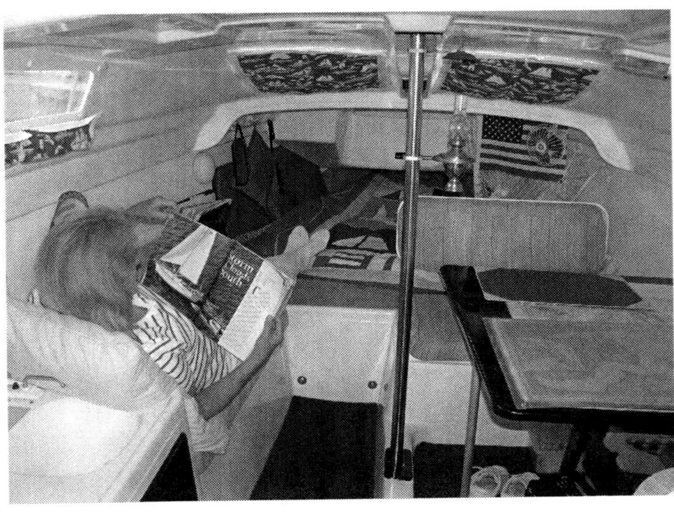

Dang! The answer to that question required no words on my part. I just got up, opened the door to the head, and started working on the situation.

We've had our porta potty longer than we've had some of our children, and now all the kids are grown up and moved away, if that tells you anything. In all those years of potty ownership, no other member of the crew has ever volunteered to share in the joy of maintaining this essential appliance. The privilege has been mine alone, and I have performed the task so many times I couldn't even begin to guess at the number. Actually, I shouldn't whine — it's a simple (although disgusting) process, and if one's brain is engaged even just enough to hold your breath for a minute without passing out, nothing can go wrong. At least that's what I thought. Evidently, something about high ambient temperature promotes enthusiasm inside a full potty holding tank. Whatever is in there (and I don't want to dwell on that question) must enjoy the warm sunshine as much as I do. It does make one want to burst out laughing, strip to one's skivvies and run down the beach. In other words, go crazy. And if the sunshine and warm temperatures will do that to me, maybe the potty feels the same way. Who knows? I don't pretend to understand all these things.

All I know is something unusual happened inside the potty on this warm and beautiful day. I reached down and unlocked the top half of the porta potty. That's the part that holds the freshwater used for flushing. I lifted it off and set it aside, then inspected the lower compartment. This is the disgusting compartment. It has a slide valve you open manually when it's time to flush, then you slide it back shut to lock all the nasty stuff in the holding tank below. Invariably, a little bit of water (or something that looks like water) collects on the top of this slide valve. So when it comes time to empty the tank, I always open and close the valve quickly to drain this moisture into the tank so it won't slosh when I pick up the lower half of the potty and carry it to the disposal site.

There is a button on the porta potty. I never used to pay any attention to this button, but after the events of this day, I investigated its function and discovered it operates a pressure-relief mechanism. Now that you know that bit of information, I'll tell you what happened next. Oh, by the way, I now operate that button. Live and learn.

So, on this warm and wonderful day, I bent over the lower half of the potty, looked at the offending moisture, took a good grip on the slide handle, and gave it a tug. The handle worked perfectly, as it always did. The valve opened, as it always did. But then something new happened. All the enthusiasm (or whatever) building inside the holding tank suddenly rushed for the door as if someone had yelled "fire" in a crowded theater. There was a "Whoosh" and, before my sunny-day-mellowed brain could react enough to close my mouth, I had moisture (and who knows what else) all over my face.

"Aargh!" I jumped back, knocking my head on the door.

"What happened?" Becky sat up and set her book aside.

"The potty exploded," I sputtered, reaching for a paper towel.

"You're kidding!" She laughed.

I could feel the humor drain out of my eyes as I turned to face her. "Does this look like I'm kidding?" I pointed to my dripping mug.

"Wow!" she said. "Has that ever happened before?"

"No." I continued wiping my face and spitting into the paper towel. "Not only that, I knocked my head on the door," I whimpered, hoping for some sympathy.

"Well, don't ask me to kiss you better," Becky said, lying back down and opening her book again. "I'm not touching those lips."

Chapter Twenty-Seven
The Night of the Deadly Dock

I've often thought about where the safest place is for a small boat like ours during a storm. It wasn't until we had owned our boat for seven years that I received an answer to my question. Unfortunately, some answers come in the form of a live demonstration that can curl the hair in your nose. The good news is, I lived through the experience and had a chance to get rid of nose hair I didn't want anyway.

We had launched *Three Eagles* the afternoon before a planned voyage. Because we wanted to get an early start the next morning, we decided to put the boat in the water and tie it up at a state park dock. With our annual marine state park pass, we could moor for free, so it seemed like a logical plan. We went back home to spend the night.

Early that evening, the wind started to blow. Something in the back of my mind told me I needed to go back down to the state park and check on our boat. Having learned over the years not to ignore whoever lives in the back of my mind and badgers me, I told Becky I'd be back in a little while. I drove to have a look at how the boat was doing.

Conditions on the bay were getting stirred up, but nothing serious. Still, I decided to place all our fenders on the port side between the boat and the dock, just for the extra protection in case the waves started to push the boat around. At the same time, I added two more docklines, to serve as spring lines. "Now you won't go anywhere," I said to the boat.

What? You thought maybe you were the only one who talks to your boat?

Satisfied she was secure, I left *Three Eagles* and returned home. Thankfully, we live only about six minutes from the marina and ten minutes from the state park. But as the evening wore on, the wind increased until it was pushing the trees around, and I started feeling uneasy again. "I'm going to go check on the boat," I said to Becky. "I'll take the cell phone, just in case."

"Good idea," she said, kissing me as I went out the door.

It was just about dark when I pulled into the parking space at the head of the state park dock and got my first view of the beating *Three Eagles* was taking. The wind was out of the north, and the state park is almost all the way at the south end of the bay. The wind-driven waves had a few miles of open water in which to build. The floating dock pitched and rolled under the influence of the waves, but *Three Eagles* was virtually jumping right out of the water!

I raced down the pier, down the ramp and along the dock to where she was tied. Up close, the scene was even worse than I imagined. *Three Eagles* pitched violently, stretching the docklines tight as steel cables. The problem was made worse by the fact that the dock and the boat pitched in opposite directions, being out of rhythm with each other. The fenders were the only salvation, and all six of them were still in place and doing their jobs—all except one. The fender positioned at the fattest part of the beam had exploded. As I watched the violent motion of the boat and how it literally tried to mount the dock, I could see how that fender was crushed beyond its capacity to withstand a beating.

But my problem now was what to do. The fury of this sudden storm was likely to last the rest of the night, and I could see all too plainly if I left *Three Eagles* on that dock, she would be in pieces by morning. In fact, as I watched in horror, I was surprised real damage hadn't already occurred. It seemed a miracle none of the deck cleats had pulled out, or the docklines hadn't broken. She was taking a terrible beating, jumping like a bucking horse being held down by a puny man holding a halter rope. This couldn't go on much longer before something failed.

Right at that moment, the dock was our worst enemy—a physical barrier against which the boat would pound itself into fragments. At least if *Three Eagles* had been riding on a mooring buoy or at anchor, she wouldn't be committing suicide like this. I had to do something, and I had to do it right now.

I pulled out the cell phone and made a call. I needed help getting the boat off the dock and up the bay to the marina where she would be safe behind the breakwater. Dialing the number as fast as I could, I got a weird-sounding busy signal. Maybe I misdialed, I thought, and tried the number again. Same thing. I tried a different number, a friend who might be able to come and help me. Busy. I tried a third number. Busy. I tried one more. Busy.

In frustration, I thrust the phone back in my pocket. The cell system must be out, I thought. Probably knocked out by this storm. The wind intensified now, and waves rolled across the bay toward us like a series of freight trains out of control.

With nobody to help, I made the decision to save the boat by myself. Maybe not the smartest or the safest plan, but I didn't have much choice and I wasn't willing to sit there and watch *Three Eagles* get smashed to bits. But how in the world could I get her off this dock, with the waves smashing her from the off-dock side?

Quickly, I unzipped the side curtain of the cockpit enclosure and jumped aboard. Fumbling with the hatch lock, I finally got it open, slid the companionway cover forward and removed the hatchboards. I grabbed the ignition key from its hook, and inserted it in the motor's remote control. I reached back and pulled the choke knob, then turned the key. Instantly, the reliable Honda jumped to life. I checked to make sure the cooling water was flowing, let the motor warm up for a minute, then punched the choke knob to the open position.

With the motor purring and ready for action, I climbed off the boat and studied the four docklines I had strung—one from the bow forward, one from the stern rearward, and two springlines crossing each other in the middle. The springlines first, I figured. Untying them suddenly allowed the boat to move more freely, and the situation looked even uglier than before. Now the boat could jump and run and smash with more momentum. No time lose—I had to get off this dock before it was too late and I lost the boat.

The wind and waves hammered into us from just forward of the beam, so I decided to release the stern line next—but not completely. I untied it, took a quick loop around the dock log (no cleats on these state park docks; they use a raised log beam to wrap the dockline around) and back to the stanchion near the open side curtain. That way I figured I could release that line from inside the boat, as I was at the helm and pulling away. Would it work? I didn't know for sure, but this was the only thing I could think of.

I took a deep breath, and untied the bow line. The wind and waves pushed the bow into the dock anyway, so *Three Eagles* didn't try to blow away. The stern line kept us from blowing backward into the pier pilings that were less than 15 feet behind the boat.

Quickly as I could move, I jumped through the open side curtain, taking the end of the bow line with me. I gave it a quick turn around the stanchion so it wouldn't go over the side, drag beneath the boat and foul the prop.

When purchasing the bow lines, we purposely selected a length that wouldn't allow the tail to get into the prop, even if the line were fully strung out under the boat. Good planning, for times like this.

I jumped behind the wheel and throttled up, praying the motor wouldn't stall. The Honda has never done that to us, but you know what they say about Murphy's Law. Thankfully, Murphy was taking the night off. The motor roared to a higher form of life, and I felt the boat surge forward. I spun the wheel away from the dock and grabbed the quick-release knot I'd tied in the stern line. Everything was going my way—the knot slipped free and I tossed the tail of the dockline back onto the dock so it could easily feed around the log and come free.

Then a moment of fear caught in my throat. The stern line was long enough to get itself wrapped around the prop. If that happened, I'd be blown back into the boat-eating pilings that were still too close for comfort.

I threw the throttle back and shifted into neutral to stop the prop from turning. With arms and elbows flying, I reeled in the stern line, keeping one eye on the pilings that grew closer as furious wind and waves pummeled the boat.

Stacking the wet line on the cockpit seat, I grabbed the control once more, squeezing the shift lock release button and throwing the throttle handle forward. Without a whimper, the Honda roared as loud as a little 9.9 can roar, and we escaped the grinding destruction that threatened us only moments before.

You know how it is when you feel like you've cheated death? Well, that's how I felt, as I watched the waves break over the dock I'd just left. Motoring into the wave train, *Three Eagles* took water over the bow, but the dodger and enclosure kept me dry and warm. I let out a whoop and a holler that would make a rodeo rider proud. In twenty minutes, I'd be pulling in behind the marina breakwater, and I was happy about that.

It was fully dark now, so I switched on my navigation lights. Not that I expected anyone else to be out on the bay on such an insane night, but you never know what kind of nut might be out there doing the same thing I was doing. After all, I hadn't expected to be out there either.

Once again, I pulled out the cell phone and gave our home number a try, so I could let Becky know what I was up to. Busy. I tried again. Busy. I tried one other friend. Busy. "Aarrgh!" I screamed into the night. "How in the world can every phone in Sequim be busy at the same time?" Obviously, the cell system had been knocked out by the storm. This taught me why it isn't a good idea to rely solely on cell phones when you're out on a boat.

Half an hour later, after snuggling down in the peace and calm of the marina, I looked around to find a way back to my truck and then home. What happened before I got home that night is a wild and wet tale in itself, involving a long night and the rescue of another boat. Ultimately, I learned a valuable lesson — weather can be dangerous for your boat, even when you're not out sailing. Close to home, trailerable sailboats can be pulled out of the water. But if you're away from your home port (and your trailer), make sure your mooring is calm and secure. After this night on the deadly dock, I decided I'd rather be anchored in a protected cove or tethered to a mooring buoy than lashed to the windward side of a dock that can tear the hull apart.

Chapter Twenty-Eight
Floating the Floorboards

I suppose I could try to claim the incident I'm about to confess was a science project — an investigation of the law of physics pertaining to water's invariable search for the lowest point. Alas, it was not. It was just an embarrassing oversight that filled the bilge with sea water. On any other day, I would prefer to just file this information in a dark spot at the bottom of my wastebasket, but maybe this will be valuable for someone who, like me, might let things get out of hand.

The scene was innocent enough. We were launching our boat the same way we had dozens of times before. The routine was easy enough. So why did I forget to close the water ballast tank valve and put the stopper back in the air vent hole? Good question.

I think the answer might have something to do with the fact that in all our prior experience, we never had a single drop of ballast water come up out of that vent hole. So what went wrong this time? I still have no idea. But here's what happened: We launched the boat and tied her to the end of the floating dock and opened the water ballast valve and vent so the boat could ballast herself while I went and washed the saltwater off the trailer, then drove to the far end of the marina to park. It was a long walk back, and all the while the ballast tank was filling.

When I got back to the boat, nothing looked unusual, so we prepared to cast off and sail to a favorite marine state park for the first night of our planned week-long voyage. With lines stowed and fenders aboard, we made a perfect run between the other boats coming and going from the marina and escaped into the open waters of the bay. Since we had gotten a late start, we had planned for a first-night's destination only an hour away. And, as luck would have it, we were at about the point of no return when we had one of those unfortunate "oops" moments.

"Oh my gosh!" I exclaimed. "I forgot to close the ballast valve,"

I said, as I reached over the stern to shut the slide. Bet I forgot the vent plug, too," I said to Becky. "Would you please check it?"

Being an excellent crew (actually, she's the Admiral), she peeked through the companionway hatch and saw that, indeed, the step had not been replaced over the vent hole (in our MacGregor, there is a removable step over the vent). And there lay the plug, on its side, idly rolling back and forth with the motion of the boat. And there was a bit of water around the vent hole.

On that day we established a new rule on our boat — if you see a little water around the vent hole, stop everything and investigate. Becky mopped up the spill, inserted the plug and gave the tightening mechanism a twist. Because our destination was within sight, we decided to wait until we were tied to the dock at the state park to proceed with the investigation.

Before long, we were securely tied to the lonely dock. At this state park, there were good shoreside facilities we wanted to make use of — thereby extending the operational schedule of our onboard porta potty, if you know what I mean. So we walked up the ramp, stopped to fill out the overnight registration slip and deposit it in its box, then visited the other amenities of the park.

About half an hour later, we moseyed back to the boat. There was no hurry, in our minds, because we thought the only problem associated with the vent plug and the bit of water we'd found around it was minor and already resolved. Nevertheless, as we walked back down the ramp toward our boat, I noticed she was resting a little lower than normal on her waterline, and listing to starboard. At first, I thought this was because we had loaded a lot of extra supplies for our voyage, but quickly dismissed that excuse and decided to look deeper into the situation.

The area beneath *Three Eagles'* cockpit is wide open and can be used for sleeping and/or storage. After removing all the stowed items from the space, I rolled back the carpet and lifted off one of the removable floor panels that open to the bilge. Yikes! I was shocked to see it full of water — and I mean FULL.

Becky and I immediately went to work with a bucket and bailing scoop. When the bucket was full, Becky poured the water into the sink, which drained overboard — this kept us from having to haul the heavy bucket up to the cockpit to pour it over the side. Twelve buckets later, I started to see the bottom of the hull. It had never looked so good. Something about sucking 25 gallons of saltwater out of the bilge makes the dry inside of the hull look much more appealing. I have to admit I'd never appreciated a dry bilge as much as I did right then.

Other parts of the bilge, extending forward of the section I was bailing, were deeper and, therefore, still flooded. So we bailed and bailed and used towels to dry the nether reaches. Soon, our towels draped over the lifelines and looked like something out of The Grapes of Wrath. We were glad we had the dock to ourselves, 'cause we made the place look sorry.

And wouldn't you know it, right about then a big, fancy, three-story-tall motor yacht cruised out of the sunset and took position just ahead of us. The owners stepped out on their upper deck to play in their starched-white shorts, nautical shirts with embroidered ships wheels over the chest, and stylish caps at a jaunty angle. They spread reclining lounge chairs all over their deck patio, started up a residential-sized barbecue ... and then they saw me.

I took note of their wardrobes and other toys as I crawled up out of the bilge to hang another wet towel over the lifeline. None of our towels matched, of course. One was green, another sort of purple and yellow, another used to be white (more or less), and I had the orange one in my hands when those fine yachts persons spotted me. They looked at me with a modicum of horror on their shiny, clean faces. That's when I became self-conscious about the saltwater-soaked rags I was wearing, my hair looking like it had be sucked through a shop vac, and our boat had taken on the appearance of a third world slum.

Becky was busy pouring a bucket of saltwater down the sink. As it drained out the thru-hull with the familiar tinkle sound, the folks on the other boat stopped what they were doing, stared at the drain, looked at each other, stared back at me with widening eyes that seemed to get stuck right about there.

What could I do? I smiled, shrugged, hung my towel, then ducked back below. That was the day I decided what is acceptable to one class of people may be unacceptable to another. We were sailors, cruisers (pocket cruisers, to be exact), operating on a limited budget, living with minimal luxury, handling life's little adventures as they came, and trying hard to smile about it all. They, on the other hand, were yachties. Huge difference.

We did all we could to dry out the boat that evening, fixed a simple dinner, then went to bed. The next morning, I examined the bilge again and found it had refilled overnight. Aargh! I removed the step and took a look at the vent plug. A trickle of water flooded in around it and drained off into the bilge through a small space designed into the boat between the inner liner and the hull. I'm sure this problem is the reason the factory designed the boat with the convenient escape route for water overflowing from the vent hole. In a later version of this boat, MacGregor came up with a complete redesign of the vent system and eliminated the potential for this problem.

"Honey," I said to Becky, "inside the spare parts bin is a brand new replacement plug. Can you please get it for me?" Well, that's as close as I can come to a cleaned-up, panic-free version of what I actually said. Like a good Admiral, she dove into the spare parts and came up with the right thing. I would have gotten the plug myself, except I was busy applying direct pressure to the boat's version of a punctured artery.

We did a quick swap of plugs, sopped up the mess, hung another couple towels, and waved good-bye to the departing motor yacht. They didn't wave back.

That morning was spent bailing and evaluating the situation. The new plug stopped the leakage. (Turns out the original plug tightening mechanism had corroded, preventing the thing from expanding into the hole and stopping the flood.) So at least we were in no danger of taking on any more water. But we did have a wet boat. And we were still close to our home port. So we decided to abandon plans for the voyage, return to the marina, put the boat back on the trailer, take it home, strip it naked and thoroughly clean it up and dry it out.

And that's exactly what we did. Since saltwater infiltrated the bilge, I thought we should flush it with freshwater a couple times to rinse all salt residue away. With every last thing stripped out of the boat, we brought in the garden hose and started washing. When the bilge filled with freshwater, we bailed out as much as we could, then used the wet mode of a shop vac to suck out the rest. Then we repeated the process. More bailing, more sucking, more towels, until everything was dry. We placed a few electric fans down in the bilge and in the cabin, opened everything up and let the air blow-dry the boat for three days. After all that, we went to work with fiberglass polish, figuring we might as well clean up all the visible parts of the boat's interior as long as there was nothing in it.

And with a fresh appreciation for things like valves and plugs, I overhauled every component of the ballast fill/drain system.

That accomplished, we took inventory of everything we had in the boat, and decided we could do without a lot of the things we had accumulated over the years of sailing.

What we ended up with, because of a stupid leaking plug (right, blame it on the plug, not the guy who was supposed to maintain stuff like that, or the guy who forgot to put the plug back in the hole in the first place), was a totally cleaned, overhauled and resupplied boat.

A week later, we went sailing.

It was a voyage we'll never forget.

Chapter Twenty-Nine
Diving the Warhawk

Fire broke out, and the next thing everybody knew, the legendary Warhawk was lying on the bottom of Discovery Bay. A hundred and twenty years later, we dropped anchor from *Three Eagles*. Our son Ryan and I donned our scuba gear and slid down the anchor line to visit what's left, while Becky remained topside to tend the boat.

I had been there before; twice. Once with our oldest son Eric on somebody else's boat. But this was the first time we had tried to use our sailboat as a dive platform. Trailerable sailboats don't make ideal dive boats, primarily because they are too small in the cockpit and it's not particularly easy to get back on board after a dive. But we figured out how to make it all work.

One of the important tools, when you're looking for an underwater wreck, is a good depth sounder. In this case, we used a Garmin fish finder that showed a representation of the bottom, as well as showing us where the fish were. Knowing the depth is important before dropping anchor, because then you can plan how much rode (anchor line) you need. The rule of thumb is a minimum of five times the distance from your anchor line cleat to the bottom. When the wind is blowing, increase that to seven times the distance.

But when you're planning to dive on a wreck or reef, the fish finder will also show you when you're in the right place. From historical records, we knew the Warhawk rested on the bottom at a depth of about 35 feet (depending upon the tide). So we crept along the 35-foot depth line until the contour of the wreck showed up on the fish finder screen. Then we stopped and lowered the anchor. As it turned out, on this day the anchor fell directly on top of the wreck and actually hung up on one of the old wooden ship's ribs.

Ryan and I got into our gear and giant-strided over the side, while Becky remained on board to make sure nothing went wrong with the boat—like drifting away, for example. This is called maintaining a live boat, and it's a good idea. There's nothing quite like coming back to the surface and finding the boat gone.

While we were on the bottom, exploring the remains of the wreck, Becky went to work making soup and hot drinks, so we'd have something to warm us up after the dive. After that, she hunkered down with an exciting novel ... *Jaws*, did she say? Hmmm.

The trickiest part of the whole adventure was getting our scuba gear back on board. This stuff is heavy, and our boat has a high freeboard, so we couldn't just toss it up onto the boat. For those of you who are divers, you'll appreciate the difficulty we had getting back aboard.

After surfacing, we swam around to the stern, removed the lead weight from our buoyancy compensation vests (BCs) and handed them up into the well where the outboard motor goes when it tilts up. Next, we inflated our BCs all the way, and took them off so they could float the tanks. I stripped off my fins, tossed them aboard and climbed up the swim ladder. That left Ryan still in the water tending the gear.

I went to the mast, disconnected the main halyard from the head of the sail and lowered it over the side, where Ryan caught it and attached it to a lifting strap on the top of the BC. Then I winched the heavy load up and into the cockpit, guiding the tank so it wouldn't abuse the side of the hull. Ryan took off his fins, handed them up and climbed the ladder.

Some trailerable sailboats may make this process easier or more difficult, depending on the configuration of the cockpit. Our MacGregor, with its steering pedestal, makes it a challenge to move around the cockpit with a bunch of scuba gear. But it can be done.

* * * *

For those of you who are history buffs, here's an excerpt from pages 82 to 84 in the book Shipwrecks of the Pacific Coast, by James A Gibbs Jr., published in 1957 by Binsfords & Mort, Portland.

"A night fire which lighted up Discovery Bay and brought every living soul within a radius of ten miles to its shores, occurred at 1 a.m. on April 12, 1883. The victim was the proud old clipper ship Warhawk, which after a brilliant career, was consumed by flames.

"The Warhawk had arrived at Discovery Bay from San Francisco and was in the process of loading lumber for the return voyage when fire of undetermined origin broke out. Scarcely a soul was aboard, the crew for the most part being at the saloon in the little mill town. When flames fanned her aging timbers, all hands were rousted out of the 'gin mill,' along with everybody else in town. All were needed to form a bucket brigade, should the fire spread to the lumber mill. Dark forms danced about before the orange flames, trying in vain to put out the fire.

"The ship's mooring lines were cut and she drifted away like a flaming torch. Captain Ruben Connor, master of the Warhawk, and some of his crew had managed to board her but found the decks unbearably hot. The soles of their shoes were smoking. The seacocks were opened in a last-ditch effort to save the ship. But the stay of the boarding party was brief, as they ran the risk of being encompassed themselves by the inferno.

"The burning ship slowly settled as the water poured into her, causing a gyration of steam. As her main deck began to flood she slipped over on her beam ends and then went to the bottom, with only the stubs of her charred masts breaking the surface. The fire had blackened her almost beyond recognition before she sank and there was only $9000 insurance to cover the loss of the 1067-ton vessel.

"The Warhawk was adjudged a total loss. Her obituary was short.

In her last role as a coastal lumber carrier, many had forgotten her brighter years. Built in 1855 at Newburyport, Massachusetts, she took part in the great clipper ship era when America ruled the seas. She made many splendid passages in both the Cape Horn and China trades.

"In 1871 she was sold at San Francisco to S. L. Mastick to engage in the coastwise lumber service. Here she fell into competition with another of the famous old clippers, the Dashing Wave. The Warhawk set an all-time record in the trade, leaving San Francisco on February 19, 1872, and arriving at Port Discovery on February 23, four days out. The entire round-trip was made in 23 days, including the loading of 750,000 board feet of lumber, which itself required 15 days.

"When one considers her only motive power was sail, he can readily see the remarkable feats performed by this graceful square-rigger of old. Needless to say, she made considerable money for her owners throughout her career and had frequently showed her heels to steam-powered craft.

"Shortly before World War II, the U.S. Maritime Commission launched a program of building modern freighters in an endeavor to bolster the sagging merchant marine. Most of the new ships were named for the fabulous clipper ships which in the mid-19th century had brought America to the fore as a maritime nation.

"As a part of this far-sighted program, the 12,000-ton C-2 type cargo vessel Warhawk was built at Oakland, California, in 1943, to honor its predecessor. She went immediately into the war effort. After the armistice she took the banner of the Waterman steamship Corporation and entered merchant service. On frequent occasions she steamed down the Strait of Juan de Fuca past the final resting place of her namesake at Port Discovery. No salute was given, however, as the years had slipped hastily by and nobody on the new ship was aware of the grave of the old clipper. The original Warhawk had faded away but the new counterpart left its silvery wake across the oceans of the world, carrying the American flag to far-flung ports."

Chapter Thirty
Cruising the Land of the Ancient Ones

Lake Powell is a primordial place, timeless as the vertical stone cliffs embracing deep blue waters. This land deserves to be explored without the encumbrance of a schedule, so the first thing to go was my wristwatch. It came off, was stowed in a convenient cubby, and my left wrist started to become monocolor for the first time in years.

When you live in the land of the Anasazi—an ancient culture of this region that reckoned seasons but probably not the precise time of day—who needs a wristwatch? The sun would wake us up in the morning and put us to sleep at night. Abdominal growls signal meal time, and everything else takes care of itself.

Sometime during the second week, we didn't know what time it was, the day of the week, or whether the month was still May. We finally achieved perfect harmony with this timeless land.

With tight canyon waterways and unpredictable winds, Lake Powell isn't the finest body of water for sailing. But in every other regard this is a place that must not be missed in one's lifetime. The towering buttes, quiet coves, and the sheer enormity of it all bring a sense of reverence to those who are sensitive to such things. Coming here can be a life-changing experience. It is a land that has a spirit and personality, a vigor and mood. And if you listen quietly, you hear its voice.

This is a cathedral built by Mother Nature, altered by the hand of man through the construction of a dam across the Colorado River on the Arizona/Utah border, and is now available for exploration by boat. There is no other place like it on Earth.

We didn't let Lake Powell's shortcoming as a sailing lake bother us. *Three Eagles'* quiet and efficient Honda 9.9 moved us along just fine when the wind wasn't right. And when the conditions allowed, we hoisted main and 150% Genoa and carved silent wakes across broad bays. Wind or no wind, we weren't here only for the sailing, but to experience this fascinating land and waterscape. We were here to exhale deeply, peel off layers of stress, let tense muscles relax, and soak up the warmth of this living land.

The wristwatch wasn't the only change that took place in our lives. Hair grew on my face where it had never been before (and never will again, because it is not in my genes to produce a worthy beard). I gave it every opportunity for ten days, but then had to declare the facial fuzz a dead issue. Finally, on an impulse to save the world from one more poor excuse for a beard, I stepped into the lake and learned just how painful it can be to shave a 10-day growth with cold water and a dull razor. Yowch!

We came to terms with nature in new ways. One morning, an enormous tarantula hawk wasp, beautiful with its shiny black body and orange wings, decided to take up residence on the beach right where we stepped off the stern to reach land. At first, we perceived her as a threat. My gosh, these things are huge! But as we observed her, and she apparently watched us, we seemed to come to an understanding. After a time, she even allowed me to move in close enough for some macro photography. Later in the day, perhaps camera shy, she moved camp and we never saw her again.

This is snake and lizard country. Scurrying lizards darted from shade to shade in pursuit of things only a lizard understands. Rattlesnakes live in the area, but we never saw one. Snakes do most of their work at night and hunker down during the day in deep shade where they are safe from the deadly heat. Still, we knew they were out there and we took precautions as we hiked among the bushes and towering rock formations. Feet and hands never went anyplace we couldn't clearly view and verify no snakes were present. I carried a long stick and beat the base of bushes we needed to pass close by during our wanderings, to stir up serpent activity before stepping into range.

At night, gnats and other flying insects seemed to enjoy hanging out around our anchorage. As we kicked back in the cockpit to enjoy the cool evening breeze, Becky took up arms with a fly swatter to keep the buzzing visitors at bay. Then she noticed the bats, sweeping low, dodging through the night sky, and her concern switched from the bugs to the bats.

"Mother Nature's bug zappers," I commented. "Don't worry about them, just think of all the bugs they're eating, and enjoy the show."

We learned how to deal with the extreme heat — something we'd never faced before as we sailed the lakes near our home in the high mountains of eastern Idaho. Life took on new patterns related to the heat — up early to enjoy some exploring in the cool morning hours and an always-spectacular sunrise, then either go swimming or crawl into the cool cabin to read or play games during the hottest part of the day, only to re-emerge early in the evening to enjoy the scenic wonders.

Morning and evening were for hiking, fishing, and doing all the strenuous chores (right - like what?) related to the cruising lifestyle. During the heat of the day we swam to cool off, then climb back aboard under the shade of our bimini and let the water evaporate from our bodies, putting nature's air conditioning system to work.

To shield the open companionway hatch, we improvised a makeshift boom tent out of a blanket, tied down to lifelines on both sides, using bungee cords and whatever else we could find, including a pair of Vice Grip pliers. We started out using clothespins, but the gusty winds ripped away the blanket one day, and in our effort to reinvent the tie-down system, the Vice Grips were pressed into duty. After this voyage, we bought some small but powerful clamps to secure the perimeter of the boom tent on future trips. We also replaced the boom tent blanket with reflective tarps to turn away the power of the sun before it can invade the boat. In the heat of this desert wonderland, erecting a shade tent over the boom is an important daily ritual.

With no interior curtains yet, we draped towels over the outside of the boat's windows, held down with clothes pins attached to various lines, and the system kept the boat interior relatively comfortable. A great deal of care was taken to prevent any direct sunlight from entering. With judicious use of the forward hatch for ventilation, our 12-volt fan kept us comfortable, even though outside temperatures were in the upper 90's every day. Later, we put up curtains that both beautified the interior and protected against the sun. We also hung easily removable white fabric side curtains around the bimini to shade the cockpit. Before our next trip, we plan to install Phifertex mesh exterior shades over the windows to turn away the sun while still permitting us to see out.

We drank a lot of water. Knowing we wouldn't be able to resupply easily, we took 30 gallons of purified drinking water in half a dozen 5-gallon containers for ease of handling. At the end of the trip, we had little left, even though we had been extremely conservative about washing dishes and using the water for cooking. None of our potable water was used for something as frivolous as bathing or washing clothes. For that, we jumped in the lake and used biodegradable wash products. In this arid, hot climate you need all the water you can carry just for drinking. Even then, it's important to hunker down and "play lizard" during the heat of the day to avoid excessive perspiration.

Every voyage is a learning experience, and our trips to Lake Powell are no exception. After returning home, we made a few purchases to help satisfy needs for future trips. One item we bought to ensure an abundant supply of purified water for drinking and cooking is a PUR Explorer water filter system compact enough for easy stowage, yet effective enough to remove giardia and cryptosporidium, bacteria, and other harmful substances from a freshwater supply.

There are commercial resupply points at Lake Powell, but they are spaced out about 50 miles apart, so they aren't exactly convenient stops for a midnight snack. Fast runabouts and ski boats can make impulse shopping trips, but not us wind cruisers. The three marinas are Wahweap, near Page, Arizona on the west end of the lake—Dangling Rope Marina, 50 miles up-lake (basically east) from Wahweap—and Bullfrog Marina, another 50 miles east. You can get general supplies at any of the three, whether it's food, drinks, ice, fuel, sunscreen, or a place to empty your porta potty.

And on that note, at various locations along the lake are remote, floating potty stations where you can dock to pump out a holding tank, dump a portable, or just walk in and use the toilet.

To find your way to Lake Powell, look at the extreme lower part of a map of Utah. The lake straddles the Utah/Arizona border. Launch ramps are located at Wahweap and Bullfrog. Neither of these places is on a freeway through downtown anyplace, and you'll enjoy spectacular travel scenery through some of America's most awesome desert and mountain country just to reach the launch ramp.

Marine charts with depth soundings of the lake are not available, but you can pick up a good map of the lake at any of the marina stores. Water depth is variable, depending upon how much water is being released through the dam and how much rainfall or snow-melt is contributing to the lake.

With a shoreline exceeding the entire coastline of California, you won't run out of places to explore. Tucked away in the mysterious multi-branching side canyons are places such as Rainbow Bridge, the largest natural bridge on earth and one of the geologic wonders of the world.

Archaeological sites of Anasazi ruins with names like Defiance House or Haunted Canyon exude the spirit of their ancient inhabitants. As you walk among the ruins and study the pictographs and petroglyphs, you can almost hear the ghosts of children laughing, the women singing and the men chanting.

Cruising the cool sapphire waters flowing between towering red cliffs, you feel like a tiny speck in an enormous and ageless universe. An eagle soars overhead searching the lake for a trout to take back to her nest. The silence of an empty land cradles you in a kind of peace and calm you never knew existed.

On one trip to Powell, we discovered Secret Cove was no longer a secret. After a couple days alone, we were invaded by a traffic jam of houseboats and jet skis piloted by college kids on vacation. We pulled anchor and went looking for the serenity of a quiet place. It didn't take long to find a deserted cove off Oak Bay where we had the world to ourselves. Life was back to just the two of us ... like Adam and Eve on their first morning in the garden. The view was stunning, the silence deep and peaceful.

After a morning swim, we hiked up the slope to the base of the cliff behind *Three Eagles*, where several small caves begged for exploration. At an elevation several hundred feet above lake level, we sat in the shade and looked out upon the razor-stark yet delicately beautiful landscape that makes Lake Powell so unique.

The ribbon of blue that was once only a river now fills tendril canyons in every direction from the main channel, its cool color contrasting dramatically with the burnt umber slickrock formations rising like monuments to the Creator. Watching a sunrise here, one half expects to hear an orchestra play a deeply moving piece from Tchaikovsky, but all is silence — still deeply moving, but quietly so. This is a place to heal the soul.

Legend says Native Americans once came to this awe-inspiring land on a vision quest. Today, people continue to come on their own personal quest for fun or for a chance to feel the spirit of this ancient land of mystery. One thing is certain ... once you have been to Lake Powell, you'll never be the same. The mystical spirit of this land will forever whisper, "come back."

Chapter Thirty-One
We Must Be Rich

We sailed into Port Ludlow on Labor Day weekend, hoping to find an empty slip but half expecting to find everything filled to overflowing. We talked about anchoring out in the remote and secluded bay behind the tiny islands called The Twins if the marina was full, but we were hoping to have close access to the shoreside amenities. As we cruised into the harbor, I got on the VHF and called the harbormaster, 'cause you never know until you ask.

"Port Ludlow harbormaster, this is *Three Eagles*, over."

"*Three Eagles*, this is the Port Ludlow harbormaster," came her reply.

"This is *Three Eagles*. We're a 26-footer looking for a slip for the night. Got anything in our size?"

A minute passed with no answer. Then, "*Three Eagles*, we have a slip for you at B-14."

"Great," I replied. "We'll tie up and come to see you."

"Take your time," she said, "Port Ludlow, out."

We grinned at each other. Port Ludlow is one of our favorite stops on our way up and down Puget Sound to various other destinations. To score a slip on this busy weekend was almost a miracle.

After tying up and signing in at the office, we wandered the docks—a favorite pastime—looking at all the other boats, waving to people and occasionally stopping to chat with someone. Boaters are such sociable folk and it's easy to engage in a conversation with perfect strangers who soon become friends.

That afternoon, a live band played on the grassy knoll just north of the marina. We heard the music and, like mice listening to the Pied Piper, scurried to see what it was all about. A local band with a name something like "Never Been To Utah" was warming up the crowd, playing favorites from every decade since the Fifties. They sounded good to me. When Becky and I used to play (banjo for her, guitar for me) in family-style hootenannies at the home of our friend, Tex, he used to say, "Hey, if you ain't good, at least be loud." Well, the guys who had never been to Utah were loud. Maybe they were even good.

Soda pop and barbecue sandwiches on hoagie buns were being served under a tent shelter, and people lounged around on picnic table benches, eating and smiling and tapping their toes or gyrating other body parts to the rhythm of the band. We grabbed a sandwich and a can of pop and kicked back to enjoy the mellow sunshine and the tunes. The longer we listened, the better these guys sounded.

Soon, I looked over at Becky, and when I caught her eye I winked. "Wanna dance?" I asked.

She winked back, ever the tease. "Sure," she smiled.

We were the only ones on the grass dance floor, but we didn't care. We just whirled and twirled and pranced to the beat of whatever song the non-Utah group played for us. And we grinned big, having the time of our lives. Then another couple, who probably couldn't stand to see us having so much fun all by ourselves, got up and started to dance. Then another. Before long, the grassy knoll overlooking the marina at Port Ludlow was host to a fantastic fresh air sock hop. The guys who had never been to Utah were in the groove, and played music that brought smiles to our faces.

We danced a while, then sneaked away hand in hand to walk the docks again while still listening to the music in the background. The sky started to pink up a bit, and the distant Olympic Mountain range began to glow. A mirror finish on the water inside the harbor reflected a perfect inverted reproduction of the breathtaking scene.

"It's like a postcard," I commented to Becky.

"Better," she said, "A perfect postcard with music."

We wandered among some million-dollar mega yachts that resembled floating condominiums, huge classic schooners and sleek racing sailboats. Our little sloop wouldn't even make a decent dinghy for some of these elegant boats.

And then it occurred to me—the owners of these stunningly expensive yachts were the same people who had been eating hoagie sandwiches, drinking pop and dancing in the grass to the music made by a bunch of guys who had never even been to Utah. They were the same folks who danced beside us, ate at the same picnic table and enjoyed this perfect evening in this ideal setting. We were all the same, at that moment, smelling the same aromas, hearing the same music, feeling the same evening breeze, witnessing the same birth of a sunset.

Something swelled in my throat and started to fill my eyes. I squeezed Becky's hand. She always has been the girl of my dreams, and here I was in paradise with the love of my life.

"Honey," I started.

She looked up at me, smiled and squeezed my hand back.

I cleared my throat so I could say what was in my heart. "You know something?" I asked.

"What?" she whispered.

"We must be rich."

And I meant every word. Being rich has nothing to do with the size of a bank account or the size of a boat. We're rich because of the blessings of living in a free land where we can go places and do things like dance on the grass and witness a perfect sunset and listen to music and be with the one we love.

We are rich because we can crash a seagull party, haul a sunstar aboard, watch the Northern Lights set fire to the sky, spit in the water to light up the critters, feel the wind and the waves lift the weight of daily life off our hearts. There are lots of ways to be rich, but for us, filling our lives with memories is the best way.

Now, we'd love to stay and talk some more, but the breeze is up and it's time to raise sail. The horizon beckons. Hopefully, we'll see you out there, too.

This is *Three Eagles* ... out.

Meet the Authors

Rich Johnson was born and raised in a tiny northern Utah town, where he learned to fish and hunt under the tutelage of his dad and grandfather. As a kid, he spent time on the far end of a two-man crosscut saw, learned to split wood for the winter stove, hunted grasshoppers in his grandma's garden for a nickel a pop bottle full, and had a dog named Tippy. Life was good.

After a stint in the Army Special Forces, Rich ended up in Los Angeles, working in the magazine industry as a writer, photographer and editor. During his 33-year career, he's written hundreds of articles and several books. His travels took him all around the country and to far-flung parts of the world. He now lives in the Pacific Northwest.

Rich enjoys sailing, scuba diving, fishing, camping, rock climbing, kayaking, golf, backcountry skiing and just about anything else that can be done outdoors. He has more than 30 parachute jumps to his credit, rappelled from helicopters, and holds a Frequent Faller card as a bungee jumper.

Rich served as a volunteer firefighter and emergency medical technician.

Becky Johnson is a freelance writer and photographer whose work has appeared in travel and outdoor magazines for more than twenty years. She's been featured in such publications as Lifestyles, Trailer Life Magazine, MotorHome Magazine, Four Wheeler Magazine, Holidays, and others. Her columns Becky's Corner, The Better Half, and People Going Places highlighted women's issues, the lighter side of life, and travel and adventure. She also worked as a copy editor and managing editor.

Becky and her husband Rich live in Washington State and have shared many adventures together — including a year-long wilderness project that involved living in a cave. Today, they enjoy traveling the country with their trailerable sailboat Three Eagles. From their home office, they work together doing research and photography for their books and magazine projects.

Becky enjoys hobbies in aromatherapy using essential oils, sailing, reading, gardening, and volunteer work in her church organization. She has a daughter, three sons and ten grandchildren.

Sailing Experience

Rich and Becky have owned a 26-foot trailerable sailboat for more than 13 years, sailed extensively in the intermountain West and the Pacific Northwest (Puget Sound, San Juans, Canadian Gulf Islands). Twice, Rich crewed for post-season delivery of commercial fishing vessels down the Inside Passage from Alaska to the Puget Sound area. His duties included standing wheel watch, navigation and other onboard work.

As a member of the Coast Guard Auxiliary, Rich served as Qualified Boat Crew and Instructor for public education courses, as well as member training. He completed the following specialty courses for AUXOPS qualification:
- Advanced Coastal
- Navigation Seamanship
- Communications
- Weather
- Search & Rescue
- Patrols

Glossary

Aft berth — The sleeping area in the rear of a boat.

Airfoil — A shape with one curved surface that creates lift when air passes over it.

Ball mount shank — The part of the hitch equipment that holds the hitch ball.

Beam reach — Sailing with the wind coming from the side (beam) of the boat.

Bight — A bend in a rope that forms an open-ended loop, used for tying some knots.

Boltrope — A rope sewn into the leading edge (luff) and the foot of sails. This lends strength to the fabric and allows the sail to be attached to the mast and the boom.

Boom — A horizontal pole behind the mast that holds the foot of the mainsail.

Boom vang — A line or tackle used to hold the boom down to improve sail shape.

Bow pulpit — Railing at the front of the boat.

Brake actuator — A hydraulic device attached to the trailer tongue; activates the trailer brakes as the tow vehicle slows or stops.

Broach — An undesirable sideways movement of the stern, when pushed by waves approaching from behind. This shoves the boat sideways and can cause capsize.

Broad reach — Sailing with the wind coming from the rear quarter.

Bunk — 1) A sleeping area; 2) carpeted wooden supports that a boat rests on when on a trailer.

Caliper — The part of a disc brake system that holds the brake pads and moves them against the rotor when the brakes are applied.

CDI Flexible Furler — A headsail roll-up system made by CDI. This system allows the headsail to be rolled up like a window blind. It is flexible and easy to work with when the mast is raised and lowered, so it is popular on trailerable sailboats.

Centerboard — A keel-like board that pivots down from the bottom of a sailboat to prevent sideways drift. Similar to a daggerboard, except that it pivots when lowered.

Chain plate — Metal fittings at or near deck level to which shrouds and stays are attached.

Cleat — A piece of wood, metal or plastic with projecting ends, mounted to various places on a boat, to which rope can be fastened. Cleats are also installed on docks for the purpose of attaching docklines.

Clew — A metal ring attached to the lower aft (rear) corner of a triangular sail.

Coupler — The part of the trailer tongue into which the hitch ball is inserted for towing.

Cringle — A small ring (similar to a grommet) on the edge of a sail, through which a rope may be run for the purpose of reefing or other control functions.

Cunningham — A line or tackle used to pull down on the lower portion of a sail's leading edge to tighten the luff.

Daggerboard — A keel-like board that is moved vertically down from the bottom of a sailboat to prevent sideways drift. Similar to a centerboard, except that it does not pivot when lowered.

Deadman — Anything that is buried underground with a line attached, for the purpose of serving as an anchor.

Deck flange — The edge of the deck that is attached to the hull during construction of a boat.

Depth sounder — An electronic device used to determine the depth of the water.

Dockline — A rope used for attaching the boat to the dock.

Downhaul — A rope that goes to the head (top) of a sail; used to pull the sail down.

Fixed keel — A weighted fin-shaped structure on the bottom of the hull, the purpose of which is to limit sideways movement of the boat and to counterbalance the pressure of the wind on the sails.

Foot — The bottom edge of a triangular sail.

Forepeak — The forward-most part of the cabin; often used as a storage space or a sleeping area.

Freeboard — The height of a boat from the waterline to the lowest spot that will allow water to come aboard.

Furl — The method of reducing the amount of headsail by rolling it up like a window shade.

GAWR — Gross axle weight rating; the vehicle manufacturer's rating of the strength of the axle.

GCWR — Gross combined weight rating; the maximum total combined weight of tow vehicle and trailer/boat, that a tow vehicle is rated to pull.

GVWR — Gross vehicle weight rating; the manufacturer's specified maximum weight rating of a vehicle when ready for travel, including passengers, fluids and cargo.

GPS — Global Positioning System; a satellite-based system of electronic navigation.

Gelcoat — A coating for fiberglass boats, applied during initial construction to give the boat a smooth finish.

Genoa — A headsail that is larger than a jib. Usually in sizes such as 120% or 150% in relation to the size of the jib.

Genoa track — A piece of hardware on each side of the deck, where the genoa control lines are run through fore/aft adjustable blocks called genoa cars.

Gin pole — A single-pole crane for lifting.

Ground tackle — Anchoring equipment is referred to as ground tackle. This includes the anchor, chain, rope and connecting devices such as shackles.

Gybe (a.k.a. Jibe) — The act of turning the boat when running downwind, so the wind changes from one side of the boat to the other.

Halyard — The rope used for raising a sail.

Hank-on — The method of attaching a non-furling headsail to the headstay. Non-furling headsails are attached to the headstay by using clips known as hanks.

Head — 1) The top corner of a triangular sail; 2) the bathroom area; 3) the toilet.

Headstay — The wire cable that runs between the bow, and some point at or near the top of the mast, that is used to hold the mast up from the forward side.

Heeling — When a sailboat leans to one side as the wind works against the sails.

Helm — The steering and control station.

Jib — A small headsail.

Lee rail — The edge of the deck on the downwind side of the boat.

Leech — The aft (rear) edge of a triangular sail.

Lifelines — Safety lines that are run along the sides of the deck to prevent people from falling overboard. These lines are usually made of plastic coated stainless steel cable and are supported by stanchions.

Luff — 1) The leading edge of a triangular sail; 2) the action of a sail as it flaps in the wind.

Mainsail — The large sail that is attached to the mast and the boom.

Mast — The large, vertical spar that supports the mainsail.

Mast compression post — The vertical support post inside the cabin and directly beneath the mast. This post prevents the downward weight of the mast from collapsing the cabin roof.

Mast crutch — The support structure that holds the mast after it has been lowered for travel, when the boat is on the trailer.

Outhaul — The control line that applies rearward tension to the foot of the mainsail.

PFD — Personal flotation device; also known as a life jacket or life vest.

Point of sail — The direction toward which the boat is sailing.

Preventer — A system of block and tackle that is used to prevent the boom from sweeping uncontrolled across the deck during a jibe.

Provisioning — Preparing supplies for the boat, such as food, water, and other essentials to be used on a trip.

Payload capacity — The rated cargo capacity of a tow vehicle, as specified by the manufacturer.

Receiver — The component of hitch equipment into which the ball mount is inserted. Typically, a receiver will have a 2-inch square tubular opening.

Reefing — The act of lowering and securing the mainsail, to reduce the total amount of sail area that is exposed to the wind.

Rigging — All of the various lines and cables that are used to secure the sails and spars are known as rigging. Standing Rigging consists of cables that support the mast in an upright position (shrouds and stays). Running Rigging consists of the control lines for the sails (halyards and sheets).

Ring and pinion ratio — The gear ratio between the ring gear and the pinion gear in the tow vehicle differential. The higher the number (for example 4.10:1) the lower the gearing, which is good for towing a heavy load.

Roller furling — The equipment used for deploying or rolling up a headsail. This allows the headsail to be rolled up as much as needed to fit the wind conditions.

Rotor — The component in a disc brake system that is gripped between the brake pads, when the brakes are applied.

Rudder — A broad, flat underwater structure that is hinged vertically at the rear of the boat and is pivoted to steer the vessel.

Sail slug — Often made of some form of durable plastic, sail slugs are attached to the leading edge of a mainsail and used to connect the sail to the slot at the rear of the mast. This replaces the need to run the boltrope up the slot and makes raising and lowering the mainsail easier.

Sheet — The control lines (ropes) for sails.

Shoal draft — Shoal water is shallow water, so a shoal draft boat is a boat that is capable of operating in shallow water.

Shroud — Cables that support the mast from the side. A typical sailboat has both upper and lower shrouds, to lend side-to-side support at the mid-point and the top of a mast.

Slab reefing — The method of storing a lowered mainsail, in which the sail is draped across the boom in an alternating back and forth manner and then secured with sail ties.

Snubber — A rubber device that is installed on docklines. It's function is to absorb shock loads as the boat moves about while tied to the dock.

Solenoid — A switching device used to trigger an action, such as switching off the trailer brakes when backing up.

Spinnaker — A colorful 3-sided sail made of lightweight material. Spinnakers are used for sailing downwind in light air.

Spreader — Horizontal arms that protrude sideways from the mast and hold the upper shrouds.

Springline — A dockline that runs from the bow aft, or from the stern forward to a dock cleat, to prevent the boat from moving forward or back while tied to the dock.

Stanchion — Vertical posts located along the sides of the deck to support the lifelines.

Stay — Cables that support the mast fore and aft. Some sailboats have split backstays, with one running to each aft corner of the boat. The forestay or headstay is the cable that runs from the bow to a point at or near the top of the mast.

Stern — The rear of the boat.

Swing keel — Similar to a centerboard, but ballasted with lead or other weight to counterbalance the pressure of the wind on the sails, and to prevent sideways drift.

Tack — A metal ring attached to the lower front corner of a triangular sail.

Tacking — When sailing toward the wind, tacking is the act of turning the boat in such a manner as to change the direction of the wind from one side of the bow to the other. If the wind is coming over the starboard (right) side, it is said to be on a starboard tack. On a portside tack, the wind comes from the port (left) side.

Tie down eyes — Metal eye-bolts used in conjunction with tied-down straps for securing the boat to the trailer for transport.

Tiller — A long-handled control arm that is connected directly to the rudder, and is moved from side-to-side to steer the boat.

Toe rail — A low strip that runs along the edge of the deck on some (but not all) sailboats, to provide a degree of safety and keep those on deck from slipping overboard.

Tongue jack — A vertical jack mechanism attached to the trailer tongue and used to raise or lower the front of the trailer.

Trailer harness — The electrical wiring connections between the tow vehicle and the trailer. This may also refer to the wiring used to power the trailer lights.

Transducer — The electronic sending and receiving unit that works in conjunction with instruments such as the depth sounder, speed, and water-temperature displays. The transducer is often installed underwater below the transom.

Transom — The flat portion of the stern.

Trim — Trimming the sails is done by either tightening or slacking the sail control line (sheet) to adjust the angle of the sail to the wind.

Water ballast tank — Sailboats that have no ballasted keel employ the weight of water in a ballast tank (inside the hull), to give stability to the boat, and to counterbalance the pressure of wind on the sails.

Whisker pole — A lightweight pole used to hold the headsail out to one side of the boat, to improve downwind sailing.

Wing and wing — Sailing directly downwind with the mainsail angled to one side, and the headsail angled out on the opposite side.

Index

CPSIA information can be obtained at www.ICGtesting.com
Printed in the USA
235620LV00011BA/177/P